BAPTIZED IMAGINATION

The imagination has been called, 'the principal organ for knowing and responding to disclosures of transcendent truth.' This book probes the theological sources of the imagination, which make it a vital tool for knowing and responding to such disclosures.

Kerry Dearborn approaches areas of theology and imagination through a focus on the 19th century theologian and writer George MacDonald. MacDonald can be seen as an icon whose life and work open a window to the intersection of word, flesh and image. He communicated the gospel through narrative and image-rich forms which honour truth and address the intellectual, imaginative, spiritual, and emotional needs of his readers. MacDonald was also able to speak prophetically in a number of areas of contemporary concern, such as the nature of suffering, aging and death, environmental degradation, moral imagination and gender issues. Dearborn explores influences which shaped him, along with the wisdom he has offered in the formation of significant Christian writers in both the nineteenth and twentieth centuries. Authors such as C.S. Lewis, G.K. Chesterton, Dorothy Sayers, J.R.R. Tolkien, W.H. Auden, Frederick Buechner and others attribute to MacDonald key paradigm shifts and insights in their own lives.

A study of MacDonald does not offer a formulaic approach to theology and the imagination, but the possibility of gleaning from his rich harvest relevant nourishment for our own day. It also provides a context in which to assess potential weaknesses in imaginative approaches to theology.

Ashgate Studies in Theology, Imagination and the Arts

Series Editors:

Trevor Hart, St Mary's College, University of St Andrews, Scotland
Jeremy Begbie, Ridley Hall, UK
Roger Lundin, Wheaton College, USA

What have imagination and the arts to do with theology? For much of the modern era, the answer has been, 'not much.' It is precisely this deficit that the proposed series will seek to redress. For, whatever role they have or have not been granted in the theological disciplines, imagination and the arts are undeniably bound up with how we as human beings think, learn and communicate, engage with and respond to our physical and social environments and, in particular, our awareness and experience of that which transcends our own creatureliness. The arts are playing an increasingly significant role in the way people come to terms with the world; at the same time, artists of many disciplines are showing a willingness to engage with religious or theological themes. A spate of publications and courses in many educational institutions has already established this field as one of fast growing concern.

This series taps into a burgeoning intellectual concern on both sides of the Atlantic and beyond. The peculiar inter-disciplinarity of theology, and the growing interest in imagination and the arts in many different fields of human concern, afford the opportunity for a series which has its roots sunk in varied and diverse intellectual soils, while focused around a coherent theological question: How are imagination and the arts involved in the shaping and reshaping of our humanity as part of the creative and redemptive purposes of God, and what roles do they perform in the theological enterprise?

Many projects within the series have particular links to the work of the Institute for Theology Imagination and the Arts in the University of St Andrews, and to the Theology Through the Arts programme in Cambridge.

Other titles in the series:

The Passion in Art
Richard Harries

Faith and Beauty
A Theological Aesthetic
Edward Farley

Baptized Imagination
The Theology of George MacDonald

KERRY DEARBORN
Seattle Pacific University, USA

ASHGATE

Published by
Ashgate Publishing Limited
Gower House
Croft Road
Aldershot
Hampshire GU11 3HR
England

Ashgate Publishing Company
Suite 420
101 Cherry Street
Burlington, VT 05401-4405
USA

Ashgate website: http://www.ashgate.com

British Library Cataloguing in Publication Data
Dearborn, Kerry
    Baptized Imagination: The Theology of George MacDonald. – (Ashgate Studies in Theology, Imagination and the Arts). 1.MacDonald, George, 1824–1905 – Religion 2.MacDonald, George, 1824–1905 – Criticism and interpretation. 3. Christianity in literature. I.Title
    823.8

Library of Congress Cataloging-in-Publication Data
Dearborn, Kerry, 1950–
    Baptized Imagination: The Theology of George MacDonald / Kerry Dearborn.
        p.   cm. – (Ashgate Studies in Theology, Imagination, and the Arts)
    Includes bibliographical references (p.) and index.
    1. MacDonald, George, 1824–1905 – Criticism and interpretation. 2. MacDonald, George, 1824–1905 – Influence. 3. Theology in literature. 4. Spiritual life in literature. 5. Christianity and literature
    – Scotland – History – 19th century. 6. Fantasy fiction, Scottish – History and criticism. 7. Christian fiction – History and criticism. I. Title. II. Series.
    PR4969.D43 2007
    823'.8–dc22
                                           2006008828

ISBN-13: 978-0-7546-5516-9
ISBN-10: 0-7546-5516-4
This book is printed on acid-free paper.

Printed and bound in Great Britain by TJ International Ltd, Padstow, Cornwall, UK.

Contents

Acknowledgments

This study derives initially from doctoral research which I submitted to the University of Aberdeen in Scotland in 1994, and subsequently from research conducted while teaching at Seattle Pacific University (SPU). I am grateful for a sabbatical and research grants from Seattle Pacific University, including a Lilly-SERVE grant, without which I could not have completed this project. The Marion E. Wade Center's award of a 2005 Clyde S. Kilby research grant for this book has also been a source of encouragement.

Many people have offered significant influence and assistance throughout the course of researching and writing this book. Professor James B. Torrance's profound insights and worshipful approach to theology inspired me to pursue advanced theological studies. Dr. Trevor Hart, my supervisor at Aberdeen, was a caring and supportive guide through the PhD process. Dr. Alan Torrance, Dr. Jeremy Begbie, and my theology colleagues at SPU have been supportive friends and inspiring theological mentors. I am grateful to Dr. Christopher Mitchell, Marjorie Lamp Mead, and Heidi Truty for their gracious assistance and generous provision of resources at the Marion E. Wade Center. The George MacDonald Society and its publication of *North Wind*, and Barbara Amell, editor of *Wingfold*, have contributed immensely to making excellent resources and scholarship on MacDonald available. Fellow George MacDonald scholars Dr. David Neuhouser, Robert R. Trexler, and Kirsten Jeffries Johnson have offered much-needed encouragement and insight along the way. I am especially grateful for David and Robert's willingness to read a draft of this book and offer crucial reflections and corrections to it. Lauren J. Ten Harmsel has been a diligent and much-appreciated research assistant in recent months. I also want to express my deep gratitude for the prayers and support of my small group, Julie Anderton, Roger and Astrid Feldman, Ross and Pam Hayes, and my husband, Tim.

Most importantly, my family has been a vital source of insight and encouragement. My mother, Alice C. Peterson, has modeled a life of joyful gratitude in the midst of significant sorrow and loss. Tim, our three daughters, Alison, Andrea and Bethany, and Alison's husband, Greg, have offered much encouragement, understanding and support.

Finally, there is no one to whom I own a greater debt than to my husband, Dr. Tim Dearborn, to whom this book is dedicated. Without his tireless help, profound wisdom and steadfast support, there would have been no book.

Abbreviations

Unless noted otherwise, all works cited are by George MacDonald.

AF	*Alec Forbes of Howglen*
CW	*Castle Warlock*
DE	*David Elginbrod*
DG	*Donal Grant*
DO	*A Dish of Orts*
DOS	*A Book of Strife in the Form of a Diary of an Old Soul*
EC	G.E. Sadler (ed.), *Expression of Character*
GCC	G.E. Sadler (ed.), *Gifts of the Child Christ*
GMAW	Greville MacDonald, *George MacDonald and His Wife*
HA	*Home Again*
HG	*The Hope of the Gospel*
ML	*The Marquis of Lossie*
MM	*Mary Marston*
PF	*Paul Faber, Surgeon*
PW	*The Poetical Works of George MacDonald*
RF	*Robert Falconer*
SF	*Salted with Fire*
SG	*Sir Gibbie*
SP	*The Seaboard Parish*
US	*Unspoken Sermons*
WM	*What's Mine's Mine*

Introduction

The Baptized Imagination and Theology

The imagination has been called, 'the principal organ for knowing and responding to disclosures of transcendent truth.'[1] This book probes the theological sources of the imagination, which make it a vital and reliable tool for knowing and responding to such disclosures. It approaches this study through focus on the theologian and imaginative writer George MacDonald. As a nineteenth-century pastor and writer, MacDonald contributed significantly in fostering theological understanding of the imagination. He also modeled an imaginative way of communicating theological truth with transforming power to shape human lives, communities, and the discipline of theology. Furthermore, through his theological sensitivity to the imagination, he was able to speak prophetically in a number of areas of contemporary concern, such as the nature of suffering, aging and death, environmental degradation, moral imagination, and gender issues.

MacDonald's marriage of imagination and theology emerged from his belief in God as loving creator and redeemer and his desire to follow Jesus Christ in all things. He was convinced that a fruitful imagination finds its inspiration drinking from the wellsprings of God's infinite creativity. Christ's image-rich manner of conveying his Father's nature and ways was compelling for MacDonald. He was concerned that theology had often become abstracted from imaginative forms and vision, producing husks that were not only hard to digest, but also offered little nourishment for an obedient pilgrimage of faith.[2]

MacDonald wrote to offer people true food which could empower them to return to the loving Father, feast at God's table and be strengthened to share in God's kingdom work. Because he conveyed his theological convictions in such a refreshing and dynamic way, C.S. Lewis describes his first encounter with MacDonald's writing as converting, even baptizing his imagination.[3] Though a young atheist at the time, Lewis was captivated by the way goodness and even death were presented in *Phantastes*. MacDonald later became significant in Lewis's pilgrimage of faith and inspired his own richly imaginative expressions of theology.[4]

---

1   James Fowler, 'Future Christians and Church Education,' in Theodore Runyon (ed.), *Hope for the Church* (Nashville, TN, 1979), p. 104.
2   MacDonald, *What's Mine's Mine* (London, 1883), p. 106; hereafter cited as *WMM*.
3   C.S. Lewis, 'Preface,' *George MacDonald: An Anthology* (London, 1955, orig. 1946), p. 21.
4   Ibid., pp. 20–21.

Though MacDonald never used the phrase, 'baptized imagination,' themes of cleansing death and renewal of one's imagination pervade his work. Of the over fifty books that he published, only five were written in a more standard theological mode (books of sermons).[5] Even these were rich with biblical imagery. His writing is not a systematic body of material to be mastered, but an invitation into a richer way of knowing and being. He resists theological categorization, for 'He was to his own age shockingly liberal, and to ours he is amazingly orthodox.'[6] Though he responded to and was impacted by the influences of his predecessors and his contemporaries, his deepest desire was to be molded by Christ's own Spirit. He yearned to see God in everything and rejoice in everything as God's holy gift: '… that was my part towards heaving the weight of sin, which, like myriads of gravestones was pressing the life out of us men off the whole world.'[7]

His literary importance has been both acknowledged and contested. On the one hand he was granted high honors, like the Civil List pension by Queen Victoria for his 'services to literature,'[8] and has been compared with Charles Dickens for the extensiveness of his popularity at one point in Europe and America.[9] On the other hand, writers have criticized his work for being at times too full and didactic.[10] MacDonald's priority was not that truth should serve art, but that art should serve the Truth. Contrary to the impetus of Scottish Calvinism which at times 'straight-laced the muse,'[11] MacDonald saw the arts as being gifts from God which could be used graciously to penetrate through the thick spectacles of certain rigid forms of theology to present an alternate and more truly *theo*logical perspective. He was therefore unapologetic when criticized for using literary means to preach and to teach, rather than for entertainment or to demonstrate his own artistry: 'People,' he once remarked', 'find this great fault with me - that I turn my stories into sermons. They forget that I have a Master to serve first before I can wait upon the public.'[12]

---

5   See MacDonald, *Unspoken Sermons*, Vol. 1 (1867), Vol. 2 (1885), Vol. 3 (1889); hereafter cited as *US*. *The Miracles of Our Lord* (1870), *The Hope of the Gospel* (1892).

6   Louise Collier Willcox, 'A Neglected Novelist,' *North American Review*, 183 (September 1906), p. 403.

7   MacDonald, *The Seaboard Parish* (Whitehorn, CA, 1995, orig. 1868), p. 500; hereafter cited as *SP*.

8   William Raeper, *George MacDonald* (Tring, 1987), p. 340.

9   Michael Phillips, *George MacDonald: Scotland's Beloved Storyteller* (Minneapolis, MN, 1987), p. 275.

10 See G.K. Chesterton in his introduction to Greville MacDonald, *George MacDonald and His Wife* (London, 1924), p. 15; hereafter cited as *GMAW*. See also Richard Reis, *George MacDonald* (New York, 1972), p. 47.

11 H. Escott, *In My Father's House* (London, 1943), p. 17.

12 *GMAW*, p. 375. Later he became very impatient with people who came to hear him speak in Casa Coraggia, his home in Bordighera, who desired for him to be more entertaining, 'so that he had continually to respond: "I don't in the least care to amuse people; I only want to help them"'; MacDonald, in Frances M. Brookfield, 'George MacDonald at

He embraced the platform provided for him as a writer, grateful that through it 'he found himself touching the hearts and stimulating the consciences of a congregation never to be herded in the largest and most comfortable of [churches].'[13] Because he felt his first calling was to serve his Master, he did not set out first to build a literary reputation. The similarity in many of his stories, and the final denouements which exalt truth and convey the triumph of good over evil, have for some made him an inferior writer.[14] He believed, however, that for a writer not to show goodness prevailing, to have written such that 'vice may have the best of it, would be to teach them that there is no God.'[15]

Some have argued that he resorted to novels and to other literary means to communicate his message out of sheer financial need, having been squeezed out of normal parish ministry. There is strong evidence against this assumption, however, namely that the 'best of his novels were written not on necessity's terms, but on his own.'[16] Furthermore, there was a lengthy gap between the advice of his publisher, George Murray Smith, to write novels because 'Nothing but fiction pays' and his first novel, *David Elginbrod* in 1863.[17] Even in the midst of his early pastorate in Arundel, MacDonald incorporated literary materials into his sermons and writings. He expressed eagerness to increase his literary focus.[18] His literary-theological orientation was in part responsible for his dismissal from Arundel, and was that which he knew kept him from being sought after by other churches.[19]

His primary goal was to preach, and to preach in such a way that it would be life-transforming. This called for an integration of form and content, such that truth would be reflected in every way, regardless of literary convention or theological restrictiveness. Thus, in an age which called for much ornamentation, MacDonald advocated greater simplicity.[20] MacDonald's application of this seems questionable when the length of his books is evaluated, but in that way he does reflect consistency

Bordighera,' *Sunday Magazine*, 34 (April 1905): 401–5, cited in Rolland Hein, *George MacDonald: Victorian Mythmaker* (Nashville, TN, 1993), p. 395.

13 Ronald MacDonald, *From a Northern Window* (London, 1911), p. 67.

14 Reis, *MacDonald*, p. 47.

15 MacDonald, *Donal Grant* (London, 1884), p. 47; hereafter cited as *DG*.

16 D. Robb, *George MacDonald* (Edinburgh, 1987), p. 28.

17 *GMAW*, p. 320, and Robb, *MacDonald*, p. 28.

18 MacDonald, 'Letter of 4 November' (1850, to Charles from Arundel), cited in Muriel Hutton, 'The George MacDonald Collection,' *Yale University Library Gazette*, 51 (1976): 83.

19 'I know my ways of thinking as so very different from those of any churches, that, it is doubtful whether I shall ever find a church already formed that will choose me. If one should, I shall hold myself in readiness to be turned out very soon. At the same time as far as now shows itself to my mind, preaching is my work and preach I will somehow or other'; MacDonald, 'Letter to John Godwin' (24 June 1853), ALS Yale, cited in Raeper, *George MacDonald*, pp. 98–9.

20 See MacDonald, 'On Polish,' *A Dish of Orts* (Whitehorn, CA, 1996, orig. London, 1893), pp. 186–7; hereafter cited as *DO*.

with the literary conventions of his age. MacDonald did not want to sacrifice artistic quality, but his commitment to truth was primary.

Though he has been criticized for reasons of style and didacticism, those who are sympathetic and open to his message have praised him both for his content and his form. Thus, for example, A.J. Scott commented that his style was good, and that especially in *Phantastes* he used language which was of 'purity and delicate beauty.'[21] C.S. Lewis, though critical of MacDonald's writing as 'at times fumbling.' found that the novels' obviousness could be a devotional asset.[22] MacDonald is praised for his realism, which 'saved him from idealizing his characters,' kept him from overly villainizing others, and insured that he never lost sight of the common aspects of everyday life.[23]

Because of his imaginative style and methodology, MacDonald has been taken less seriously in theological than literary circles. For the systematic theologian, he is often perceived as not being systematic enough, and his imaginative approach is seen as having a weakening and sentimentalizing affect.[24] MacDonald was well versed in theology and understood 'all the great historical theological controversies, such that it would be quite easy to build up from his works a system of theology and ethics ....'[25] However, he was determined as much as possible to avoid mere abstraction, as truth for him was primarily a person, Jesus Christ, who established a condition of truth for people in terms of their entire being and relationships. 'In its deepest sense, *the truth* is a condition of heart, soul, mind, and strength towards God and towards our fellow – not an utterance, not even a *right* form of words; and therefore such truth coming forth in words is, in a sense, the person that speaks.'[26] The Truth of Christ was not something to debate, but something to 'be beheld.'[27] MacDonald staked his entire life on this Truth, and 'would rather die the death' than believe false notions about God.[28] He sought to communicate theological truth not just in words, but through his entire being. 'Maurice, Tennyson, and Carlyle proclaimed the writer as priest and prophet, but MacDonald *was* the writer as priest and prophet.[29]

---

21 A.J. Scott, 'Testimonials to George MacDonald,' for Candidate for Chair of English Edinburgh (Brander Library, Huntly, 1865), p. 32. See also F.D. Maurice, 'Testimonials to George MacDonald,' for Candidate for Chair of English Edinburgh (Brander Library, Huntly, 1865), p. 13; John Dyer, 'The New Novelist,' *The Penn Monthly Magazine*, I(6) (June 1870), pp. 217, 219, 220, cited in Phillips, *MacDonald*, p. 273.

22 Lewis, 'Preface,' *George MacDonald*, p. 14, and Catherine Durie, 'George MacDonald,' in W. Raeper (ed.), *The Gold Thread* (Edinburgh, 1990), pp. 165–6.

23 Mary McDermott Shideler, *George MacDonald* (Grand Rapids, MI, 1972), p. 2.

24 See Thomas Gunn Selby, cited in Robert Lee Wolff, *The Golden Key* (New Haven, CT, 1961), p. 259.

25 Joseph Johnson, *George MacDonald* (London, 1906), p. 80.

26 *US*, 1, p. 103.

27 *DO*, p. 205.

28 MacDonald, *Life Essential: The Hope of the Gospel*, ed. Rolland Hein (Wheaton, IL, 1974), pp. 35–6; hereafter cited as *HG*.

29 Wolff, *MacDonald*, p. 378.

MacDonald's ability to open windows theologically has been a common theme among those who know of his work. Thus is it said that 'He helped to enlarge the religious spirit of Scotland from the cage of a bitter if tonic Calvinism – and to set it free in the right direction.'[30] His is called 'a sunnier and less austere type of theology,'[31] one which 'did not let the devil have all the bright colours.'[32] Chesterton saw MacDonald standing for 'a rather important turning-point in the history of Christendom, as representing the particular Christian nation of the Scots. As Protestants speak of the morning stars of the Reformation, we may be allowed to note such names here and there as morning stars of the Reunion.'[33] The *Scotsman*, in 1857, states of MacDonald's writing: 'The dogmatist, if he lingers there, will find the tightly-wound coil of his prejudices unwinding he knows not how and the child-heart, somewhere hidden in the breast of every living man, awaken and yearn toward the truth.'[34]

He was able to open windows and soften prejudices because he had no interest in defending or in attacking systems. As Hein writes, 'he is singularly free from the cultic mentality.'[35] His supreme interest was in retaining faithfulness to the Truth, as had been revealed in Jesus Christ. His message was acclaimed by the Rt. Rev. Phillips Brooks as being 'a message from God' which stood out from all the other sermons he had heard. 'Here was a gospel. Here were real tidings, and you listened and forgot the preacher.'[36] John Ruskin commented about his *Unspoken Sermons*, Volume I: 'They are the best sermons – beyond all compare – I have ever read, and if ever sermons did good, these will.'[37]

MacDonald's vision of the Kingdom of God was pervasive in his life and in his work. The resonance of another realm can be felt in all that he wrote, not in a utopian or escapist manner, but in a way which is able to bring 'to life the latent desire of his readers to face up to reality.'[38] His son, Greville, calls it 'a singleness of vision' flowing from 'the open road between him and God.'[39] With this vision, everything has meaning and greater depth than what is readily observable.[40] As Chesterton remarked, MacDonald 'did really believe that people were princesses and goblins and good fairies, and he dressed them up as ordinary men and women.

---

30 H.J.C. Grierson, 'George MacDonald,' *The Aberdeen University Review*, 12(34) (1924), p. 12.
31 Harry Escott, *A History of Scottish Congregationalism* (Glasgow, 1960), p. 107.
32 G.K. Chesterton, Introduction to *GMAW*, p. 14.
33 Ibid., p. 13.
34 *The Scotsman* (12 August 1857); cited in *GMAW*, p. 281.
35 R. Hein, *The Harmony Within* (Grand Rapids, MI, 1982), p. 154
36 Phillips Brooks, *Lectures on Preaching* (1904), p. 16; cited in *GMAW*, p. 423.
37 John Ruskin, cited in *GMAW*, p. 337.
38 Elizabeth Saintsbury, *George MacDonald: A Short Life* (Edinburgh, 1987), p. 111.
39 *GMAW*, p. 378.
40 Chesterton called MacDonald 'a St. Francis of Aberdeen, seeing the same sort of halo round every flower and bird'; G.K. Chesterton in Introduction to *GMAW*, p. 14.

The fairy-tale was the inside of the ordinary story and not the outside.'[41] This vision made MacDonald very passionate about his work and his life, which overflowed in his writing and in his preaching.[42] It also challenged him to affirm in times of deep discouragement and in the most dire of circumstances that 'nothing will do ... but an absolute enthusiastic confidence in God.'[43]

MacDonald perceived and was able to convey the radical inversion of kingdom values. He willingly condemned riches, arguing that 'God will not give us little things to spoil our appetite for great things.'[44] He revealed a noble gentleman hidden in the circumstances of a pauper, or a fisherman. An old woman, who to some seems a witch, became the symbol of divine intervention and grace. 'It is so silly of people,' she tells Irene, 'to fancy that old age means crookedness and witheredness and feebleness and sticks and spectacles and rheumatism and forgetfulness ... The right old age means strength and beauty and mirth and courage and clear eyes and strong painless limbs.'[45] That which is seen as destructive (for example, the North Wind) is portrayed as that which nurtures and is life-giving. That which was considered foolish was shown to be true wisdom (for example, Diamond). His vision of the kingdom was so strong that C.S. Lewis claimed: 'radiance was incarnate in his work.'[46] It was so all-consuming for him that he had difficulty putting it into dry formulations: 'If it is true that we are made in the image of God then the paramount, absorbing business of our existence is to know that image of God in which we are made and to know it in the living Son of God, the one and only ideal Man. The older I grow, the more absolutely convinced I am of this; I have no words strong enough to put the statement in.'[47] That is why he chose to communicate this vision through narrative, poetry, hymns, sermons, so that it could be woven into the very fabric of life. It is possible to hear MacDonald speak through his characters as well as his non-fiction work, for he firmly believed that 'A man's own nature ... must lie at the heart of what he does.'[48]

It is not the object of this book to impose a system on his thoughts. Rather, the aim is to reveal in the midst of the inherent harmony of his work, MacDonald's own apprehension of the Eternal Word, along with some of the implications of this apprehension particularly for a theology of the imagination. Though 'he distrusted all

---

41   Ibid., p. 11. Cf. C.S. Lewis, 'The Weight of Glory,' in *The Weight of Glory and Other Addresses* (Grand Rapids, MI, 1975), p. 15

42   See Samuel McComb, *Preaching in Theory and Practice*, cited in *GMAW*, p. 49.

43   MacDonald, 'Letter to Ann Ross' (2 January 1856), cited in Raeper, *MacDonald*, p. 134. MacDonald struggled with doubts throughout his life, and at times felt desolate, but he saw these as times of growth, pushing him (like his novel character, Ian) onto the 'higher truth he was always seeking'; *WMM*, p. 62.

44   MacDonald, *Proving the Unseen*, ed. William Petersen (New York, 1989), p. 6.

45   MacDonald, *The Princess and the Goblin* (London, 1949), p. 106.

46   C.S. Lewis, cited in E. Saintsbury, *MacDonald*, p. 106.

47   MacDonald, *Proving the Unseen*, p. 12.

48   MacDonald, *Marquis of Lossie* (London, 1927, orig. 1877), p. 200; hereafter cited as *ML*.

abstract systems of thought, and he avoided systematizing his own ... his convictions are thoroughly consistent with each other, and quite comprehensive theologically.'[49] Simultaneously, the hope is to demonstrate the strength and legitimacy of his more imaginative approach to theological pursuit and communication. If there is merit in allowing Christ to be the systematizing center of one's theology in both content and imaginatively rich forms of communication, then it is worthwhile to attend to one who sought to order his ways and his writing by Christ.

In an effort to explore MacDonald's contributions as a theologian, seven specific areas out of many will be addressed. It is illuminating to understand the influences on his thinking which helped to shape him in a distinctive way. Chapter 1 will explore the early influences of Scottish Calvinism and his Celtic heritage. Second, much has been made of the influences of literary thinkers on MacDonald's literary approach, but far less of their impact on his theology. Thus, Chapter 2 will explore classic and literary writers who influenced both his theology of the imagination and his image-rich approach to theology. Third, the group of theologians whom MacDonald counted as among his closest and most respected friends, A.J. Scott, F.D. Maurice, and to a degree Thomas Erskine, have not been adequately considered in their pivotal relationship to MacDonald's theology. These influences will be addressed in Chapter 3.

Much of the reticence toward MacDonald theologically has derived from especially two areas which are viewed as controversial: his theology of the atonement and his theology of and incorporation of the imagination. Both of these areas have been used to discredit him as a theologian. Chapter 4 will present a discussion of MacDonald's theology of the imagination. Chapter 5 will deal with MacDonald's perspectives on the imagination and the way he used it to offer alternative visions of God, particularly through a reconsideration of the atonement. Finally, specific theological insights he gained from this basis which are relevant to his view of the nature of humanity will be discussed in Chapter 6, and to the issues of suffering, aging and death in Chapter 7.

Many factors make MacDonald a worthy subject for the series *Ashgate Studies in Theology, Imagination and the Arts*. One factor is his influence in the formation of significant Christian writers in both the nineteenth and twentieth centuries. In addition to C.S. Lewis, other writers such as G.K. Chesterton, Dorothy Sayers, J.R.R. Tolkien, W.H. Auden, and Frederick Buechner attribute to MacDonald key paradigm shifts and insights in their own lives.

A second factor is that his prophetic voice resonates with many contemporary concerns, and he demonstrates ways to address these concerns both imaginatively and with theological acumen. These prophetic insights are explored in this book, including:

- his embrace of the imagination as a gift from God that is able to receive and communicate theological truth

---

49 Hein, *The Harmony Within* (1982), p. 25.

- his discernment about ways to detect and challenge distortions of the imagination
- the way in which form and content were harmonious in his work
- his balanced portrayal of God, using both masculine and feminine imagery anchored firmly to God's self-revelation in Jesus Christ
- his relatively egalitarian thoughts about women and their capabilities
- his willingness to combine deep conviction and love of God in Jesus Christ with openness to learn from people of all traditions
- the challenge of his teaching about money and his actual lifestyle in times of relentless poverty which were expressions of total dependence on God for his daily bread (and for the sustenance of his wife and 11 children)
- his attitudes about creation and the call for Christians to honor God's gift to us of the natural world
- his wisdom about aging, suffering, and death
- the utter confidence in God which framed his thinking about all of theology and all of life.

A third factor is the value of a book which examines intensively the life and thought of one individual. Intrinsic to artistic expression is 'the scandal of particularity' – the way in which the particular can convey universal insight. Intrinsic to Christian theology is the recognition that truth is personal and relational. MacDonald can be seen as an icon who through his life and work opens a window to the intersection of word, flesh and image. He communicated the gospel through narrative and image-rich forms which honor truth and address the intellectual, imaginative, spiritual, and emotional needs of his readers. It is appropriate in a series on 'Theology, Imagination and the Arts' to explore through MacDonald the way in which the imagination calls 'old bones' to new life, so that people can feel the impact of truth that is embodied in metaphors, parables, persons, and narratives. Obviously his work is anchored in a particular context, and while conveying far-reaching insight, also reflects idiosyncrasies of his age. A study of MacDonald thus offers not a formulaic approach to theology and the imagination, but the possibility of gleaning from his rich harvest relevant nourishment for our own day. It also provides a context in which to assess potential weaknesses in imaginative approaches to theology.

Chapter 1

Calvinist and Celtic: MacDonald's Context and Early Influences

It is a law with us that no one shall sing a song who cannot
be the hero of his tale, who cannot live the song he sings.[1]

George MacDonald did not consider himself heroic, but he did aim for consistency between his life and the truth of his 'tales.' He struggled to discern the very nature of truth, which for him centered on the question 'Who is God?' His struggle was intensified by the divergent views of God presented to him, and the conflicting implications of these views for the arts and for life itself.

Two dominant and polar forces are reflected throughout his writing. These can largely be traced to the Federal Calvinism of his context and the Celtic influences of his Gaelic heritage. MacDonald wrestled deeply with their differing views of God. Though he came to conclusions that were out of step with his age, he believed them to be grounded in scripture, ancient tradition, his own heritage, and the presence and nature of Jesus Christ. Rejected by many for his alternate vision, he was also heralded as a prophet of challenge and liberation. Because MacDonald was willing to wrestle and persevere regardless of the cost, his life and theology were forged in the fires of both suffering and faith. Thus it has been said: 'MacDonald's work is the best revelation of his character. He has lived the songs he sang. He is the best he wrote.'[2]

This chapter will explore MacDonald's life and the early influences that shaped him into the person, writer, and theologian that he became. MacDonald was grateful for his heritage, and wrote: 'Surely it is one of the worst sins of a man to turn his back upon the rock whence he was hewn.'[3] The first section will explore Federal Calvinism, which provided the early scaffolding of his faith. Aspects of this tradition remained vital to MacDonald, while others felt like a cage from which he yearned to escape. The second section will explore his Celtic heritage which inspired him to discover truth indigenous to his Gaelic roots. The polar influences of Calvinist

---

1   George MacDonald, from The Parable of the Singer, 'Within and Without,' *The Poetical Works of George MacDonald* (2 vols., London, 1893), Vol. 1, p. 52; hereafter cited as *PW*.

2   Johnson, *George MacDonald*, p. 277.

3   MacDonald, 'Written in reply to a review printed in The Spectator' (11 July 1867), in Glenn Sadler (ed.), *An Expression of Character: The Letters of George MacDonald* (Grand Rapids, MI, 1994), p. 159; hereafter cited as *EC*.

and Celtic thought created a faith crisis for MacDonald which peaked during his university years and led him to a renewed vision of Jesus Christ. His discovery of Christ at the heart of all things and the impact of this discovery on his life and understanding of the nature of truth will be discussed in the third section. Integral to Celtic thought is a sacramental perspective which is willing to honor truth from a variety of cultures, artistic sources, and from nature. Thus Chapter 2 will go on to explore those influences which MacDonald embraced from Classic, British Literary and European theological and literary sources, respectively.

1. Federal Calvinist Influences

George MacDonald was born in 1824 in Huntly, a town in northeast Scotland. Though he was proud of the Celtic heritage of his clan, he acknowledged his birthplace as a 'border region in which the tide of Gaelic had ebbed away.'[4] He was the second of five surviving sons, and his mother died when he was eight years old. With her death, his paternal grandmother assumed a dominant role in his life. She represents one major pole in his religious education, that of a more rigid Federal Calvinism reinforced by his Church, the predominant culture, and his primary school teacher.

Federal Calvinism had developed from Calvinist theology in the late sixteenth and seventeenth centuries, and became a dominant expression of Christianity in Scotland. The word 'federal' derived from the emergent political philosophy of the day which affirmed that a contract (*foedus*) between the sovereign ruler and his/her constituents could ensure greater freedom.[5] A contractual perspective shaped the way the biblical term 'covenant' came to be viewed. Rather than understanding covenant to be rooted in God's unconditional love for humanity, it was perceived as more contractual. The obligations flowing from grace came to be seen as the conditions of grace. Thus, rather than affirming God as the Father who loves all of humanity and who freely forgives all through Jesus Christ, Federal Calvinists believed that God's love and forgiveness had to be purchased by the payment of Christ's sufferings on the Cross. God, as the ultimate monarch, was sovereign over all things and had chosen to love only the elect. Thus Christ's death purchased forgiveness for the elect alone.

This first pole of influence in MacDonald's life had a duality about it which is obvious in his work. He felt the need to distinguish between the 'faith … found in the old Scottish manse,' with which he had 'true sympathy,' and 'many of the forms gathered around that faith' which he opposed.[6] Thus this first pole includes both those aspects of Federal Calvinism that he absorbed as implicit pillars of strength in his faith and those which he explicitly and continually challenged. The latter aspects involved belief in a God of wrath who from all eternity had arbitrarily chosen to

---

4   Ibid., p. 159.
5   For further study, read James B. Torrance, 'Introduction,' in John McLeod Campbell, *The Nature of the Atonement* (6th edn., Grand Rapids, MI, 1996).
6   'Letter to an Unknown Lady' (1866), in *EC*, p. 153.

damn some to eternal punishment and elect others for salvation. The only way one could know where one stood in this selection process was to examine one's life for evidences of being among the elect. Thus, though salvation was understood as a gift of unmerited grace, works were the way one might confirm one's election. This produced a great sobriety in religion that distrusted the imagination, frowned on the arts (especially theater and music) and enforced a strict Sabbatarianism.

MacDonald's grandmother epitomized this perspective for him, for she was a staunch Federal Calvinist who had a fiery personality and believed intensely in a severe, wrathful God. MacDonald later came to question how much her view of God correlated with God's self-revelation in Jesus Christ. She burned the contents of the old MacDonald family chest because it contained remnants of the family's Catholic heritage. She also burned her son's fiddle, condemning it as a satanic snare. MacDonald portrayed aspects of his own grandmother in the novels *Robert Falconer* and *What's Mine's Mine*.[7] Though he grieved the lack of joy that he saw in his grandmother, he readily acknowledged warmth coming from her faith, especially in her response to the needy.

MacDonald's autobiographic allusions through Robert Falconer convey his hunger throughout his early years for light and for windows to let in fresh air. MacDonald's early education contributed to this feeling of being enclosed, for his primary school teacher, Colin Stewart, was also a rigid Federal Calvinist. Stewart forced his students to memorize the catechism from the Westminster Confession (1647) and recite it on Saturday mornings. If they failed, they were kept from going out to play and would instead have to remain under his eagle eye until they mastered the required material. Stewart's punishments were so fierce that MacDonald's younger brother's death was linked with one of his whippings. The teacher in *Alec Forbes* (Murdoch Malison) is created after MacDonald's memory of Colin Stewart.

MacDonald did not find the worship in Federal Calvinist churches particularly inspiring. He observed: 'One grand aim of the reformers of the Scottish ecclesiastical modes, appears to have been to keep the worship pure and the worshippers sincere, by embodying the whole in the ugliest forms that could be associated with the name of Christianity.'[8] Church itself was 'weariness to every inch of flesh upon his bone.'[9] People hurried from the church when the service was over 'as if they could not possibly endure one word more.'[10] A strict Sabbatarianism prevailed such that 'the sending out of a child to fetch milk on a Sunday morning was condemned – and while Sunday walking may have been disapproved of by other churches, among the Missionars it was absolutely forbidden.'[11] He is able to joke about it in his novels.

---

7   *Robert Falconer* is fairly autobiographical about MacDonald's earlier years and his struggles with Federal Calvinism.

8   MacDonald, *David Elginbrod* (London, 1863), p. 36; hereafter cited as *DE*.

9   MacDonald, *Robert Falconer* (London, n.d., orig. 1868), p. 274; hereafter cited as *RF*.

10 MacDonald, *Alec Forbes of Howglen* (London, n.d., orig. 1865), p. 168; hereafter cited as *AF*.

11 Raeper, *MacDonald*, p. 26.

One of his characters who is criticized for picking a flower on the Sabbath justifies his action on the basis of the flower's own defiance of the day. 'To think o' a weyd like that prankin' itself' oot in its purple and its spots upo' the Sawbath day!'[12] Yet MacDonald saw it as a heavy and grievous burden to bear, which affected him throughout his life: 'such an embodiment of profound but sad peace as in my mind will more or less for ever be associated with a Scotch Sunday.'[13]

His own particular ecclesiastical experience derived initially from a Missionar Kirk in Huntly, which had seceded from the established Church of Scotland in 1733. The Missionar Church expressed a vision for reaching out both in overseas and home missions. Its zealousness, according to David Robb, instilled in MacDonald 'his fervent outreach to all men, the evangelistic spirit in which he wrote, and his sense of the ideal Christian community – small, organically alive.'[14] However, one of the central issues which MacDonald continually confronted was the distortion he saw in the Calvinism of his youth, particularly what he saw as a warped, almost manicheistic view of God and hell.

The Scottish Calvinism of MacDonald's youth remained a lingering presence in his life and theology, like gray fog resting on the North Sea. In part he struggled to distinguish between Calvin's theology and subsequent Federal Calvinism.[15] Though 'Calvin's theological centre is Christ and union with Christ,' later Calvinists such as Beza and Perkins became preoccupied with God's election and sovereignty.[16] They downplayed Calvin's emphasis on God's loving, rational will, and instead emphasized God's will as power and arbitrariness toward God's fallen creatures. The atonement was interpreted in forensic terms. The holiness of God combined with the total depravity of humanity required the sacrifice of Christ, before God's wrath against sin could be appeased and humanity could be forgiven. Jesus was conveyed as the legal means by which the elect escape punishment, though not necessarily the revelation of God's character and nature. Thus the grandmother in *Robert Falconer* explains: 'But laddie, he cam to saitisfee God's justice by sufferin' the punishment due to oor sins; to turn aside his wrath an' curse; to reconcile him to us. Sae he cudna be a'thegither like God.'[17] MacDonald would later describe Federal Calvinism as a 'theology which crushed the hearts of men by attributing injustice to their God.'[18]

---

12 *AF*, p. 375. Cf. *DE*, p. 36.

13 MacDonald, *Castle Warlock* (London, n.d., orig. 1882), p. 273; hereafter cited as *CW*. Cf. *AF*, p. 377.

14 Ibid., p. 8.

15 For example: 'The cause of this degeneracy they share in common with the followers of all other great men as well as of Calvin. They take up what their leader, urged by the necessity of the time, spoke loudest, never heeding what he loved most; and then work the former out to a logical perdition of everything belonging to the latter.' See *DE*, p. 37.

16 Roger Newell, 'Participatory Knowledge,' Vol. 1, unpublished Ph.D. Thesis (Aberdeen, 1983), pp. 39, 40.

17 *RF*, p. 354.

18 MacDonald, *Paul Faber Surgeon* (Whitethorn, CA, 1998, orig. London, 1879), pp. 50–51; hereafter cited as *PF*.

Through the *fencing of the table*, only those whose lives demonstrated evidence of salvation were allowed to participate in Communion. The need for signs of salvation weighed heavily on MacDonald when young and upon first becoming a Church member. 'I consented but with fear & trembling ... I do not think Christ will allow me to go to his table unworthily although I should not have come forward so soon had not the Dr. [Morison] urged me ... My greatest difficulty always is "How do I know that my faith is of a lasting kind and such as will produce fruits."'[19]

The Scots Confession (1560), which he was forced to memorize along with the Westminster Confession, was crucial to many positive aspects of MacDonald's later faith. 'We confess and acknawledge ane onelie God, to whom onelie we must cleave, whom onelie we must serve, whom onelie we must worship, and in whom onelie we must put our trust ....' MacDonald was molded by this assertion of the uniqueness and the utter sovereignty of God, who alone deserves human devotion. Furthermore, its statement of acknowledging God rather than conceiving God pointed MacDonald early in life toward a humble approach of receiving God's revelation rather than a dogmatic one claiming full comprehension. MacDonald adopted wholeheartedly the confession's emphasis on God's gracious initiative, the radical distinction between Creator and creature,[20] and the utter rejection of all idols, including the most insistent one – the self.

The priority given to God in all things held him fast against the full tide of Romanticism, and Cartesian self-assertion, which Barth would claim 'failed to hear the warning of the Reformed confession ... and has thought fit to exchange the mediaeval conception of the world as geocentric for the much more naive conception of the world as anthropocentric.'[21] In addition, it urged in MacDonald a hunger to know this one and only God and the freedom to challenge any system which would set itself up as absolute. MacDonald found any airtight theological system suspect, like 'a vault of stone around the theorist whose very being yet depends on room to grow.'[22]

Though MacDonald would reject some of the basic tenets of Federal Calvinism, its lasting influence, he felt, was preferable to paganism: 'Surely it is something more to stand with Moses upon Mount Sinai, and see the back of God through ever so many folds of cloudy darkness, than to be sitting down to eat and drink, or rising up to play about the golden calf, at the foot of the mountain.'[23] He saw the value of this faith even in his own grandmother, who in addition to raising nine children of her own, also adopted four beggar children.[24] MacDonald retained belief in God's

---

19 'Letter to his father' (8 November 1845), in *EC*, p. 11.
20 See MacDonald, 'The Imagination: Its Functions and its Culture,' in *DO*, pp. 1–42.
21 Karl Barth, *The Knowledge of God and the Service of God*, trans. J.L.M. Haire and Ian Henderson (London, 1938), in R. Ellmann and C. Feidelson (eds), *The Modern Tradition* (New York, 1965), p. 942.
22 MacDonald, *Malcolm* (London, 1887, orig. 1875), p. 296.
23 *AF*, p. 111.
24 See Kathy Triggs, *The Stars and the Stillness: A Portrait of George MacDonald* (Cambridge, 1986), p. 4.

sovereignty and supreme wisdom, both of which were instilled in him through his Calvinistic training. Because of these influences in his theology, MacDonald emphasized the need to face and eradicate sin from one's life. Thus he avoided the common pitfall of cheap grace in which one embraces unconditional grace without the corollary of unconditional obedience.[25]

2. Celtic Heritage

If his grandmother signifies the Federal Calvinist pole, the other pole of MacDonald's life is characterized by his father. George MacDonald, Sr. is portrayed as wise, loving, and merciful. C.S. Lewis described MacDonald's relationship with his father as 'almost perfect.'[26] MacDonald wondered how the Creator and Redeemer could be described by the Church as less loving and just than his own father seemed to be. Thus, as a child he began to associate God with his father's character more than with the wrathful God of his catechesis. He agonized to think of God as a tyrant supremely concerned about God's own glory and thus establishing a system of limited atonement.[27] Certainly his father was more mature and caring than that. In *Weighed and Wanting* he describes feeling as a child that he preferred for God not to love him unless God also loved all people in the same way.[28]

MacDonald's father also embodied many attributes associated with Celtic Christianity. He affirmed an egalitarianism which bred generosity toward all people and a desire for unity rather than sectarianism within the Church. Thus MacDonald wrote: 'I find my Scotch clannishness a most elastic material, & think of it as only one form of a rudimental form of love to all men.'[29] George Sr.'s emphasis on cooperation rather than competitiveness was based on confidence that Truth would prevail, and it strengthened MacDonald to rise above controversy and debate: 'There is no triumph for the Truth but that [the enlightenment of souls to see the truth]. She knows no glorying over the vanquished, for in her victory the vanquished is already of the vanquishers.'[30]

George, Sr. embraced the mystery of the gospel. He rejected the extreme points of both Calvinism and Arminianism along with the tendency to tear the gospel 'to

---

25 James Hogg wrote a parody on the way a Federal Calvinist perspective at times led to expressions of cheap grace; *The Private Memoirs and Confessions of a Justified Sinner* (London, 1926 edn), p. 24.

26 Lewis, *George MacDonald: An Anthology*, p. 10.

27 James Torrance points out that 'not all federal theologians taught this doctrine of God,' as is evident in the work of Robert Rollock in 1596. Even so, 'within a few years limited atonement became the widely accepted federal view in Scotland'; James Torrance, 'The Incarnation and 'Limited Atonement,' *Evangelical Quarterly*, 55 (1983): 83–94.

28 MacDonald, *Weighed and Wanting* (London, 1882), p. 20.

29 'Letter to Josiah Holland' (27 May 1851), in *EC*, p. 176.

30 *DE*, p. 335. George MacDonald, Sr. is the model for the character David Elginbrod; see *GMAW*, p. 323.

pieces by those who believe there is no mystery in the Scriptures and therefore attempt to explain away what is evidently for the hour of God to conceal.'[31] Thus it is no surprise to read his son George's subsequent letter to him claiming, 'I am neither Arminian nor Calvinist ....'[32] George Sr.'s openness to learn from others, including those he called 'the new faith folks,' and his deep confidence in God were obvious influences on MacDonald, and are expressed in all of his writing.[33] The 'new faith folks,' one of whom preached near Huntly, gave MacDonald hope that one could see more than just the back of God on Mt. Sinai. Their affirmation of the universal atonement of Christ would have profound significance in MacDonald's ability to trust and devote his life to God.

Throughout MacDonald's work, one hears echoes of his father's hopeful faith, 'We have ground for confidence in our God, the author of all blessings that He who spared not His only son, but delivered him up to the death for us all, will with Him also *freely give us all things.*'[34] Much of the colorfulness of MacDonald's youth, evident in a panoply of later illustrations, is due to the liberality of his father, whom he said gave him all that he asked for and of whom he writes:

Thou hast been faithful to my highest need ...
Yet most I thank thee, not for any deed,
But for the sense thy living self did breed
Of fatherhood still at the great world's core.[35]

Greville MacDonald summarized the Celtic influences in his father's life: 'George MacDonald inherited all the characteristic virtues; and the clan-system, a social law built upon Faith rather than Competition, may in large measure explain his rooted fidelity to God and man.'[36] Greville also attributed to the Celtic tradition MacDonald's 'devotion to the soil, his love of liberty, his intolerance of injustice, his eloquence and love of learning.'[37] The Celtic love of the poetic was part of his inheritance as well, and he expressed great pride in the Bardic traditions which communicated history, law, and worship in verse.[38] MacDonald observes: 'For had not Scotland a living literature, and that a high one, when England could produce none, or next to

---

31 George MacDonald, Sr., 'Letter to His Son, George' (Huntly, 31 May 1850), in *EC*, p. 34.
32 MacDonald, 'Letter to His Father' (Arundel, 15 April 1851), in *EC*, p. 51.
33 George MacDonald, Sr., 'Letter to His Son George' (Huntly, 31 May 1850), in *EC*, p. 34.
34 George MacDonald, Sr., 'Letter to His Son George' (Huntly, 24 May 1850), in *EC.*, p. 34.
35 *PW*, 1, p. 134.
36 *GMAW*, p. 39. Cf. 'Letter to his Father' (5 April 1853), in *EC*, p. 57.
37 *GMAW*, p. 39.
38 See ibid., p. 38.

none – I mean in the fifteenth century?'[39] Thus MacDonald claimed 'to be proud of my Celtic birth,' and included numerous references to things Celtic in his writing.[40]

The Celtic sensitivity to the supernatural can be seen as shaping some of MacDonald's interests and writing. He alluded many times to the belief in 'Kelpies,' Scottish spirits or demons, and to the Celtic 'second sight' which his own father was said to have experienced.[41] For a time he was drawn into Professor Gregory's interest in spiritualism and mesmerism at the University of Aberdeen. However, he concluded that dabbling in occult practices was something to be avoided, whereas 'second sight' was more of a pure gift.[42] Mechanical manipulations of spirituality were disdainful to MacDonald, who valued so highly the freedom of the will in submission to the *Chief* alone.

Many themes that are part of Celtic Christian tradition emerge in MacDonald's stories and sermons. A central theme is of pilgrimage in which the protagonist moves from a flattened and enclosed worldview to a more sacramental embrace of life and creation. Like Celtic heroes, called *peregrini*, the wanderer commits to a living martyrdom by leaving kin and relinquishing security and control.[43] Ultimately the living martyrdom in MacDonald's Celtic-like stories includes a willingness to die to oneself for the sake of others. Through dying to oneself, one develops the character and strength to be a true witness (*martyr*) to the nature of love which is at the heart of the universe.

Whether Irene or Curdie in the *Princess* books, Anodos in *Phantastes*, Vane in *Lilith*, or Robert Falconer, to name just a few examples, MacDonald's protagonists often gain some form of Celtic sacramental vision. They perceive meaning and music in nature they have not previously noted. They grasp the interrelatedness of all of creation, and see beauty at the heart of all things. They experience a baptism of sorts from a feminine personage, which cleanses, heals, and engenders joy in living. And through the pilgrimage of relinquishment, suffering, and 'death,' these heroes and heroines experience an enlivening of imagination that leads to greater empathy with others, along with greater creativity and courage in the face of need. Such Celtic Christian perspectives as the feminine characteristics of the divine, the value of beauty and the arts, the importance of the Trinity, the dignity and worth of the stranger, the significance of community, and a love of God's creation are evident throughout MacDonald's work.

---

39 *AF*, p. 107.

40 MacDonald, 'Written in reply to a review printed in The Spectator,' in *EC*, p. 159.

41 'Book of the Day: *George MacDonald. A Centenary Volume*,' *London Times* (20 May 1924), p. 10.

42 See David Robb, 'George MacDonald and Animal Magnetism,' *Seven: An Anglo-American Literary Review*, Vol. 8 (1987), p. 10. *DE*, pp. 323–4.

43 Celtic heroes like St. Patrick, St. Columcille, and St. Ninian were people of pilgrimage, called *peregrini*, who left the land they loved to carry the love of God to a new region. According to John M. Jones, the phenomenon of Celtic pilgrimage abroad was curtailed by the late eighth century, after which the emphasis became more the 'pilgrimage of the heart'; see J.M. Jones, *With an Eagle's Eye* (Notre Dame, IN, 1998), p. 83.

MacDonald loved Scotland and pined for even its least desirable season when in Italy: 'Oh, that awful gray and white Scotch winter – dear to my heart as I sit and write with windows wide open to the blue skies of Italy's December!'[44] Though for health reasons he was not able to spend much of his adult life there, some of his best novels are the Scottish novels. The inclusion of much Scottish dialect was justified on the basis of its greater vitality and proximity to reality.[45] Chesterton saw the national character of the Scottish as vivid and colorful, 'intensely romantic and passionate.'[46] One perceives this influence in MacDonald's willingness to express greater literary freedom than many of his contemporaries in depicting romance and in including sexual allusions.[47]

The second Celtic pole was somewhat threatened by MacDonald's early education in Federal Calvinism. Chesterton noted the irony of the Calvinist and Celtic conjunction of thought in Scotland. In spite of their colorful heritage, 'by a queer historical accident … [they] have been forced to "wear their blacks" in a sort of endless funeral on an eternal Sabbath.'[48] MacDonald himself marked this paradox, writing that 'dear old Scotland … has the sweetest songs in its cottages and worst singing in its churches, of any country in the world.'[49]

3. Christ the Center

University in Aberdeen was a time of deep wrestling for MacDonald. The polarities of Calvinism and Celtic Christianity in his childhood left him with many questions. His education was rigorous, with three hours a day of Greek and one hour of Latin in addition to other courses. Though his major studies were primarily in the area of Natural Philosophy, much of his time was spent in spiritual turmoil.

Theological turmoil was brewing around him. One of the *new faith folks*, James Morison, had come to believe in universal atonement through the reading of 1 Corinthians 15:3–4. Morison was expelled from the Church with his father and two others in 1843.[50] Kennedy, MacDonald's minister while at the University of Aberdeen at Blackfriars Church, was very critical of the Morisonion movement. Kennedy mentored MacDonald, exposing him to urban ministry and to his first experience of large-city squalor and poverty. He trained him to teach in his Sunday

---

44 *CW*, p. 65.

45 See ibid., p. 115, and Raeper, *George MacDonald*, p. 192.

46 G.K. Chesterton, 'Introduction,' in *GMAW*, p. 13.

47 *Phantastes* and *Lilith* are very striking examples of this, but it is also evident in his novels, in which sensual allusions to ankles, feet, and hands are common.

48 Chesterton, 'Introduction,' *GMAW*, p. 13.

49 *DE*, p. 294.

50 Raeper, *George MacDonald*, p. 51.

School for eight hundred children. Yet when MacDonald's Morisonian leanings were discovered, he was denied further responsibility with the ministry.[51]

In the midst of many questions and doubts, MacDonald took long lonely walks along the Aberdeen coastline with the wind and the North Sea to heighten his sense of the world around him. He prayed fervently that he would know the true character of the living God.[52] The fog finally lifted for him through reading the New Testament and focusing on the person of Jesus. He encountered Jesus as the true revelation of God's nature. He rejoiced to discover that Jesus did not come to purchase but to express God's love for humanity.[53] MacDonald describes the theological development of an old minister in *Paul Faber Surgeon*, which resembles his own spiritual evolution:

> He sought [Jesus'] presence, and found Him; began to think less of books and rabbis, yea even, for the time, of Paul and Apollos and Cephas, and to pore and ponder over the living tale of the New Covenant; began to feel that the Lord meant what He said, and that His apostles also meant what He said; forgot Calvin a good deal, outgrew the influences of Jonathan Edwards, and began to understand Jesus Christ.[54]

In contrast to his Calvinist training, he came to see that God's grace in creation and redemption was more determinative ultimately than the fall. Human depravity was no longer the defining reality of life and faith, for he saw Christ as the Alpha and Omega who created all things in grace, defeated sin and death on the Cross, and is at work to bring all people into God's redeeming and transforming love. He wrote to his father: 'Can anyone fear the wrath of God, who really believes that he is one with that only Saviour?'[55]

MacDonald's sense of God's redeeming love greatly impacted his perspective on nature and the arts. He wrote a letter to his father saying: 'One of my greatest difficulties in consenting to think of religion was that I thought I should have to give up my beautiful thoughts and love for the things God has made.'[56] However, in reading his Bible he came to see that Christ, the source of all, could use all things to draw people to himself. 'If [the gospel of Christ] be true, everything in the universe is glorious, except sin.' Thus he went on in his letter, 'I love my Bible more – I am always finding out something new in it – I seem to have had everything to learn over again from the beginning all my teaching in youth seems useless to me – I must get it all from the Bible again.'[57] Rather than viewing the imagination and the arts

---

51 See ibid., pp. 51–2, and also *Huntly Express* (6 October 1905). Greville describes the Morisonian influence as 'the offer of release from some of their mental chains … greatly to Dr. Kennedy's concern'; *GMAW*, p. 79.

52 Raeper, *George MacDonald*, pp. 41–54, and Phillips, *George MacDonald*, pp. 99–136.

53 See Phillips, *George MacDonald*, pp. 124–36.

54 *PF*, p. 52.

55 MacDonald, 'Letter to His Father' (8 February 1855), in *EC*, p. 84.

56 MacDonald, 'Letter to GMD senior' (11 April 1847), ALS Yale, in Raeper, *George MacDonald*, p. 237. Cf. Colossians 1:15–20.

57 Raeper, *George MacDonald*, p. 237.

as satanic snares, MacDonald began to consider them as intimately connected with God's good creation. As will become apparent, he not only saw the imagination's potential to harmonize with God's creative ways, but also to convey something of God's nature.

Over the next few years, MacDonald's vocation gradually took shape. He had initially wanted to become a doctor, but his family's finances were insufficient. While tutoring in London, he felt called to pastoral ministry. He desired to help others experience the lifting of the darkness that he had experienced and to know that 'the difficulties I met with in the bible – were phantoms and no realities in themselves.'[58] It was at this time that he also met his future wife, Louisa. After studying for the ministry at Highbury College, he accepted his first church at Arundel in England. Before he could start, he almost died of pneumonia, yet he faced this with both humility and determination. In a letter to his father, he wrote:

> All that I know is that when I have work to do, I will try to do it with God's help, and then if I fail, it is not my fault. But I am not unhappy about it … Perhaps such attacks might come and go … for some years. But I have no idol of chance, as many Christians seem to have. All will be well with me. I know you would give me my heart's desire if you could. And I know God is better than you - and it was Christ himself that taught us to call him Father. If I were to die tomorrow, I would thank God for what I have had, for he has blessed me very abundantly: I could say 'I have lived.'[59]

MacDonald recovered for the most part from this attack, but his lungs were a source of struggle and weakness for him throughout his life. Still he was able to embark on his ministry call to Arundel. His theological perspectives were somewhat at odds with his congregation, and thus he was not able to sustain this position beyond three years.[60] The rest of his life, he earned his living by teaching, occasional preaching, writing, and odd jobs. The imagination became his ally in communicating theological ideas that had been rejected when preached directly. Novels and stories became his pulpit through which he could fulfill his call to preach the good news of Jesus Christ.[61] Endeavoring to support 11 children became very trying, for MacDonald was often ill, and his family was frequently near utter poverty.

There were times when he vacillated in his faith with periods of intense doubting and 'a considerable depression of spirits.'[62] For the most part, he sought to have as the core of his entire life the reality of God as his Father who was utterly to be trusted.

---

58 MacDonald, unpublished testimonial as part of his application to Highbury College, London (8 August 1848), in *EC*, p. 23.

59 *GMAW*, p. 147.

60 The Church's objections to MacDonald included his hope that eternal life could extend to animals and salvation to the heathen after their death, his willingness to challenge parishioners about 'mammon-worship and cruelty,' his teaching on Sabbath-keeping, and his being tainted by German thought; *GMAW*, pp. 156–7, 177–81. See also MacDonald, *What's Mine's Mine* (London, 1883), p. 61; hereafter cited as *WMM*.

61 See MacDonald, 'Letter to his father' (Manchester, 17 October 1853), in *EC*, p. 67.

62 MacDonald, 'Letter to Mrs. A.J. Scott' (27 May 1851), *EC*, p. 52.

MacDonald clung to the belief that God would, in love and justice, use everything in his life to make him more like Jesus. Thus, through extreme poverty, the death of four children, and professional rejection, he was able to express the humility of a child longing to hold firmly and trustingly to the Father's hand. He remained grateful that God was holding fast to him to lead him through the trials and to use them all for good. At some points his family was in such poverty that they literally did not know how they would obtain their next meal. As a way of earning money and also that they might minister to others as a family, the plays which they had enacted for their own pleasure, such as *Macbeth* and *Pilgrim's Progress*, became productions under the direction of Louisa, MacDonald's wife. The MacDonalds became a drama troupe in their own right, performing in Britain and in Italy, where they lived in part because of MacDonald's health problems.[63]

He could condemn all expressions of anxiety with credibility for he had much cause for anxiety in his life had he submitted to the tyranny of circumstances. 'His peace of mind came from resting in the Holy Present not any kind of escapism,' wrote C.S. Lewis.[64] He loved all of life, and reveled in the beauty of nature, song, and friendships; and because he lived with such open hands, even in poverty his home was open to all. He was deeply opposed to all expressions of materialism, greed, and hoarding:

> The heart of man cannot hoard. His brain or his hand may gather into its box and hoard, but the moment the thing has passed into the box, the heart has lost it and is hungry again. If a man would have, it is the Giver he must have ... Therefore all that He makes must be free to come and go through the heart of His child; he can enjoy it only as it passes, can enjoy only its life, its soul, its vision, its meaning, not itself.[65]

Though he loved finery (he was known in college to dress rather colorfully and elegantly) and things of beauty, he could not understand how one could intelligently choose material possessions over following Jesus, and he was clear that one had to choose. This was not much of a contest for MacDonald, as he believed that 'God is so beautiful, and so patient, and so loving, and so generous that he is the heart & soul & rock of every love & every kindness & every gladness in the world. All the beauty of the world ... comes out of his heart first.'[66]

His contributions were manifold. He wrote over fifty books (including novels, poetical works, books of sermons, and theology). Through his writing he endeavored to show forth the greatness of God and the impact God could have on individual

---

63 For a thorough description of the MacDonald performances of *Pilgrim's Progress*, see Rachel Johnson, 'Pilgrims: The MacDonalds and John Bunyan's The Pilgrim's Progress,' *North Wind*, 21 (2002), pp 15–25.

64 Lewis, *George MacDonald: An Anthology*, pp. 13–14.

65 George MacDonald, *The Seaboard Parish* (Whitethorn, CA, 1995, orig. 1868), p. 443; hereafter cited as *SP*.

66 MacDonald, 'Letter to His Daughter, Mary Josephine MacDonald' (3 August 1869), in *EC*, p. 170.

lives. He endeavored to draw people into a hunger for goodness, for holiness, for communion with their Father and with one another, and for the window of their lives to open to the fullness of God's gift of life to them.

In addition, he was involved in social reform with John Ruskin and Octavia Hill, who endeavored to improve housing in the tenement areas of London, and to enable success in job training and procurement. MacDonald and some of his children would visit, speak, and perform musically for groups of people in these areas, as well as invite them into his own home. His inside knowledge of such situations is evident in *Robert Falconer* and *Weighed and Wanting*.

His deep commitment to the idea that God would be Father to all people urged him into activity not only with the poor, but also with women's causes. MacDonald held a fairly egalitarian approach, which cohered with the Celtic Christian traditions of his ancestry. He felt women should receive proper education and in fact taught in a ladies' college, convinced that women should be free and responsive to God's call for their lives as well.[67]

In his seventies he determined to keep his mind active and to distract himself from the constant physical discomfort he felt, so he established a regime of reading, including Spanish, Italian, Dutch, and German as well as English.[68] He lived until he was 81 years old, hungering at the end to join his deceased wife and children, and most of all to meet the Father of his being. Thus he wrote in *Diary of an Old Soul*:

> Lord, till I meet thee thus, life is delayed;
> I am not I until that morning breaks,
> Not I until my consciousness eternal wakes.[69]

MacDonald's son, Ronald, wrote: 'There has probably never been a writer whose work was a better expression of his personal character.'[70] The polar influences of his early life stretched him into prophetic greatness, for it helped him to focus his primary attention on Jesus Christ and to hold fast to the priority of seeking to know God in accordance with divine self-revelation. He was likened to St. John, for:

> There was in him that gentleness and humanity and strength - a depth of fire below the surface in spite of all his sweetness - that I fancy were characteristics of the disciple Jesus loved ... I saw, I felt, his holiness and nearness to God, and yet I should not have been afraid to confess to him most secret sins ... He would not cast me out ... I can hear him now. But after all, whatever help or comfort any one may try to give you, it is but to follow

---

67 Ironically, only MacDonald's sons received a formal education, which may have been due to financial constraints.

68 Kathy Triggs, *The Stars and the Stillness: A Portrait of George MacDonald* (Cambridge, 1986), p. 157.

69 George MacDonald, *A Book of Strife in the Form of a Diary of An Old Soul*, 28 December (London, 1882), p. 263; hereafter cited as *DOS*.

70 Ronald MacDonald, 'George MacDonald, a Personal Note,' *From a Northern Window* (London, 1911), p. 58.

the advice of Jesus ... put out your heart to God - get down on your knees - He will help you as no one else can, and will give you an answer of peace.[71]

Theologically, MacDonald sought Jesus' help above all else in his understanding of God, all the time aware of how limited his own understanding was. To A.J. Scott he wrote: 'I feel as if I had good brains but not enough of them.'[72] His goal was in no way to exalt himself, but rather to be rid of himself, for 'To be rid of self is to have the heart bare to God and to the neighbour - to *have all* life ours, and possess all things.'[73] 'MacDonald never claims for himself the spiritual maturity that is, in his system of thought, the *sine qua non* for complete understanding.'[74] 'But indeed the business of the universe is to make such a fool of you that you will know yourself for one, and so begin to be wise.'[75]

For MacDonald, the business of the theologian is first to *be* true, that one may be able to speak the truth. A central conviction was that one's vision of the truth becomes clearer as one becomes increasingly true in one's own being. The character of the theologian and the character of theology are thus interdependent. MacDonald exhorts the seeker: 'what you call riddles are truths, and seem riddles because you are not true.'[76] Much of his own credibility theologically is based on his own *trueness* as a person, and the reality of his life, which, like his theology, was not based on refractions of the truth, but focused primarily on the source of Truth. He was not afraid to admit his doubts because he had found that 'doubt is the hammer that breaks the windows clouded with human fancies, and lets in the pure light.'[77]

---

71 Rev. John Rooker, in *GMAW*, pp. 537–8.

72 MacDonald, 'Letter to A.J. Scott' (Hastings, 17 May 1858), H.M. 6334, Huntington Library, San Marino, California.

73 MacDonald, 'Letter to John Stuart Blackie' (11 November 1984, National Library of Scotland), in Raeper, *George MacDonald*, p. 388.

74 Hein, *The Harmony Within* (1982), p. 154.

75 MacDonald, *Lilith* (Tring, 1986, orig. 1895), p. 26.

76 Ibid., p. 45.

77 MacDonald, 'Letter to an Unknown Lady' (1866), in *EC*, p. 154.

Old books, new facts, they preach aloud –
Their tones like wisdom fall:
I see a face amid the crowd
Whose smile were worth them all.
… Nor claim I thus a place above
Thy table's very foot;
'Tis only that I love no love
That springs not from the root;
… My soul with truth clothe all about,
And I shall question free:
The man that feareth Lord, to doubt,
In that fear doubteth thee.[78]

MacDonald's quest was to discern Truth and serve Truth passionately without fear of the possible consequences of such utter abandonment. 'While others often wrote what they considered fashionable and acceptable to their readers, George wrote what his heart and soul directed.'[79] He recognized the fickleness of public acclaim, asserting that 'the praise of one generation may be the contempt of another, perhaps of the very next, so that the repute of his time could assure him of nothing.'[80]

In seeking truth, he endeavored to avoid controversy and defensiveness about his perspectives, valuing truth for its own sake, and not as something he could ever own or possess: 'I wish to be in a condition in which I can do my work for the Truth's sake, without any reference to others who oppose my teaching. We ought never to wish to overcome because WE are the fighters, never feel THAT IS MY TRUTH.'[81] Because of the mysterious and meta-logical nature of Truth, MacDonald believed the imagination to be a powerful means by which God's self-revelation could penetrate into the mind and heart of a person.

MacDonald's desire to allow the Eternal and Living Word to shape his understanding of the Truth is expressed throughout his work. It freed him to be somewhat detached from other norms and fearless in his theological pursuit. His is a theology of apprehension of the Truth by passionate involvement with the Truth, and a willingness to wait on God for self-disclosure, affirming that 'trust is better than foresight.'[82] Theology was reasonable for MacDonald when it was utterly relational, and he yearned for the time when his 'whole soul is *filled* with love to him, which is only a reasonable thing.'[83]

---

78 MacDonald, 'The Disciple,' selections in *GMAW*, p. 87, also in slightly varied version in *PW*, Vol. 1, pp. 189–217.

79 Elizabeth Saintsbury, *George MacDonald: A Short Life* (Edinburgh, 1987), p. 79.

80 George MacDonald, *Home Again* (London, 1900, orig. 1887), p. 18; hereafter cited as *HA*.

81 MacDonald, 'Letter to Louisa' (29 November 1853), in *EC*, pp. 71–2.

82 George MacDonald, *Flight of the Shadow* (London, 1891), p. 190.

83 MacDonald, Application to Highbury Theological College (1848), in Raeper, *George MacDonald*, p. 53.

MacDonald wrote that the one 'who will order his way by the word of the Master shall partake of his peace, and shall have in himself a growing conviction that in him are hid all the treasures of wisdom and knowledge ....'[84] In this way, MacDonald was able in part to rise above the limitations of his own age to a prophetic stature which anticipated theological insights of the twentieth century, yet insights which remain anchored in the earliest Christian traditions and revelations.

---

84 MacDonald, 'Letter to an Unknown Lady' (1866), in *EC*, p. 154.

Chapter 2

Classical and Literary Influences on MacDonald's Life and Thought

The combination of MacDonald's diverse interests, varied education, aptitude for languages, love of reading, and humble willingness to learn from everyone meant that those who influenced him came from many orientations and disciplines. MacDonald sought to discern the Truth in each person whom he read or encountered. He endeavored to be 'liberal' in the sense of being 'able to see the good and true in people that differ from you – glad to be roused to the reception of truth in God's name from whatever quarter it may come, and not readily finding offence ....'[1] His rudder and his destination were ever Jesus Christ, whom he saw as God's true self-revelation, but the winds of many traditions and people were received by him also as God's gifts which could propel him in God's purposes.[2]

1. Classical Influences

Most likely, it was at university that MacDonald was first exposed to Plato and Greek thought through his studies of Greek language. The influence of Plato on MacDonald is evident throughout his writing.[3] What appealed to MacDonald in Plato was his emphasis on Goodness as an ideal which is most real. MacDonald's belief that the world is the antechamber of the greater reality of the Kingdom of God was redolent of Plato.[4] His view that suffering can serve a positive end may be traced in part to ancient thought.[5] Also evident is the Platonic idea that participation in the eternal light of God by grace is the basis of human knowing. For MacDonald, participation in divine nature was not an abstract concept. It was part of the ontological transformation brought about in and through Christ. Finally, MacDonald's dialogical

---

1   *SP*, p. 308.
2   'That is the heart of my hopes by day and my dreams by night. To behold the face of Jesus seems to me the one thing to be desired'; *SP*, p. 42.
3   See, for example, *SP*, pp. 314, 424, and *The Marquis of Lossie* (London, 1927), p. 307; hereafter cited as *ML*.
4   An obvious example of this can be found in 'The Golden Key,' in which Mossy and Tangle walk through the shadowlands and tearfully yearn for 'the country from whence the shadows fell'; Glenn Sadler (ed.), *The Gifts of the Child Christ* (Grand Rapids, MI, 1996), p. 272; hereafter cited as *GCC*.
5   See Peter Kreeft, *Making Sense out of Suffering* (London, 1986), p. 72.

orientation, integral to his views on education and his own writing style, finds traces in the Socratic tradition. However, though he readily acknowledged the influence of Greek thought, and the comfort Plato was at times to him, he made it clear that it was in Christ that his centre of truth and comfort fully abided.[6]

MacDonald seemed to disregard Plato's distrust of the artist and his exaltation of reason over the imagination.[7] Plato valued reason as the necessary vehicle for arriving at the transcendent, impersonal essences of Truth, Goodness, Beauty, and Justice. It is ironic that MacDonald would come to challenge the very rationalistic tradition which Plato heralded. Rationalism's increasing influence on intellectual life in the West shaped a way of knowing based on ordering, analysis, and efforts to gain mastery and control. Devaluation of the mythic element and the rise of empiricism concerned MacDonald greatly. The Greek ideal of Beauty (*kalon*) as an 'other-worldly universal' would have a profound impact on the realm of aesthetics and also became foundational in the Kantian 'tendency to abstract aesthetic experience from physical reality.'[8] MacDonald would contend against this tradition that the imagination and the Christian faith offer a way to integrate aesthetic experience and physical reality. Just as MacDonald was convinced each person (including himself) grasped only a part of the whole and thus conveyed both truth and falsehood, he could honor what he held as wisdom from Plato and disregard that which seemed inconsistent with the central truths he held.

2. British Literary Influences

The vastness of MacDonald's exposure to British literature is evident in his book *England's Antiphon*, in which he takes the reader on a tour of six hundred years of poetry. He offers a theological context for this overview, with central focus on worship. As *Antiphon* 'means the responsive song of the parted choir,' MacDonald saw himself as the 'Choragus, or leader of the chorus' in relation to the singers of his nation.[9] Poetry's 'music' was a metaphor for life, with God as the 'one who makes the joy the last in every song,' in every life, no matter how tragic.[10]

---

6   See, for example, *ML*, p. 310.

7   Plato, *The Republic*, Book X (New York, 1956), pp. 387ff. Because the material world was for Plato an imperfect representation of the world of Forms, and the imagination created representations of the material world, the fruit of the imagination was considered to be two or more stages removed from the truth. This separation of truth from art and the relegation of art to imitation had a lasting impact. Other divergent voices had emerged within Classic tradition, such as Plotinus, who highly esteemed the poet as a creator and not just imitator, but these became the weaker voices.

8   Jeremy Begbie, *Voicing Creation's Praise* (Edinburgh, 1991), pp. 157, 163, 191.

9   George MacDonald (ed.), *England's Antiphon* (London, n.d.), pp. 2, 3.

10 'Letter to his Father' (3 June 1855), in *EC*, p. 86. As Robert Trexler suggests, this is most likely a reference to the fourth movement of Beethoven's Ninth Symphony (1823), which is inspired by Schiller's poem 'To Joy' (1785); R. Trexler, personal correspondence (27 December 2005).

MacDonald's understanding of the interconnectedness of theology and poetry permeates the entire book. This interrelation he believed to be rooted in worship: 'If the act of worship be the highest human condition, it follows that the highest human art must find material in the modes of worship.'[11] Poetry serves a doxological purpose, for 'poetry is the first form religious utterance will assume.'[12] Under the influence of these poets, MacDonald experienced an alternative to the imbalance emerging from the Enlightenment: 'Perhaps we may find in them a sign or two that in cultivating our intellect we have in some measure neglected our heart.'[13] The grave theological consequences of this neglect were obvious to him: 'In the worship of [Christ] a thousand truths are working, unknown and yet active, which, embodied in theory, and dissociated from the living mind that was in Christ, will as certainly breed worms as any omer of hoarded manna.'[14] Thus he assembled the work of those intent on 'eternal principles of truth' in order to build something 'like a chapel in the great church of England's worship' that could foster true worship.[15]

The correlation of theology with poetry is evident as a current of Romanticism. For MacDonald it meant the freedom to embrace the aesthetic as vital to the theological as in his own Celtic background. The conviction was that:

> Theology cannot be separated from literature without weakening it *as* theology; the theologian must also be an expert literary critic, fully conversant with all the critical apparatus involved. It is no accident that the great tradition of nineteenth-century religious thinkers ... were part of a literary tradition as much as a theological one. Any attempt to understand them in narrow theological terms alone is doomed to distortion and failure.[16]

Many of the literary influences on MacDonald's life become clearer when one acknowledges their theological nature. The more obvious influences can be seen as coming from the Romantic movement in general, and from Coleridge and Wordsworth in particular. While this analysis, for the sake of space, will concentrate more on these influences, it is also important to acknowledge the influence of the seventeenth-century poets and writers whom MacDonald loved so much, and who deepened in him his faith and his own poetic ability.

In fact, 'George Herbert was MacDonald's ideal in the realm of religious verse – apart from the "shape" poems which he found affected – for Herbert managed to combine form and sentiment perfectly, as well as remaining a model pastor.'[17] Both Herbert and Henry Vaughan reinforced in him the conviction of God's goodness and love.[18] MacDonald also deeply valued Herbert's and Milton's honesty and openness

---

11 MacDonald, *England's Antiphon*, p. 1.
12 Ibid.
13 Ibid., p. 7.
14 Ibid., p. 6.
15 Ibid., pp. 5, 2.
16 Stephen Prickett, *Romanticism and Religion* (Cambridge, 1976), p. 133.
17 Raeper, *George MacDonald*, p. 122.
18 Phillips, *George MacDonald*, p. 118.

about their doubts and their anguish. Shakespeare was a model to him of keen engagement with life and truth. When MacDonald was 42 years old, he expressed his deep appreciation of Shakespeare: 'Indeed, I have studied him more than any book except the Gospels.'[19] John Bunyan's *Pilgrim's Progress* became an integral part of his family's life, for they not only cherished it as a source of wisdom for themselves, but also as that which could bring encouragement to others.[20]

Allusions to these poets and writers are plentiful in MacDonald's work. However, Coleridge and Wordsworth will be discussed, because they were able to offer a bridge to these past traditions that made sense of their own context, and without denial or escapism offered new perspective on the Enlightenment.

a. The British Romantic Movement

The Romantic Movement flowed through at least two differing but overlapping streams. Confusion arises in assessing MacDonald's place in this movement if these distinctions are ignored. The tradition of Romanticism which influenced MacDonald was not the majority Romantic tradition for the most part. The argument of this book is that the more predominant emphasis on escapism and anti-rationalism which devolved into a subjectivism that exalted feelings above all was not appealing to MacDonald.

Others, like Raeper, have argued that MacDonald adopted Romantic patterns for art, in which creativity arises from impulses of feeling and perception, such that 'the source and subject matter of a poem ... are the attributes and the actions of the poet's own mind.'[21] He cited a poem in MacDonald's, *At the Back of the North Wind*, as exemplifying such an anti-rationalistic perspective for the 'words are not there to create meaning but somehow mystically and intuitively can change hearts.'[22]

Though one can find evidence in MacDonald, as Raeper has done, of such a meta-rational approach (*meta* seems more consistent with MacDonald than *anti*), it can be argued that the aspect of Romanticism which most influenced him was that which sought a more integrating perspective on life. Here the movement was toward a deeper experience and understanding of life, rather than an escape from it. This minority tradition emphasized harmony between the inner and outer worlds, and affirmed both the subjective and the objective aspects of reality.

There are central themes associated with Romanticism which can be found in both streams of Romanticism: the yearning for *home*, the importance of the child and childhood, the fascination with the mysterious, including death and the occult,

---

19 'Letter to Rev. Dr. Macintosh' (6 May 1866), in *EC*, p. 156.

20 See Rachel Johnson, 'Pilgrims: The MacDonalds and John Bunyan's The Pilgrim's Progress,' *North Wind*, 21 (London, 2002), http://www.macdonaldsociety.org/NW21/nw21_pilgrim_progress.htm.

21 Raeper, *George MacDonald*, p. 110, citing M.H. Abrams, *The Mirror and the Lamp* (Oxford, 1953), p. 22. See also Douglas B. Hindmarsh, 'The Faith of George MacDonald,' unpublished Masters dissertation (Regent College, 1989), pp. iii, 57.

22 Raeper, *George MacDonald*, p. 124.

and the organic nature of reality and truth.[23] The difference is whether these were seen as objectively based, and important to humanity because of their ontological grounding, or whether they were viewed as expressive solely of inner states, and thus important because of their evocative nature.

It was the minority tradition with the more objective and ontological view, led by Coleridge and Wordsworth for the most part, which had a greater impact on MacDonald. Stephen Prickett identified three strands in the 'minority' Romantic tradition: (1) the 'ambiguity' of the human situation in which inner and outer worlds both harmonize and conflict, (2) the 'bi-focal' or 'stereo-scopic' nature of language which expresses this ambiguity metaphorically, and (3) the way in which this emphasis produced those who were both 'creative writers (usually poets) *and* also theologians.'[24] One can see these strands having affected MacDonald's worldview, his understanding of the nature of language, and ideas about the imagination, as well as his own particular sense of call. Though much of MacDonald's own response to this influence is described in Chapter 4, a few comments, first about Coleridge and secondly about Wordsworth, will help to clarify in part from whence MacDonald's perspective derived.

b. Coleridge (1772–1834)

> He prayeth best, who loveth best,
> All things both great and small:
> For the dear God who loveth us,
> He made and loveth all.[25]

Coleridge, who was a friend of MacDonald's father-in-law,[26] modeled for MacDonald the possibility of being both a major artist and a major religious thinker. He accomplished this in a way which highly appealed to MacDonald, such that he neither produced a movement or school of thought *per se*, nor did he systematize his thinking.[27] Prickett sees 'evidence for the influence of Coleridge [underlying] almost

---

23 On the theme of childhood, Jerome Hamilton Buckley invites a Freudian and Jungian interpretation of its presence in the work of MacDonald; see *The Triumph of Time* (Cambridge, 1966), p. 112. Robert L. Wolff applies Freudian interpretations to MacDonald's use of the themes of home – fatherhood and motherhood, and of childlikeness; see, for example, Wolff, *The Golden Key: A Study of the Fiction of George MacDonald* (New Haven, CT, 1961), p. 351.

24 Prickett, *Romanticism and Religion*, pp. 7–8. Prickett uses for his examples of such literary/theological thinkers Coleridge, Keble, Newman, Maurice, and MacDonald.

25 Coleridge, *The Poetical Works of Samuel Taylor Coleridge*, ed. James Dykes Campbell (London, 1938), p. 110. Raeper noted that MacDonald was 'obsessed' with the 'Ancient Mariner,' from which these four lines come; Raeper, *George MacDonald*, p. 112.

26 *GMAW*, p. 138. 'Letter from J. Powell to M. Brighton' (30 August 1850).

27 F.D. Maurice, *The Kingdom of Christ* (4th edn., London, 1891), p. xi.

every part of his [MacDonald's] critical essays.'[28] The three areas in which this is most evident are: (1) Coleridge's worldview, (2) his understanding of the nature of language, and (3) his view of the imagination.

1) Coleridge's Worldview

The development of Coleridge's ideas was a complex and extensive process. Central to Coleridge's later vision was the affirmation of a supernatural world beyond this world yet dialectically related in such a way as to illustrate the purposive character of the whole universe.[29] Coleridge's development of the idea of polarity challenged an assertion of unanimity between human thought and God's ways and nature, or Natural Theology. In fact, as Prickett affirms, 'Coleridge's painful disengagement from this tradition [*Naturalistic*] has been described as the great intellectual struggle of his life.'[30]

Though initially Unitarian, Coleridge came to believe that the basis of all truth was the doctrine of the Trinity.[31] Embracing the Trinity as the central key to all of reality was an acknowledgement of the radical otherness of God alongside God's chosen identification with creation. Coleridge communicated 'a symbolic tension between incompatible yet interdependent worlds' in which 'the transcendent "otherness" of a God of mystery, immanent in the world of nature and human psychology' simultaneously stands 'over against that world in judgement.'[32] In order to describe both the otherness and the relationship between them, he developed the concept of polarity. This allowed for both the distinctions between God and the world, and the dynamic between them. Polarity challenged ideas of dualism and paradox, and instead emphasized relation and reconciliation. The reconciliation of two polar realms was not understood as a facile achievement. Coleridge's concept of polarity included suffering, most profoundly the reconciling suffering of Christ on the Cross.[33]

Coleridge applied his Trinitarian philosophical gleanings about polarity to creation. In his book *The Friend*, Coleridge describes what he calls 'the universal principle of polarity': 'Every power in nature and in spirit must evolve an opposite, as the sole means and condition of its manifestation; and all opposition is a tendency

---

28 Ibid., p. 229. See also, Colin Manlove, *Christian Fantasy* (Notre Dame, IN, 1992), p. 158.

29 Prickett, *Romanticism and Religion*, p. 61.

30 Ibid., p. 80. Coleridge expressed some of the limitations of Natural Philosophy in *Biographia Literaria; and Two Lay Sermons* (London, 1894 reprint), p. 125.

31 Coleridge, 'Notes on Sherlock's Vindication of the Doctrine of the Trinity,' in *The Complete Works of Samuel Taylor Coleridge*, ed. W.G.T. Shedd (New York, 1884), Vol. 5, p. 397. Cf. Owen Barfield, 'Either: Or,' in , Charles Huttar (ed.), *Imagination and the Spirit* (Grand Rapids, MI, 1971), p. 31.

32 Prickett, *Romanticism and Religion*, p. 27.

33 As Prickett explains, 'Tragedy is a perpetual possibility; as the crucifixion reminds us, there is no easy reconciliation'; Prickett, *Victorian Fantasy* (Brighton, 1979), p. 187.

to re-union.'[34] Relationship becomes central to the very nature of existence, with *One* being manifest through the co-existence of an *Other*.[35] The dynamic relationship between the two forces implies the presence of a third 'something' which Coleridge described as 'an interpenetration of the counteracting powers, partaking of both.'[36] He used the word *coinherence* to describe the interpenetration, or the differentiated unity.[37] Viewed from a Trinitarian perspective, differing realities do not necessarily oppose, negate, or absorb each other, or stand in logical abstraction as in the case of paradox. Rather they may enhance each other and the dynamic between them then becomes a third reality – a process of interrelationship and interdependence. Polarity allows for distinctiveness without separation, and unity in diversity.[38]

Coleridge's thoughts about polarity also formed the basis for his thinking about inspiration, obedience, and the organic nature of reality. If there is a twofold nature to reality and the potential of interpenetration between these distinct realms, then revelation and inspiration become realistic possibilities. For Coleridge, the contingent nature of the created realm places demands upon humanity for openness, growth, and imagination. In this way, the Truth of the eternal realm, with all of its 'otherness,' may break through.[39] Thus, he asserted: 'Too soon did the Doctors of the Church forget that the heart, the moral nature, was the beginning and the end; and that truth, knowledge, and insight were comprehended in its expansion.'[40] This dynamic rather than static vision of life called for discovery prior to definition, for the universe was seen as 'implicit with hidden meaning' which must be unveiled to be understood.[41] The imagination is vital in approaching and comprehending meaning. Creativity is possible, for humanity is gifted with the power to participate imaginatively in the meaning and purpose of this ever-changing and growing universe.

---

34 Samuel Taylor Coleridge, *The Friend: A Series of Essays to Aid in the Formation of Fixed Principles in Politics, Morals, and Religion* (London, 1866), p. 55n.

35 Coleridge, 'Letter to his Son, Hartley,' in Owen Barfield, *What Coleridge Thought* (Middletown, CT, 1971), pp. 181–2.

36 Coleridge, 'Biographia Literaria,' in H.J. Jackson (ed.), *Samuel Taylor Coleridge* (Oxford, 1985), p. 310.

37 Coleridge, *Aids to Reflection*, ed. Henry Nelson Coleridge, Esq. (Burlington, VT, 1840), p. 157n. Wayne Corapi writes: 'Coinherence is a favorite word of Coleridge's (the Latin translation of *perichoresis*) that signifies a differentiated unity,' Corapi, 'History and Trinitarian Thought: The Impact of Samuel Taylor Coleridge's Understanding of History on His Conversion to Trinitarian Orthodoxy,' unpublished thesis (Regent College, 1997), p. 87.

38 Coleridge stress on interdependent distinctiveness is reminiscent of the Chalcedonian affirmation of the perichoretic nature of the Trinity – without confusion, conversion, division, or separation.

39 Coleridge, *Aids to Reflection*, p. 120.

40 Ibid., p. 193.

41 Prickett, *Romanticism and Religion*, p. 53.

2) *Coleridge's Worldview and the Nature of Language*

Coleridge's worldview offers numerous implications for understanding language, symbol, and Scripture. Language emerged from relationships, community, and culture, rather than from self-evident ideas. He stood in opposition to the logical-positivist assertion that one begins with premises and definitions, and asserted rather that 'we conclude by *discovering* them.'[42]

Language reflects the twofold nature of reality, and is itself 'stereoscopic' or 'bi-focal.' Coleridge was aware that 'the language of great literature expresses more than we can know at any one time or place.'[43] This was supremely so in the Scriptures, whose histories are the 'educts of the imagination' with its 'reconciling and mediatorial power,' which 'gives birth to a system of symbols, harmonious in themselves, and consubstantial with the truths, of which they are the conductors ... Hence ... the Sacred Book is worthily entitled the Word of God.'[44] He found in both biblical facts and persons twofold significance, of temporal and eternal, particular and universal, unified and diverse, past and future relevance.[45] The Scriptures are symbolic of universal truths in their embodiment of such polarity, and their ability to reconcile that which seems contradictory.

He viewed the Bible organically, applying to it the metaphor of the circulatory system through which inspiration flows, but from which passages may not properly be amputated and used as proof texts for the propping up of various systems of thought.[46] He embraced both its uniqueness and sacred nature as that through which the transcendent is mediated.[47] Yet he was careful to avoid fundamentalism or literalism, which seemed to him superstitious and insensitive to the nature of language.[48] Genuine faith allowed for the Bible to be exposed to literary criticism and historical scholarship, recognizing that it is through the very material of the temporal that the eternal is revealed.

The fact that Scripture evidences correspondence between the sign and the signified established for Coleridge a basis from which to understand all that is symbolic. One comes to an understanding of poetic language via religious language, rather than the reverse.[49] Understanding revelation in a stereoscopic sense, including both the historical aspects of the prophets and of Christ and the corresponding inner, personal assent of the individual believer gave clarity to the meaning of the symbol for Coleridge. He attributed to the poetic symbol, real revelation in the sense that it gave evidence of 'the translucence of the eternal through and in the temporal.'[50]

---

42 Ibid., p. 11.
43 Ibid., p. 28.
44 Coleridge, *The Statesman's Manual*, in *Biographia Literaria*, pp. 321–2.
45 Ibid., p. 322.
46 Cf. British Museum, MS. 47 532, p. 32, in Prickett, *Romanticism and Religion*, p. 51.
47 Coleridge, *Confessions*, ed. H.N. Coleridge (1849), p. 9, cited in Prickett, *Romanticism and Religion*, p. 29.
48 Prickett, *Romanticism and Religion*, p. 45. Cf. Reardon, p. 82.
49 Prickett, *Romanticism and Religion*, p. 33.
50 Coleridge, *The Statesman's Manual*, p. 322.

Poetry did not mean isolation from reality into the realm of fantasy and illusion, but rather was based on real epiphanies of truth which shone forth from the prism created by the convergence of polarities such as the concrete and abstract, particular and universal, temporal and eternal: 'It [the symbol] always partakes of the reality which it renders intelligible; and while it enunciates the whole, abides itself as a living part in that unity, of which it is the representative.'[51] The symbol opens up reality and the imagination.

3) Coleridge's Worldview and the Imagination

While Coleridge was convinced that truth could be perceived and communicated more fully through the imagination, he was careful to distinguish imagination from fancy. Fancy has to do not with reality, but with 'apparitions ... Alas for the flocks that are to be led forth to such pastures.'[52] Not only does the fancy lead one away from reality, it is itself, '"mere dead arrangement" of "fixities and definites": a scissors-and-paste job of the mind.'"[53] In contrast, the imagination in the primary sense was seen as 'a repetition in the finite mind of the eternal act of creation in the infinite I AM' and 'the living power and prime agent of all human perception ....'[54] Imaginative creativity was seen to flow from truth and reality, and to so re-present it that one's pleasure in and one's awareness of that reality was enhanced.

The imagination was for Coleridge the supreme poetic gift, and art could mediate between nature and humanity.[55] Nature is 'for the religious observer the art of God.' Art is meant to convey the thought present in nature, and was deemed to be 'rich in proportion to the variety of parts which it holds in unity.'[56] This unity is not one that is imposed, but rather one perceived, via the imagination, and the mystery of this unity between humanity and nature is that 'which itself should suffice to make us religious: for it is a problem of which God is the only solution ....'[57] As the original Artist creates with purpose, human art should seek to reflect and harmonize with what is revealed of God's purpose.

Coleridge embraced the imagination as that which makes apprehension of polarity possible – that alone which offered a way out of dualistic 'either/or' thought patterns.[58] Through this insight, Coleridge provided a basis for metaphorical thinking

---

51 Ibid., p. 322.

52 Ibid.

53 Prickett, *Victorian Fantasy*, p. 6, citing Coleridge, *Biographic Literaria*, ed. J. Shawcross (Oxford, 1902), Vol. 1, p. 202.

54 Coleridge, *Biographic Literaria*, p. 144.

55 Coleridge, 'On Poesy or Art,' *Miscellanies, Aesthetic and Literary*, ed. T. Ashe (London, 1892), p. 42.

56 Ibid., p. 44.

57 Ibid., p. 47.

58 It is interesting to note that Paul Ricoeur in his writing on metaphor leans on Coleridge's understanding of the imagination in its role of creating reciprocity and growth in the midst of bipolar tension; P. Ricoeur, *The Rule of Metaphor*, trans. Robert Czerny (Toronto, Ontario, 1977), p. 249.

which discerns and maintains harmony between form and content, between medium and message, and between inner and outer worlds.

The way in which 'polarity' is used interpretatively for nature, for human thought, as well as in divine apprehension, raises the question of whether the principle of polarity is granted too heavy an epistemological burden. Does this framework create too close an alignment between the creation and the Triune Creator? As a principle, it is effective in reconciling much that seems in opposition. As *the* principle, it may run the risk of claiming Christ's central and unique role in Christianity as the self-revelation of the Triune God

Though Coleridge's ideas on polarity are evident in MacDonald, the latter does try to modify them by giving central importance to the Persons of the Trinity, rather than the *principle* of the Trinity. Even with this danger, of which Coleridge seemed aware,[59] he offered a vital new approach to the imagination, and with it to philosophy and theology, which worked to offset Kantian dualism and Cartesian anthropocentricism. Coleridge had inherited what he called 'A hunger-bitten and idea-less philosophy,' and was convinced that it 'naturally produces a starveling and comfortless religion.'[60] He yearned to reveal faith that goes beyond the dead letter and mechanical understanding, which by the aid of the imagination can offer its sheep authentic pastures in which to feast and lie down. Thus he wrote: 'In the Trinity all the *Hows?* may and should be answered by *Look!*'[61] His influence is evident in literature, philosophy, and theology, particularly affecting literature through Wordsworth, and challenging the Church of England through F.D. Maurice, and the Catholic Church through John Henry Newman.

Coleridge's perspective on reality, language, and the imagination deeply appealed to MacDonald, for he seemed 'to have re-discovered and reaffirmed the complex symbolism that transforms the language of religious experience from easy platitude and comfortable doctrine to ambiguity and tension, to fear and trembling.'[62] MacDonald's respect for Coleridge is evident in the many references to Coleridge's writings throughout MacDonald's works (*David Elginbrod, Phantastes, 'The Wise Woman,' Thomas Wingfold, Curate, Mary Marston, The Tragedie of Hamlet, A Dish of Orts, Far above Rubies*). In *There and Back*, Richard's fascination with the many editions of 'The Rime of the Ancient Mariner' written by Coleridge between 1798 and 1817 reflects MacDonald's deep appreciation and knowledge of Coleridge's work as well. MacDonald includes compassionate remarks about Coleridge's drinking and drug problem in *Donal Grant* and *Sir Gibbie*.[63] MacDonald refers to Coleridge with

---

59 See Coleridge, *Aids to Reflection*, pp. 186–92.
60 Coleridge, *The Statesman's Manual*, p. 322.
61 Coleridge, 'Notes on Sherlock's Vindication of the Doctrine of the Trinity,' in *The Complete Works of Samuel Taylor Coleridge*, ed. W.G.T. Shedd (New York, 1884), 5, 397.
62 Prickett, *Romanticism and Religion*, p. 33.
63 MacDonald, *DG*, p. 292, and *SG*, pp. 35–6.

Wordsworth as 'The prophets of the new blessing,' and describes him as someone who offers heart, with delight and art.[64]

Coleridge shared similar concerns to MacDonald's about Federal Calvinism's emphasis on God as sovereign will rather than sovereign love.[65] Themes of beauty from ashes and of growth through failure, which were central in much of MacDonald's thinking and experience, can be seen in Coleridge's work.[66] MacDonald was also encouraged by Coleridge's freedom to learn from other scholars.[67] Through his insights on the validity of intuitive knowledge which 'for Calvin as well as Coleridge is the very opposite of subjectivity,'[68] he also opened up the possibility of harmony between the aesthetic, theological, scientific, socio-political, and philosophical arenas, which he believed all needed the renewing life-blood of faith. Coleridge inspired others, like MacDonald, who longed to address concerns in a variety of realms in light of the gospel of truth and grace. Finally, in the midst of his brilliant intellectual ability, Coleridge's emphasis on faith as a way of life requiring submission of one's will to God, became a central emphasis of MacDonald's reflections.

c. Wordsworth (1770–1850)

> Our destiny, our being's heart and home,
> Is with infinitude, and only there.[69]

Wordsworth was older than Coleridge, yet 'Coleridge had much to do with the opening of Wordsworth's eyes.'[70] The ideas of Coleridge entered 'the bloodstream' of readers through Wordsworth's poetry – and among them, George MacDonald. Wordsworth's readers encompassed a wide range of thinkers, including those who resisted his position on faith, like Matthew Arnold and John Stuart Mill; those who were part of the Evangelical movement, such as Kingsley and Hughes; others involved in the Oxford Movement, including Keble, Pusey, and Newman, as well as non-party thinkers like F.D. Maurice and George MacDonald.[71] J.S. Mill wrote

---

64 MacDonald, *Wilfrid Cumbermede*, Ch. 15, and *England's Antiphon*, p. 293.

65 Roger J. Newell, 'Participatory Knowledge: Theology as Art and Science in C.S. Lewis and T.F. Torrance,' unpublished Ph.D. thesis (University of Aberdeen, 1983), Vol. 1, p. 60, and citing Coleridge, *Aids to Reflection*, pp. 95–108.

66 The parallel of the shooting of the albatross to Curdie's shooting of the dove in *The Princess and Curdie* is obvious.

67 It was largely the influence of Coleridge which introduced German philosophy and literature to Britain; see Reiko Aiura, 'Recurring Symbols in the Fantasies and Children's Stories of George MacDonald,' unpublished M.Litt. thesis (University of Aberdeen, 1986), p. 59. MacDonald read the works of many of the same German thinkers, including Schelling, the Schlegels, Fichte, Kant, and Schleiermacher. Cf. Raeper, *George MacDonald*, pp. 239–40.

68 Newell, p. 114.

69 William Wordsworth, 'Natural Apocalypse,' in *Modern Tradition*, p. 57.

70 MacDonald, *England's Antiphon*, p. 307.

71 Prickett, *Romanticism and Religion*, p. 71.

of Wordsworth's poems as a 'medicine for my state of mind,' for in them he found 'a source of inward joy, of sympathetic and imaginative pleasure, which could be shared by all human beings.'[72]

1) Wordsworth and Coleridge

MacDonald called Coleridge a 'sage' and Wordsworth a 'seer' whose sight had been enlarged by Coleridge.[73] MacDonald alluded more to the Wordsworth's poetry in his books than to Coleridge's,[74] as Wordsworth's poetry brought into expression much of Coleridge's philosophical orientation. It bears noting that Coleridge experienced personal formation and growth during his stay in Germany, whereas Wordsworth was somewhat traumatized by his months in France during the Revolution.[75] What had seemed to him full of rich promise became deeply disillusioning, and he was eventually forced to flee France for his own safety: 'Dejected even to hopelessness for a time, he believed in nothing.'[76] Nature was his initial source of restoration, and thus became a key to his life and his reflections. Whereas Coleridge is said to have reintegrated philosophy, aesthetics, and theology for the refreshment of those parched by Enlightenment dryness, Wordsworth is noted for having taught the Victorians how to feel.[77] Coleridge and Wordsworth spent much time together and enjoyed much mutual respect and appreciation, yet Coleridge 'devoted some thousands of words in the *Biographia Literaria* to the errors of style, tone, and syntax' in Wordsworth which he felt derived from his 'indefensible theory of poetry.'[78]

2) Wordsworth – a Christian Pantheist

Because Wordsworth devoted so much of his life to reflecting on and dwelling in the nature around him, MacDonald called him the 'high priest of nature,' for 'in all things he felt the solemn presence of the Divine Spirit.' Creation was not seen just as the work of God's hands but also the 'flowing forth of his heart' and 'of his love of us.'[79]

MacDonald identified Wordsworth's orientation as 'Christian Pantheism,' but cautions that it does not follow that he was an apostle of nature who identified nature

---

72 J.S. Mill, *Autobiography* (London, 1873), p. 125.

73 MacDonald, *England's Antiphon*, p. 307.

74 For example, throughout his novel *David Elginbrod*, MacDonald demonstrated the growing sensibility of Margaret under the influence of Wordsworth's poetry.

75 In *What's Mine's Mine*, MacDonald includes a reference to Wordsworth's trauma in France: '"It was Wordsworth's bitter disappointment in the outcome of the French revolution,' continued Ian, 'that opened the door [of Nature] to him'"; *WMM*, p. 217.

76 MacDonald, *England's Antiphon*, p. 304.

77 Raeper, *George MacDonald*, p. 238.

78 William Wordsworth 'The Prelude,' in Carlos Baker (ed.), *Selected Poems and Sonnets* (New York, 1954), pp. iii–iv.

79 MacDonald, 'Wordsworth's Poetry,' *DO*, p. 247.

with God.[80] Rather, nature was seen as 'the word of God in his own handwriting' or 'the expression of the face of God' which has a 'moulding' and formative effect.[81] Because nature was considered part of the overflow of God's love, it could draw one back to a more vibrant perspective on all of life and offer a corrective to mechanistic ways of approaching relationships, theology, and life.

The priority, according to MacDonald, was God's self-revelation in the Word: 'When we understand the Word of God, then we understand the works of God; when we know the nature of an artist, we know his pictures; when we have known and talked with the poet, we understand his poetry far better.'[82] From this context, nature was to be understood not mechanically and externally ('we murder to dissect'[83]), but through involvement. All aspects of nature were part of its unity, including the seemingly socially unfit (a beggar, an 'old woman or idiot boy'[84]), who were often subjects of Wordsworth's poems.

Wordsworth's combination of naturalism, Platonism, humanism, and theism led to both confusion and creativity. Because MacDonald lived long enough to have read *The Prelude* in its entirety, Prickett argues that he had a clearer sense of Wordsworth's ability to reconcile and hold together dialectically opposing points of view, one of the essential strengths of a poetic perspective.[85] MacDonald saw Wordsworth holding together God's transcendence and immanence in a way that impacted both thought and feeling.

The interrelatedness of humanity, nature, and God, evident in Wordsworth's perspective, permeates MacDonald's writing. To do justice to Wordsworth, 'it will never do to overstress the naturalistic element in his thought as over against the humanistic and theistic components. All three conspire to fructify in his belief in the motherhood of nature, the brotherhood of man, the fatherhood of God, and … the neighbourhood of pain.'[86] He was able to maintain tension and harmony within these various foci through his use of and approach to the imagination.

3) Wordsworth on the Imagination
For Wordsworth, as for Coleridge, imagination was both a tool of creativity and discovery which enabled meaning and truth to be discerned and conveyed. His communication of the ultimate unity in God's creation was an appealing response

---

80 *DE*, p. 34. Cf. F.W. Robertson, *Lectures on the Influence of Poetry and Wordsworth* (London, 1906, reissued 1970), p. 164.
81 *DE*, p. 40. Cf. 'Tintern Abbey,' William Wordsworth, 'The Prelude,' p. 99.
82 Ibid., p. 256. This is MacDonald's interpretation of Wordsworth's position, but it seems more to be a description of MacDonald's priority than perhaps one which could be as consistently found in Wordsworth.
83 Wordsworth, 'The Tables Turned,' William Wordsworth, 'The Prelude,' p. 79.
84 Raeper, *George MacDonald*, p. 124.
85 Prickett, *Romanticism and Religion*, p. 87.
86 William Wordsworth, 'The Prelude,' p. ix. This citation is from Carlos Baker, ed., *William Wordsworth "The Prelude", Selected Poems and Sonnets* (New York: Holt, Rinehart and Winston, 1954), p. ix.

to the social chaos of nineteenth-century Britain. The imagination offered a way to transcend contradictions and philosophical conflicts, and convey the inseparability of thought and feeling.[87] An enlivened imagination was essential to perceive the living reality in all things and the meaning veiled from the scrutiny of mere scientific analysis.[88]

Wordsworth embraced the imagination as that which enhances one's vision and appreciation for even the simplest of things so as to stimulate powerful feeling that directs emotions and thoughts heavenward. He rejected the idea that this approach was merely sentimental,[89] claiming instead that it was consistent with the mind's characteristic activity – creativity. The imagination's role, he believed, is appropriate to the nature of reality in offering true referentiality.[90] An effective use of the imagination, as in poetry, required 'more lively sensibility, more enthusiasm and tenderness … a greater knowledge of human nature, and a more comprehensive soul.'[91]

Knowledge of reality emerges from one who 'looks at the world in the spirit of love' and who thus grows in sympathy and pleasure.[92] Wordsworth saw clear parallels between religion and poetry, both of which would touch the realm of the transcendent while holding fast to the immanent. Yet he felt one could do a great disservice to poetry and art through religious distortions.[93] Both must serve the truth, being true to human nature, to the natural realm and to God. In this way, the imagination would lift one's gaze to worship 'the Invisible alone.' One's sensitivity will be so heightened as to hear the 'Earth, [who] with her thousand voices, praises God.'[94]

MacDonald deeply appreciated Wordsworth's heightened sensitivity and his stereoscopic vision of reality. The idea that there was poetry to be awakened in the soul, which would help to 'break through the crust of his selfishness, and redeem him from a slow, mercenary, or sensual existence,' became integral to MacDonald's perspective.[95] He longed to expose his readers to such a vision, and thus included numerous references to Wordsworth.

MacDonald differed from Wordsworth in giving greater prominence to overt expressions of faith in his writing and in his deeper concern for theological verity than aesthetic efficacy. He also believed that 'there are regions to be traversed,

---

87 Prickett, *Victorian Fantasy*, pp. 162–3. See 'Preface to Lyrical Ballads,' in William Wordsworth, 'The Prelude,' p. 6.

88 In 'The Prelude,' Wordsworth wrote of the imagination having sparked at times a 'flash that has revealed / The invisible world.' From *The Prelude*, Book VI, lines 600–601, in William Wordsworth, 'The Prelude,' p. 305.

89 Prickett, *Victorian Fantasy*, p. 162.

90 Prickett, *Romanticism and Religion*, p. 100.

91 Wordsworth, 'Preface to Lyrical Ballads,' William Wordsworth, 'The Prelude,' p. 6.

92 Ibid., pp. 16–17. Cf. Robertson, *Lectures*, p. 78.

93 Wordsworth, 'Preface to Lyrical Ballads,' William Wordsworth, 'The Prelude,' p. 44.

94 Wordsworth, 'Hymn,' in MacDonald, *England's Antiphon*, pp. 308–10.

95 Robertson, *Lectures*, p. 19.

beyond any point to which Wordsworth leads us.'[96] Yet he saw in Wordsworth a determination which was similar to his own: '[Wordsworth] was not disobedient to the heavenly vision; he recognized the voice within him and obeyed it; and no wish for popularity, no dazzling invitations to a brighter life, could ever make him break his vows or leave his solitude.'[97] The universal nature of truth for Wordsworth and the fact that 'highest poetry represents the most universal feeling' encouraged MacDonald in his own desire to urge unity rather than sectarianism.[98] The nature of poetic feelings as described by Wordsworth kept MacDonald also from insipid sentimentalism, for these were feelings 'disciplined by Nature' and 'disciplined through the minds of the acknowledged great masters and poets.'[99]

Both Coleridge's and Wordsworth's work deepened MacDonald's already well-established interest in German literary and theological perspectives. MacDonald, ever hungry to grow in his understanding of truth, also found fruitful ground in his exploration of European writers.

3. European Theological and Literary Influences

MacDonald's exposure to European influences began early in his academic life. He worked to master German, though at the time it was not a popular language for study.[100] Windows opened for him to the writings of Novalis (Friedrich Philipp von Hardenberg) and E.T.A. Hoffman, along with Jacob Boehme and Emanuel Swedenborg, during a time when MacDonald was eagerly searching for resolution to the conflicts and questions he had about the Calvinism of his youth. In these writers he found a blend of mind and heart, of faith, imagination, and reason, of science and mysticism, of love for God and creation.

Whereas in Britain fantasy and fairy stories were relegated to the nursery, Novalis and Hoffmann, along with Tieck and De La Motte Fouqué, whom MacDonald also enjoyed, introduced the writing of adult fantasies.[101] Novalis particularly stands out as influential in his thoughts and theological development during this period of his life. Key themes can also be seen as emerging from Boehme, and Swedenborg (as well as William Law), particularly the idea of correspondences between the natural

---

96 *WMM*, p. 216.
97 Ibid., p. 151.
98 Ibid., p. 97. Cf. 'Poetry discovers good in men who differ from us, and so teaches us that we are one with them … For the poet belongs to the world rather than to his party …'; ibid., p. 103. This desire for unity and concern for all led a number of Romantic thinkers to a disdain of materialism which was viewed not only as divisive and exploitive, but also that which stifled one's sensitivity to all of life.
99 Robertson, *Lectures*, p. 129. Cf. Wordsworth, 'Letter to Lady Beaumont,' *WMM*, p. 125.
100 Raeper, *George MacDonald*, p. 49.
101 MacDonald thought *Undine* by Freidrich de la Motte Fouqué was the most beautiful of fairy tales; *DO*, p. 313.

and the spiritual.[102] Furthermore, Goethe's influence on MacDonald is evident in his establishment of the place of the hero's moral development in the real world, and his exaltation of the mystery and nobility of womanhood.[103] The focus of this section will be on Novalis, who combined many of these emphases, was a conduit for the influence of Schleiermacher on MacDonald, and who is acknowledged as among the most influential of all European writers on him.[104]

a. The Appeal of Novalis to MacDonald

MacDonald's deep appreciation for Novalis is evident particularly for his *Geistliche Lieder (Spiritual Songs)*, twelve of which MacDonald translated and gave as Christmas presents to his close friends in 1851, and which over the next forty-five years he reworked at least three times.[105] The appeal of Novalis to MacDonald is both personal and ideological. Novalis's life included struggles similar to MacDonald's: the death of a dear loved one (for Novalis, this was his fiancée, Sophie), the battle with lung disease (which overcame him at the age of 29), and the rigidity of the religion of his youth. Philosophically, the appeal was manifold, the main points of which will be enumerated with examples given primarily from Novalis' *Spiritual Songs* in MacDonald's translation (hereafter cited as S.S.).[106]

First, Novalis expressed a passionate hunger and thirst for God, and for meaning beyond this life, acknowledging the vanity of dedicating oneself to the pursuits of this world: 'Without thee, what were life or being!' (S.S. 1):

> Hero of love, oh, take me, take me!
> Thou art my life! my world! my gold!
> Should every earthly thing forsake me,
> I know who will me scatheless hold! ... (S.S. 11)

Second, Novalis depicted a God of love and grace, who by the Son enabled wandering and wayward humankind to come 'home.'[107] MacDonald could relate to his expressions of 'anguish' and 'longing,' and humankind's bondage and 'unrest.'

---

102 MacDonald alluded to these writers even in his novels, quoting Boehme's *Aurora*, for example in *DE*, p. 40. See Richard Reis, *George MacDonald* (New York, 1972), p. 38.

103 Aiura, 'Recurring Symbols,' p. 41. MacDonald's respect for Goethe is evident in the naming of his book *Diary of an Old Soul*, which so closely resembles the title of the work found in Goethe's Meister: 'Tagebuch einer schönen Seele' ('Diary of a Beautiful Soul'); John Neubauer, *Novalis* (Boston, MA, 1980), p. 129.

104 Phillips, *George MacDonald*, p. 118.

105 A.J. Scott was among the recipients of this translation of Novalis's work, and he acknowledged his own appreciation for it, saying Novalis was an 'old friend'; Raeper, *George MacDonald*, p. 89; Phillips, *George MacDonald*, p. 192

106 The following quotations from the *Spiritual Songs* are taken from MacDonald's *Rampolli* (London, 1897 and 1899), pp. 17–36.

107 Throughout his writing, MacDonald pursued this theme found in Novalis of being drawn homeward: "'Die Philosophie ist eigentlich Heimweh, ein Trieb überall zu House zu

And he rejoiced with Novalis, who proclaimed God's love, known through Christ's deliverance:

> Then came a saviour to deliver –
> A Son of Man, in love and might!
> A holy fire, of life all-giver,
> He in our hearts has fanned alight. (S.S. 1)

Third, Novalis also rejoiced in the reconciliation Christ enabled between humankind and nature: 'Let us then in God's full garden labour, / And to every bud and bloom be neighbour' (S.S. 2). From his fragments, and in his novel *Heinrich von Ofterdingen*, he revealed his belief in the relatedness of all of life, and the need for sympathy with the flower, animal, rock, and even stars. Thus the miner and the farmer were for him 'curators of spiritual values equally with the artist and the musician.'[108] This vision of creation required humility and nearness to Christ, a willingness to '… nestle/ Like children to thy knee' (S.S. 6). Humanity, having regained a sense of harmony with creation, could now awaken to the reality that Christ shines forth from all that is glorious in nature (S.S. 12).

Fourth, Novalis's views on death were shaped by his beloved's death and the belief that Christ had been overcome by death and yet had conquered it. He emphasized God's redemptive gifts through death, particularly ultimate union with God and with the beloved. Novalis emphatically believed in the Resurrection ('He lives! he's risen from the dead!'; S.S. 9) and the vicarious nature of Christ's Resurrection for humanity:

> Uplifted is the stone,
> And all mankind is risen;
> We all remain thine own,
> And vanished is our prison. (*Hymnen an die Nacht* 5)[109]

There was no longer any need for fear, for the one 'Who heeds the counsel of the Son / Enters the Father's door' (S.S. 9). For Novalis, death, and darkness and night became associated with a doorway to communion with his beloved and with Christ.[110]

Fifth, the belief that death had been overcome gave new meaning to suffering for Novalis. Toward the end of his own life, in the midst of grave suffering, he wrote: 'The Lord's will be done – not mine … Patience and surrender to the will of God are

---

sein."' ('"Philosophy is really home-sickness, an impulse to be at home everywhere"'); Novalis, cited by MacDonald in *Rampolli*, p. 15.

108 Bruce Haywood, *Novalis: The Veil of Imagery. A Study of the Poetic Works of Friedrich von Hardenberg (1772–1801)* ('s-Gravenhage, 1959), p. 151. MacDonald reflects this perspective in depicting his hero, Curdie, as both miner and poet, and in his portrayal of heroes as associated with farming (for example, David Elbinbrod, Alister Macruadh).

109 Novalis, as translated and cited in MacDonald, *Rampolli*, pp. 13, 14.

110 Haywood, *Novalis*, p. 140.

the best remedies.'[111] Entries in his diary in his final year of life reveal that he saw his own illness as 'years of apprenticeship towards a higher art of life.'[112] Thus he believed suffering distinguishes humankind from animals and plants: 'man is born to suffer.'[113] The courage and faith with which he faced the loss of his fiancée and his own physical suffering drew MacDonald close to Novalis. Peace was possible for Novalis because in his anguish he had experienced answers to his cry for God, 'Oh but then God bends him o'er us! / then his love comes very near! ... Life's cup fresh to us he reaches; / Whispers comfort, courage new ...' (S.S. 13).

Sixth, Novalis espoused the universal nature of Christ's atonement and the unity of all people, particularly Christians, which also appealed to MacDonald. Novalis left the Moravian Church and became Roman Catholic, in part to regain a sense of the 'catholicism' of the faith. He was critical of Protestants for having 'wrenched themselves loose from the universal Christian community, through which and in which alone was possible the true, the enduring rebirth.'[114] But he also criticized the Catholic Church for having become a 'corpse' such that the 'actual rule of Rome ... silently came to an end ... long before the violent insurrection.'[115]

He acknowledged Luther's positive corrective and Protestantism as a rightful protest 'against every arrogant seizure of an irksome and wrongful-seeming power.' Yet he denounced Protestantism for provincializing and dividing the Christian world, and for placing it under the authority of princes and principles hostile to religion. The proper role of Christendom was that of 'the creation of peace' which would both unify and individualize.[116]

Seventh, unity and individuality are possible because of the centrality and the nature of Christ, who was for Novalis all in all. At times, as Barth suggested, Novalis treats Christ, Mary, and the beloved as somewhat interchangeable.[117] But especially in the *Spiritual Songs*, written at the end of his life, Christ emerges as the One on whom humankind is utterly dependent for life and growth.

---

111 *Novalis, Schriften*, Richard Samuel, ed., Verlag W. Kohlhammer Stuttgart, (1960), Volume 4, p. 57.

112 Ibid. (3, 667), cited in Neubauer, *Novalis*, p. 158.

113 Ibid. (3, 684), cited in Neubauer, *Novalis*, p. 158.

114 Novalis, *Hymns to the Night and Other Selected Writings*, trans. Charles E. Passage (Indianopolis, IN, 1960), p. 49.

115 Novalis, in G. Schulz (ed.), *Novalis in Selbstzeugnissen und Bilddokumenten* (Reinbek bei Hamburg, 1969), p. 503, cited in H. Küng and W. Jens, *Literature and Religion*, trans. Peter Heinegg (New York, 1991), p. 158.

116 Novalis, *Hymns*, p. 50.

117 Karl Barth, *From Rousseau to Ritschl*, trans. Brian Cozens (London, 1959), pp. 264–5.

If I him but have,
If he be but mine,
If my heart, hence to the grave,
Ne'er forgets his love divine –
Know I nought of sadness,
Feel I nought but worship, love, and gladness. (S.S. 5)

Of all of Novalis's writing, it is these poems which seem to have most deeply impacted MacDonald.

Eighth, Novalis' desire to reinstate a proper balance between reason and faith, science and art, and his experience as both a scientist and a poet encouraged MacDonald.[118] Novalis believed that humanity had for too long succumbed to the secular religion of rationalism, which failed to answer the most penetrating questions of existence, particularly as related to death and what lies beyond the grave.[119] Faith had been allowed to shrivel under the spirit of rationalism, which Novalis symbolized as an icy blast driving over a frozen world. He strove to challenge the hunger for 'knowledge and possessions'[120] and the denigration of imagination and emotion which had 'reduced the infinite creative music of the universe to the monotonous clatter of a monstrous mill.'[121]

Calling for a return to 'faith and love,'[122] he chose the night as a symbol of mystery, rediscovery, and death, the true nature of which has been revealed through Christ. Seeing night as the 'womb of revelation' signaled in Novalis as well as Schleiermacher and Hölderlin (who also used this image) a turn away from the objective and toward the subjective.[123] Rejecting mind/body dualism, Novalis turned to intuition and imagination as the way of reconciliation and harmony. Yet he recognized the need to attend to objective reality: 'A man will never achieve anything excellent in the way of representation so long as he wishes to represent nothing more than his own experiences, his own favourite objects, so long as he cannot bring himself to study with diligence and to represent at his leisure an object wholly foreign and wholly uninteresting to him.'[124] He desired an equilibrium for society which he saw as the ability to remain 'poised on the crest' by an 'attraction toward heaven.'[125] Both science and poetry share common goals of pointing to the ethical verities behind nature, revealing the harmony among all things, and returning humankind to intimate communion with creation and the Creator.

---

118 'Novalis was, next to Goethe, probably the scientifically best educated poet of his age'; Neubauer, *Novalis*, p. 50.
119 Haywood, *Novalis*, p. 67.
120 Novalis, *Hymns*, p. 48.
121 Ibid., pp. 53–4.
122 Ibid., p. 48.
123 Haywood, *Novalis*, p. 67.
124 Ibid., p. 67.
125 Ibid., p. 56.

Ninth, flowing from this emphasis, Novalis's resistance to human systems would have also struck a melodic chord for MacDonald. He stated adamantly that: 'The more limited a system is, the more it will please the worldly wise.' Under the influence of Hemsterhuis, Novalis affirmed the priority of understanding relations rather than isolated facts.[126] Thus he advocated a new approach to philosophy characterized by 'freedom and infinitude' which would result in a 'lack of system brought under a system.'[127]

Many of these emphases were expressed poetically in Novalis's work, incorporating themes and symbols that not only excited MacDonald, but also influenced his work. Themes particularly evident in MacDonald's work are good aspects of death, the philosophical urge toward home, the harmony of all of life, and the proximity of the transcendent. *Phantastes* especially reflects the ideology of Novalis and his embracing of dreams and imagination as vehicles of truth. MacDonald quotes Novalis at the end of *Phantastes*: 'Unser Leben ist kein Traum, aber es soll und wird vielleicht einer werden.'[128]

b. Difficulties in Novalis

In the midst of these similarities, there are theological difficulties which appear in MacDonald that bear the influence of Novalis, and areas in which MacDonald diverges from Novalis. Küng discourages one from judging Novalis too harshly for some of his theological weaknesses, as he was a person in process whose life and thought were cut short on earth.[129] Even so, awareness of them and their impact on MacDonald may enhance understanding and representation of MacDonald's theology.

1) Novalis's Epistemological Subjectivity

Epistemologically, the balance for Novalis shifted to a more subjective basis of discovery and knowledge. The infinite was seen as openly accessible to the finite: 'Nothing is more accessible to the mind than the infinite.'[130] The artist was gifted as the one who understands and communicates such truth.[131] This resulted in a kind of aesthetic elitism: 'Anyone who does not immediately know and feel what poesy is can never have any conception of it instilled into him.'[132] Barth argued that in this way the *hubris* and *absolutism* of the Enlightenment were actually carried forth into Romanticism.[133] Art became *the* place of freedom and discovery, the bridge between

---

126 Neubauer, *Novalis*, p. 32.

127 Novalis (2, 289), in Neubauer, *Novalis*, p. 25.

128 'Our life is no dream, but it ought to become one, and perhaps will'; Novalis, in MacDonald, *Phantastes*, p. 182.

129 Jens and Küng, *Literature and Religion*, pp. 162–3.

130 Novalis, *Hymns*, p. 71.

131 See Novalis, *Miscellaneous Fragments*, cited in ibid., p. 69.

132 Novalis (Fragment, I, 887), in Barth, *From Rousseau to Ritschl*, pp. 234–5.

133 Barth, *From Rousseau to Ritschl*, p. 247.

infinity and the finite. Knowledge derived from creativity and human effort: 'We know only inasmuch as we fabricate' (*machen*).[134] This epistemological approach is symbolized in Novalis's 'Hyazinth und Rosenblütchen.' The key to lifting the veil of divine knowledge, which the goddess expressly discourages, is to become immortal oneself. Thus, Novalis wrote: 'Religion arises when the heart, withdrawn from all single real objects, feels and makes itself an ideal object.'[135] The unveiling revealed the beloved, 'Rosenblütchen,' poetry, art, religion, and ultimately, writes Novalis, 'What did he see? He saw – wonder of wonders – himself.'[136]

Novalis's attitude toward the Bible and its epistemic role flowed from this perspective. Novalis was critical of 'the absolute accessibility of the Bible to the people' via Protestantism, for 'now the inadequate contents, the rough, abstract sketch of religion in these books, became all the more obvious' and literalism became a deadening weight on the spirit of holiness.[137] Even so, the Bible was considered 'the archetypal book,' the proper model of book which could encapsulate the universe. Novalis studied it to derive a theory upon which he could create 'a scientific bible, a real and ideal model, and the seed of all books.'[138] He did not see why the Bible could not itself grow, nor why it should be given unique status: 'If the spirit sanctifies, every real book is a Bible.'[139]

2) Novalis's Christology
When Novalis's kind of aesthetic priority is carried into Christology, the outcome tends to be more anthropocentric than theocentric. Yet, in a real sense Novalis embraced and exalted Christ. Schleiermacher was deeply moved by Novalis's vision of love for Christ and Christian community in *Spiritual Song* 6.[140] Novalis wrote of the pre-eminence of Christ, bringing illumination to Greek and Hindu thought.[141] Yet with all of this there is delimitation expressed in which Christ is not the sole intermediary between God and humanity. Barth identified Novalis's position as closer to pantheism, for he understood him to be saying: 'everything can be the organ of the Godhead, the intermediary, if I exalt it to that position.'[142] Novalis chose Sophie to be his mediator, and perceived in Christianity the '"total capability [*Allfähigkeit*] of all earthly things to be wine and bread of eternal life.'[143]

In this way, Christ, like the Bible, becomes a sort of impersonal archetype. Redemption remains an intimately personal experience, yet 'Christ becomes a passive

134 Novalis (II, 378 and 589), in Neubauer, *Novalis*, p. 31.
135 Novalis, cited in Hindmarsh, pp. 85–6.
136 Novalis (Fragment, 439), in Barth, *From Rousseau to Ritschl*, p. 234.
137 Novalis, *Hymns*, p. 50.
138 Novalis (III, 363), in Neubauer, *Novalis*, p. 57.
139 Novalis, *Hymns*, pp. 71, 69.
140 Neubauer, *Novalis*, p. 114. See also Novalis, *Hymns*, p. 91.
141 Haywood, *Novalis*, pp. 69–70.
142 Barth, *From Rousseau to Ritschl*, p. 245.
143 Neubauer, *Novalis*, p. 89, citing Novalis (3, 523).

spirit that transfuses and sanctifies all parts of the world.'[144] Questions remain about the extent to which Christ mediated an ontological gap between God and humans, or merely a psychological gap. Here it is that Novalis, like Schleiermacher, remains Romantically anchored, for the abyss, or separation of humans from God, is more that of 'heavy guilt-illusion' than guilt, more the 'Fear of Law's sword' than violation of the Law, more 'Sin's old spectre' than sin and evil itself (S.S. 1).[145] Here the death which he overcame was not illusory, but the evil and rebellion which occasioned such death are diminished in contrast to the heightened prominence given to *feelings* of gloom, despair and hopelessness. This explains why it seems that redemption is received without a great degree of struggle or contrition.

3) Novalis's Ecclesiology

Novalis's ecclesiology was significantly shaped by his commitment to unity. Rather than submit to rationalist compartmentalization, he argued for the interdependency of philosophy and art, history and nature, love and religion. Barth felt that in this Romantic attempt at integration of these diverse areas there was a sense in which they seemed to disappear into each other, or to be subsumed under the principle of a 'Romantic synthesis.'[146]

Küng viewed the urge toward unity in Novalis and fellow Romantic thinkers at Jena as expressive of a 'post-modern paradigm,' rather than being dreamily nostalgic or reactionary. Their longing for a new basis of peace, their search for 'the blue flower' or a 'final home' propelled them toward a vision of religion that integrated faith and reason.[147] This religion would offer an umbrella under which 'denomination and ideologies – including the Freemasons' could be reconciled.[148] Thus he called for 'a visible Church which will take into its bosom all souls athirst for the supernatural, and willingly become the mediatrix between the old world and the new.'[149] In Novalis's vision of the Church, the artist is given a priestly role as a 'guide along the inner way'[150] to lead the Church toward greater unity and toward a sense of harmony with the universe.

Like Schleiermacher, Novalis allowed Christ's centrality to be overshadowed by humanly divined principles of love, peace, and unity, in which revelation is achieved through poetry and intuition. In contrast to Schleiermacher, Novalis asserted that God's intervention was required for human liberation. Yet God's truth must conform to human notions of love and unity, as well as human mystical feelings. With Novalis, the role of the imagination and art has risen to heights loftier than MacDonald would grant.

---

144 Novalis (1, 174), in Neubauer, *Novalis*, p. 115.
145 See ibid., p. 196.
146 Barth, *From Rousseau to Ritschl*, p. 248.
147 Jens and Küng, *Literature and Religion*, pp. 155–63.
148 Ibid., p. 161. F.D. Maurice revealed, however, that in reality this is not a broader but a narrower basis of the Church, for it is founded on human opinion rather than on the Trinitarian God who is Lord of all.
149 Novalis, *Hymns*, pp. 62–3.
150 N. Saul, *History and Poetry in Novalis and in the Tradition of the German Enlightenment* (Bithell Series, University of London, 1984), Vol. 8, p. 79.

c. MacDonald's Response to Novalis

MacDonald reflected aspects of Novalis' theology, though Calvinist influences encouraged greater emphasis on God's sovereignty.[151] Like Novalis, poetry for MacDonald was a higher expression of truth than didactic propositions. The imagination was the means of perceiving deeper meaning, but in a more contingent way. There was only one God and one mediator, who was Jesus Christ. What for Novalis were at times mediators, were for MacDonald metaphors, given by God to bring reality more into focus and to foster greater obedience to God's will.[152] He envisioned the artist as performing a priestly role, in being a purveyor of such a vision from God; but this role was not exclusively held by artists. Many of the wise and 'priestly' types in his books are not poetic (though as their closeness to Christ increases there is a sense in which creativity is increased). For MacDonald, knowledge of God was not based on creativity, but obedience.[153] The infinite is accessible as God's gift to humankind through Christ and through conformity with Christ by his Spirit.

Like Novalis, he rejected the systematic byproducts of abstract philosophizing, but went further to assert that God's truth could never be contained by our systems or opinions, and could never be subsumed under any other category, even that of love or unity. Unlike Novalis, MacDonald's humility kept him from the presumption that he could write a new, more contemporary Bible. Though MacDonald did not view other books as equally revelatory as the Bible, he agreed with Novalis that they could also be inspired. MacDonald expressed concern about the idolatry of those who exalted the Bible as the living Word of God rather than Jesus Christ: 'Jesus alone is the Word of God' and it is discipleship to him that is the highest calling.[154] In his movement away from overly literal interpretations of the Bible, there are times when his arguments about specific passages seem expanded a bit to conform to his theology, as with his greater emphasis on humanity as God's offspring than as God's adopted ones.[155] MacDonald's idea of greater human proximity to God derives in part from the influence of Novalis.[156]

MacDonald's Calvinist background called him continually back to a commitment to the utter uniqueness of the 'self-existent God' who is the one Lord, and who must be approached through the death and life of Christ, and the death and new birth of the believer. In contrast to the depersonalization of God at times by both Federal Calvinists and Romantics like Novalis, MacDonald maintained a consistently personal and relational understanding of God through his vision of God as Father, Son, and Spirit. Like Novalis, he desired that a relationship with God be experienced ecumenically and universally, but viewed this hope as God's creation and under the Lordship of Jesus

---

151 See Wolff, *The Golden Key*, p. 44.
152 See Hindmarsh, 'The Faith of George MacDonald,' p. 91.
153 For example, Janet in *Sir Gibbie*, and Janet in *David Elginbrod*.
154 'Letter to an Unknown Lady' (1866), in *EC*, p.154.
155 MacDonald adopted the term 'offspring' from Acts 17:29.
156 In contrast to Raeper's argument, however, it did not take MacDonald away from a God of judgment to a God who only expressed love; Raeper, *George MacDonald*, p. 49. See, for example, 'Consuming Fire,' *US*, 1, pp. 27–49.

Christ: '... All my hope, all my joy, all my strength are in the Lord Christ and his Father ... all my theories of life and growth are rooted in him; ... his truth is gradually clearing up the mysteries of this world.'[157]

Barth affirmed the power and insight of Novalis and Schleiermacher, and admired their heartfelt love of God and efforts to challenge abstract expressions of theology. However, he challenged the presumption of the 'Romantic synthesis' and efforts to unveil the divine, revealing human religious reflections and 'ideals' to which God must conform. MacDonald's response to this endeavor can be seen symbolically portrayed in *Phantastes*. Anodos desperately longs to lift the veil on his 'Isis' and see the goddess beneath. His singing and adoration bring her form into view, but his attempt to grasp her results in disaster which reveals her utter helplessness and sends him into a land of despair. She is no goddess, but a sort of poetic ideal, and he has learned only of his own selfishness and its damaging effect on that which he loves. Humanity cannot create a bridge across to God nor lift any veil by which humans may grasp and master the divine. And for MacDonald, it was especially the poems of Novalis which express God's initiative in Christ and human dependency on him, those poetical works of his last years which broke through to him and brought refreshment to his soul and to his theology.

Because MacDonald took God's will so seriously, his ethical concern was more prominent, such that even his fantasies dealt with moral development. In contrast, 'Novalis is more concerned with the development of his character's poetic rather than their moral sensibilities.'[158] Still, MacDonald respected him deeply and looked forward to the day when '"somewhere, somehow," [he would] clasp the large hand of Novalis and, gazing on his face, compare his features with those of Saint John.'[159]

To close this section on the influence of European thinkers on MacDonald, it is important to remember that he was asked to resign his pastorate at Arundel partly because of exposure to German thinking.[160] He had translated Novalis's poems and had given them as Christmas presents, and so was considered tainted with all the faults of German Theology.[161] It has not been openly recognized that among the Germans whom MacDonald read and appreciated, Luther was also very significant, though he is not mentioned so overtly as Novalis in his other books. Still, in his anthology of European poems and hymns, *Rampolli*, Luther's works occupy over one fifth of the book (65 out of 302 pages). MacDonald's hunger to know more of God made him a humble learner from those of every denomination, wherever he heard truth in which he could see the face of Christ.

---

157 'Letter to An Unknown Lady' (1866), in *EC*, p.154.

158 R. Hein, 'Faith and Fiction: A Study of the Effects of Religious Convictions in the Adult Fantasies and Novels of George MacDonald,' unpublished thesis (Purdue University, 1971), p. 119.

159 *DO*, p. 230.

160 See footnote 60 in Chapter 1.

161 *GMAW*, pp. 179–80.

Chapter 3

British Theological Influences

In MacDonald's adult life, the most extensive influences on his theological content came from friends who were considered theologically unorthodox and even heretical. Each of these men suffered job loss and/or criticism because of their theology. At times MacDonald wondered if they were all part of a 'new kind of reformation.'[1] Those with whom he developed close friendships include Frederick Denison Maurice, Alexander John Scott, and to a less intimate degree Thomas Erskine and John MacLeod Campbell.[2] Their relationships with Edward Irving meant that he also had an influence on MacDonald, though more indirectly, as no direct contact with him is mentioned in accounts of MacDonald's life.

All of these friends were fellow Scots, except Maurice. They shared a common distrust of human systems and abstract 'notions' (particularly as applied to religious understanding).[3] They also expressed disregard for popular opinion[4] and a willingness to question the traditions 'received from their fathers,' for the sake of believing in 'the Lord God of their fathers.'[5] Though they were all theologically suspect for these and other reasons (MacDonald called them and himself 'heterodox'),[6] they were drawn together by that which they held to be true more than by that which they opposed. Their theological perspectives were closer to the Celtic Christian influences of his own heritage, and thus formed a profound basis from which MacDonald could celebrate and express the gift of the imagination. After a very brief overview of the history of their relationships, the focus of this chapter will be on their primary theological distinctives that so deeply impacted MacDonald.

---

1   Raeper, *George MacDonald,* p. 96. Cf. Nicholas R. Needham, *Thomas Erskine of Linlathen: His Life and Theology* (Edinburgh, 1990), p. 526n.
2   A letter of MacDonald's documents a friendly visit he received from Campbell when he was in Glasgow on 7 January 1869; Hein, personal correspondence (10 October 2005). Cf. Hein, *George MacDonald*, pp. 208–9.
3   See Ellen Flesseman-van Leer, *Grace Abounding* (London: King's College, F.D. Maurice Lectures, 1968), p. v; John B. Logan, 'Thomas Erskine of Linlathen: Lay Theologian of the "Inner Light,"' *Scottish Journal of Theology*, 37 (1984): 23–40; Raeper, *George MacDonald,* p. 242.
4   See Frederick Denison Maurice, *Doctrine of Sacrifice* (London, 1879), p. xxxviii, and Raeper, *George MacDonald*, p. 242.
5   Maurice, *Doctrine of Sacrifice*, pp. 120–21.
6   'MacDonald to his Father' (n.d.), in *GWAW*, pp. 197–8. MacDonald after being asked to resign from Arundel: 'my heterodoxy has driven me out …'; 'MacDonald to Louisa' (1 July 1853, The Beinecke), cited in Hein, *George MacDonald*, p. 91.

1. A Brief History of Relationships

MacDonald was at least a generation younger than each of these men. The relationships between Campbell, Scott, and Erskine began around 1826.[7] Campbell wrote of this meeting forty-three years later, still in amazement that each of them 'and each separately – [had] come to the same light of the divine love in which I was rejoicing. A friendship begun in its light of life.'[8] Irving, soon after through a discussion with Campbell and Scott, adopted belief in 'the doctrine of the universal love of God.' Irving wrote that prior to acknowledging God's unlimited love, 'I was always finding myself striking against something or other, like a fish in a tub; but now I am in the ocean.'[9] Maurice treasured in Irving that which stands as the center point for this entire group of theologians: '… that unless we begin from God – unless we start from the conviction, that *the thing which is done upon earth He doeth it Himself* – the belief in Christ will pass into a belief in a mere Saviour for us – the belief in a Spirit will be at first a mere recognition of certain influences acting upon us, and will evaporate at last into Pantheism.'[10]

MacDonald was especially close to Scott and Maurice. He was amazed 'to have the man [Scott] whose intellect and wisdom I most respect in the world for my friend, he not being ashamed to acknowledge the relation.'[11] He expressed respect and gratitude by naming his firstborn child after him, Lilia Scott. His letters to Scott, addressing him as 'My Master,' reflect his own feelings of intellectual inferiority to him, and his hope one day to write a book good enough 'to let me ask you to allow me to dedicate it to you.'[12] The book, *Robert Falconer*, was completed and dedicated to Scott after his death in 1866. When Scott died, MacDonald wrote to Mrs. Scott and acknowledged her husband as 'the best and greatest of our time.'[13] Scott's tombstone epitaph, quoting Jesus in John 7:17, expresses his commitment to radical obedience as a way of knowing theological truth. This also became a central emphasis of MacDonald's: 'If any man will do His Will, he shall know of the doctrine.'[14]

MacDonald had come to admire Maurice in London during his Highbury days. He likely knew of the storm caused by Maurice's *Theological Essays*, and his consequent expulsion from King's College during 1853, the same year as MacDonald's own

---

7   Johnson, *George MacDonald*, p. 25. Raeper claims the Scott-Erskine meeting took place in 1828; Raeper, *George MacDonald*, pp. 240–41. However, Campbell's letter (see note 8) places it at an earlier date, closer to Johnson's statement.

8   Campbell, 'Letter to his youngest daughter' (26 March 1870), in Needham, *Thomas Erskine of Linlathen*, p. 471.

9   Edward Irving, cited in R.H. Story, *St. Giles' Lectures, Scottish Divines* (Edinburgh, 1883), p. 243.

10 Maurice, *Doctrine of Sacrifice*, p. xiv.

11 'Letter to his father' (August 1855), in *EC*, p. 101.

12 'Letter to A.J. Scott' (29 March 1854, Huntington Library, Manuscript HM 6336).

13 'Letter to Mrs. Scott' (9 February 1866), in *GMAW*, p. 359.

14 Johnson, *George MacDonald*, p. 31.

forced resignation from Arundel. MacDonald attended Maurice's inaugural lecture at the Working Men's College in London in 1854.[15] After the publication of *Within and Without*, he received a letter of appreciation and commendation from Maurice.[16] MacDonald wrote of having visited Maurice in 1858, who introduced him to George Murray Smith. Smith became his publisher for *Phantastes*.[17]

In 1860, Maurice was installed as the rector of the Chapel of St. Peter's in Vere Street, which became MacDonald's spiritual home after he and his family moved to London.[18] Not only did Maurice's theology continue to shape MacDonald, but Maurice also introduced him to the Christian Socialist Movement. It was through Maurice that the MacDonalds met Octavia Hill, who involved them in work with the poor of London.[19] Maurice became godfather to MacDonald's son, Maurice (named after him), and in 1865 when the Chair of Rhetoric and *Belle Lettres* at Edinburgh fell vacant, it was Maurice who wrote one of the testimonials for MacDonald.[20] Maurice and MacDonald discussed the possibility of writing a book together including sermons, prayers, and hymns, but Maurice's failing health prevented such an endeavor.

Theological commitments and approaches drew these men together, and their relationships strengthened them to face the opposition their unpopular beliefs provoked. Each of them embraced the freedom to question all human religious statements, the idea that truth could be expressed from a variety of sources, and supremely that the one consistent source of theological revelation was the Living Word of God, Jesus Christ, as revealed in the Scriptures. Though there were differences, the following discussion will focus on perspectives which they shared in common, primarily as conveyed through Maurice, who wrote more extensively than Scott and who was more influential in MacDonald's life than Erskine.

2. Theological Distinctives

a. Theological Starting Point

For these theologians, the central root of theology was that God exists in Triune communion as revealed through Jesus Christ. In Jesus, the Son of God, humankind may see into the very heart of the Father. Thus Maurice wrote: 'My desire is to ground all theology upon the Name of God the Father, the Son and the Holy Ghost; not to begin from ourselves and our sins; not to measure the straight line by the

---

15 Raeper, *George MacDonald*, p. 104.

16 *GMAW*, p. 194.

17 Phillips, *George MacDonald*, p. 254. Cf. Hein, *George MacDonald*, p. 150.

18 Hein, *George MacDonald*, p. 150. MacDonald left the Congregational denomination and became a lay member of the Church of England; Raeper, *George MacDonald*, p. 242.

19 *GMAW*, p. 368, n. 1. Maurice invited MacDonald to lecture on poetry for Working Women's Classes at which Octavia Hill was present.

20 Raeper, *George MacDonald*, pp. 227–8.

crooked one. This is the method which I have learnt from the Bible. There everything proceeds from God ....'[21]

Maurice felt that theology should not assume the form of a system, but should adapt to God's self-disclosure in Christ. To derive a coherent system, one 'must make the different parts of the scheme fit into each other; his dexterity is shown not in detecting facts, but in cutting them square.'[22] He viewed systems as human ladders even more awkwardly constructed by Protestants than by Catholics.[23] But for him, the opposite of system was not lack of system, but *method*, in which logic would serve as a handmaid rather than a tyrant.

Maurice found Plato helpful in this area, in demonstrating the utter impossibility of framing a comprehensive system which includes 'nature and society, man and God.'[24] However, Maurice resisted any attempt 'to recast Christian doctrine in a particular philosophical mould.'[25] He wrote that people may find 'in that Name into which we are baptized, the reconciliation ... the deliverance from the intellectual dogmas which had kept them asunder.'[26] He described the theological method as 'the oldest of methods. The Bible begins with it in the first Chapter of Genesis. "*God speaks, Man hears*."'[27] It is where 'All things descend from God to the creature, instead of ascending from the creature to God.'[28] For this reason he did not seek to be original as a theologian, but to be faithful. He viewed himself as a digger rather than a builder, seeking to show that 'economics and politics ... must have a ground beneath themselves, that society ... is to be regenerated by finding the law and ground of its order and harmony, the only secret of its existence in God.'[29]

Speaking as one who had come out of the Unitarian tradition, Maurice affirmed the centrality of the Trinity in God's self-communication: 'And, therefore, believing in the Trinity ... I am at the point whence all other truths radiate, and to which

---

21 Maurice, *Doctrine of Sacrifice*, p. xli.

22 Maurice, *Ecclesiastical History*, p. 222, in Alec R. Vidler, *The Theology of F.D. Maurice* (London, 1948), p. 15.

23 Maurice, *Doctrine of Sacrifice*, pp. xvi–xvii.

24 Maurice, *Moral and Metaphysical Philosophy*, Vol. I, p. 150, in Vidler, *The Theology of F.D. Maurice*, p. 16. Cf. Bernard M.G. Reardon, *Religious Thought in the Victorian Age* (London, 1971), pp. 160–69. Maurice has been called a Christian Platonist, but Flesseman-van Leer contests this. Platonist terms, such as 'Logos,' 'Word,' 'were no philosophical concepts for him but were concretely informed by the Person of Jesus Christ'; Ellen Flesseman-van Leer, *Grace Abounding: A Comparison of Frederick Denison Maurice and Karl Barth* (London, 1968), p. 2.

25 Ibid., pp. 169–70.

26 Maurice, *Lincoln's Inn Sermons*, 2, p. 143, in Vidler, p. 124.

27 Maurice, *Tracts for Priests and People* (1862 No. XIV), p. 61, in Vidler, *The Theology of F.D. Maurice*, p. 20 (my italics).

28 Maurice, *Sequel to the Inquiry*, p. 231, in Vidler, *The Theology of F.D. Maurice*, p. 20.

29 Maurice, *Life of F.D. Maurice*, Vol. II, p. 136, in Vidler, *The Theology of F.D. Maurice*, pp. 12–13.

they converge.'[30] He attacked the Bampton Lectures of Dean Mansel, in which he understood Mansel contending that God had only revealed his attitude toward humanity, and not his essential nature: 'Man can only really trust him, if he has the certainty that in no depth of his divinity is God other than as he is known to man.'[31] Similarly, Scott wrote: 'We believe in a God-Man. Plato, Socrates, confessed a God: we confess Immanuel, and His Father – such a God as no man sees, understands, knows, saving inasmuch as he sees, knows and understands the Man Christ Jesus.'[32] Thus Maurice argued vehemently for consistency to be affirmed between the immanent and economic Trinity.

1) Scriptural Basis

The centrality of the Trinity emerged for Maurice (et al.) from Scripture. They all affirmed divine inspiration of the Bible, and while being careful not to equate it with the Living Word of God, affirmed its role to be that of leading humankind to this Word. Maurice saw it as a 'history of God's acts to men, and not of men's thoughts about God,'[33] and thus he embraced it as a place where God would meet humankind to illumine the darkness and to guide them into the light.[34] The Bible was seen as a whole in the light of Christ, without contradiction between the Old and New Testament, for in both: 'everlasting life … is offered to mankind by Christ, who is the only mediator between God and man, being both God and Man.'[35] Though the possibility of error was granted, they were confident that the Holy Spirit could guide God's people into the truth and would demonstrate the authenticity of the Bible.[36]

2) The Inner Light

Confidence in God's gift of an inner light emerged from belief in illumination and guidance provided by the Holy Spirit through the Scriptures. This was not understood as a separate way of acquiring knowledge outside of revelation: 'I hold … that all our knowledge may be traced ultimately to Revelation from God.'[37] Similarly, Maurice asserted: 'I utterly deny that any sect, or any law, or any life framed in conformity therewith, can save a man. A light of nature is to me quite unintelligible. I receive, according to Scripture, Christ as the one Light of the world; and believe that all

---

30 Maurice, *Doctrine of Sacrifice*, pp. xxxv–xxxvi.

31 Flesseman-van Leer, *Grace Abounding*, p. 2.

32 Alexander J. Scott, *On the Divine Will*, extracted from *The Morning Watch*, Vol. 7 (1830): 15.

33 Maurice, *Ecclesiastical History*, p. 2, in Vidler, *The Theology of F.D. Maurice*, p. 16.

34 Maurice, *Patriarchs and Lawgivers*, p. 49, in Vidler, *The Theology of F.D. Maurice*, p. 156.

35 Maurice, *Word Eternal*, pp. 32, 33, note B.

36 Cf. Maurice, *Claims of the Bible*, p. 112, in Vidler, *The Theology of F.D. Maurice*, pp. 162–3; cf. Torben Christensen, *The Divine Order, A Study in F.D. Maurice's Theology* (Leiden, 1973), p. 154, from Maurice, *Introductory Lectures Delivered at Queen's College*, p. 25.

37 Maurice, *Sequel to the Inquiry*, p. 97, in Vidler, *The Theology of F.D. Maurice*, p. 178.

must be saved by Him.'[38] Maurice affirmed that goodness was also expressed by non-Christians, but the only possible source of this goodness could be the 'grace of Christ, and the inspiration of His Spirit.'[39]

Erskine described both subjective and objective aspects of the inner light. An inner confirmation of the truth of the gospel was only possible on the basis of the objective history of God's interactions with creation and the objective reality of the Holy Spirit. The Spirit seals God's truth to each person's heart and grants a sense of inner assurance. Both were seen as essential.[40]

3) The Early Church Fathers

Common sources of wisdom for Maurice and others within this perspective were the Early Church Fathers. Maurice justified his views on Eternal Life and Eternal Death partly on the basis that they were 'directly suggested by the Athanasian Creed.'[41] He also quoted Irenaeus in support of these views, saying: 'he supposes an immortal duration not to be natural to the soul, but a gift of God, which he can take away, and did take away from Adam and restored it again in Christ to them that believe in him and obey him.'[42] Irving found confirmation for his affirmation that Jesus Christ had assumed fallen human flesh also from the Early Church Fathers and the ancient Confessions.[43]

With God's self-revelation in Christ as their theological starting point, each of these thinkers expressed deep confidence and joy in their faith and in their understanding of its implications for humankind. This is in contrast to the lack of confidence they detected in those who placed their trust in God's decrees rather than in God's self. Thus A.J. Scott wrote: '... a confidence in God himself is high above a confidence in his decrees, as the heavens are above the earth.'[44] He spoke of this 'problem of the age' inhibiting people from understanding the full implications of the Holy Spirit dwelling in them, 'such that they are never awed, never strengthened, never raised above the world, by knowing that the Holy Ghost *is in them of a truth.*'[45] The confidence of those like Scott and Maurice, in fact, derived from the apprehension of the character of this God in Christ, who by the Spirit would dwell in them, having cleansed them of all unrighteousness through the shedding of his own blood.

---

38 Maurice, *Word Eternal*, note on note B, p. 34.

39 Ibid., p. 34.

40 See Erskine, *Election*, pp. 171–2, and *Letters*, Vol. I, p. 44, in Needham, *Thomas Erskine of Linlathen*, pp. 441, 92. MacDonald wrote about the inner light which he identified directly with the Holy Spirit: 'I could ... pray God for that inward light which is his spirit'; *SP*, p. 500.

41 Maurice, *Word Eternal*, p. 2. See also Maurice, *Theological Essays*, note on pp. 443–9.

42 Maurice, *Word Eternal*, note F, p. 38. In this note, Maurice also encouraged the reading of Gregory of Nyssa, particularly the close of *De Animâ et Resurrectione*. See also Maurice, *Word Eternal*, p. 23.

43 Mrs. Oliphant, *The Life of Edward Irving* (London, 1862), Vol. 2, p. 12.

44 Scott, 'On the Divine Will,' p. 7.

45 A.J. Scott, 'Hints on 1 Corinthians XIV,' in *Neglected Truths*, No. 1 (London, 1830): 4.

b. The Nature of God

Because of God's self-revelation as Triune, Maurice refused to apply abstract philosophical terms to God, such as 'Omnipresence' and 'Omnipotence.' Omnipotence could be equated with capriciousness and communicated nothing of 'a Father whose will Christ came on earth to manifest and to fulfil.'[46] He left the Unitarian Church, believing that the denial of the gospel that the Son of God took human flesh and died humankind's death in order to reconcile humankind to God 'empties God of His fatherly character, and robs us of the privileges of sons.'[47] Thus he affirmed the Cross of Christ as the complete manifestation of the character of God.[48]

1) The Love of God

In light of the revelation that God is Triune, even beyond God's acts of lovingkindness to humankind, Maurice (et al.) affirmed that God is love in God's innermost Being: 'In the Trinity I find the love for which I have been seeking.'[49] Scott wrote that in Christ, what is shown of the Godhead is not power, but love.[50] Central to the very character of God, this love is neither arbitrary nor capricious.[51] Rather, it is unconditional and limitless. Having confused the Creator with the creature, humankind has cast God in its own image as one who is not entirely trustworthy and who thus must be placated. In truth, Christ reveals that sacrifice is not something God demands of humankind in order to make them worthy, but is part of the very loving character of God, who alone can make them worthy.

Maurice argued that throughout history, as evident in the Bible, humankind has attempted to make sacrifice 'the minister of man's self-will, self-indulgence, self-glorification,' the means of changing the purposes of God to their purposes and ways.[52] None of the Old Testament sacrifices earn people right relationship with God. Rather, each is offered by God as a way of maintaining the relationship God had already initiated. Furthermore, Christ revealed that all true sacrifice 'proceeds from God, which accomplishes the purposes of God in the redemption and reconciliation of His creatures which enables those creatures to become like their Father in Heaven by offering up themselves.'[53] In beholding the Lamb of God that was slain, one sees the meaning of love, which is God's nature.[54] Because God's sacrificial love atones,

---

46 Maurice, *Theological Essays*, p. 287, in Flesseman-van Leer, *Grace Abounding*, p. 2.

47 Maurice, *Doctrine of Sacrifice*, pp. xxix–xxx.

48 Maurice, *Word Eternal*, p. 29.

49 Maurice, *Theological Essays*, p. 302.

50 Scott, 'On the Divine Will,' p. 16. Maurice qualified this idea by affirming Christ's own disclosure of the real essence of power: 'in obedience, humiliation, sacrifice, dwelt the mighty conquering power – that power against which no other in earth or heaven could measure itself'; *Doctrine of Sacrifice*, p. 219.

51 Ibid., pp. 28, 14.

52 Ibid., pp. xliii–xlv.

53 Ibid.

54 Ibid., pp. 220–21.

cleanses, and reconciles, sin is removed rather than accommodated and covered over. Heathen notions of sacrifice foster pride, blasphemously asserting that what is in truth God's gift of reconciliation is instead a human contrivance to bribe God into overlooking sin and revolt.[55] Rather, 'Sacrifice must proceed from the Will of God, and is perfected when the will of man is subdued to it.'[56]

2) The Righteousness of God

Maurice maintained that human notions of righteousness must make way for God's own self-disclosure. Righteousness is to be understood in terms of Jesus Christ, for whom love and righteousness were not in opposition. The righteousness and the love of God are one in 'blotting out the transgressions' and in the way 'the barrier between God and His creatures is removed by Himself.'[57] Thus he repudiated any opposition between gospel and law, stressing that 'law is a form in which God's love meets man.'[58]

This emphasis on the righteousness of God took evil and sin seriously and affirmed belief in the wrath of God. Thus, for example, the flood 'declared the unchangeableness of God's righteous order; that would bend to no transgression; that would overcome all who set up mere power and disorder against it.'[59] He viewed God's wrath as utterly appropriate to God's love and integral to the establishment of God's kingdom: 'If I did not think that God's wrath was burning, and would burn always, against that which is evil and unloving, I could have no faith in His goodness and His love; I should have no hope for the world.'[60] Christ revealed that nothing can separate humankind from God's love, which is stronger than any sin, and which can cast out any darkness.

3) Election

In the light of God's love and righteousness, Maurice affirmed election as being intrinsic to God, rather than purely extrinsic. In divine love which overflows in self-giving, God chose to be God with humanity, with Christ's blood as the 'seal of an everlasting bond that was established before the foundation of the world.'[61] In this way Maurice saw God's predestination as the decision before creation to elect humankind as sons and daughters adopted through a covenant of love. This accorded with the Calvinist doctrine of supralapsarianism in that election preceded creation and the fall.[62] It differed from Calvinism in Maurice's refusal to see the

---

55 Ibid., p. 91.

56 Ibid., p. 86.

57 Maurice, 'Sermon on Romans 3:20–27,' *Doctrine of Sacrifice*, pp. 146–60.

58 Flesseman-van Leer, *Grace Abounding*, p. 5. See Maurice, 'Sermon on Galatians 3:13–14,' *Doctrine of Sacrifice*, p. 139

59 Maurice, *Doctrine of Sacrifice*, p. 28.

60 Maurice, *Word Eternal*, p. 19.

61 Maurice made this comment in reference to Hebrews 9:19–27, cited in Flesseman-van Leer, *Grace Abounding*, p. 31.

62 See ibid., pp. 33–5.

incarnation apart from God's initial purpose in Christ, or a mere remedy for the fall. God's purpose was not frustrated by the fall, but remains guaranteed in Christ. Furthermore, for this reason he objected to both the 'exclusivism and individualism' of Calvinist doctrine.[63] Election is viewed in Christ, 'the eternal Mediator, the living Word, in whom God had created the world, in whom He has held converse with the sons of men.'[64] Thus Maurice wrote that through the Cross of Christ, Paul realized election was not arbitrary and artificial, but rather that Christ is the 'deep and true foundation of that divine election.'[65] Similarly, Scott saw in Christ an affirmation of God's eternal purposes, revealing that God is 'unwilling that sinners should perish' and refuses to be indifferent to the eternal misery of any sinner.[66]

c. The Nature of Humankind

Christ offers the determinative shape to election and human redemption; the fall does not.[67] Humanity is not known apart from Christ any more than God can be known apart from him. Maurice recognized that humanity would not be what it is outside of its relationship with God.[68] He refused to see humankind only in Adam or to build ethical systems on the basis of the fall. Rather, he viewed Christ as the head of every person. All people are claimed by Christ, created and redeemed in him.

Everything against God's will was seen as evil, and human will in opposition to God was seen as diseased and sinful.[69] Without a sacrifice for sins, communion with God would not be possible, but again the sacrifice comes from God to lead people back, not in order to rescue them from God. The Cross for Maurice was not an exemplarist act, nor was Christ a substitute as in a forensic model. Rather, he was the representative of sinful humanity, accomplishing for humanity what it could not accomplish for itself.[70] Christ's representation was twofold, for he represented both God before humanity and humanity before God. In him union was achieved between humanity and God.[71]

Thus when Maurice spoke of human righteousness, it was in terms of Christ's own righteousness. Human righteousness is possible through one's admission that one has no righteousness and that all righteousness must come from God.[72] Humanity was created to be in communion with God, and this was as true after the fall as before. The 'true human condition,' the 'original righteousness' of humankind, is the

---

63 Ibid., p. 35.
64 Maurice, *Doctrine of Sacrifice*, p. 201.
65 Ibid., p. 201.
66 Scott, 'On the Divine Will,' p. 21.
67 Maurice, *Doctrine of Sacrifice*, p. xxxiin.
68 Ibid., p. 4.
69 Maurice, *Epistle to the Hebrew*, p. cxv, in Vidler, *The Theology of F.D. Maurice*, p. 109.
70 Maurice, *Doctrine of Sacrifice*, p. 262; Reardon, pp. 178, 189, 191.
71 MacDonald's development of this view of the Atonement will be explored in detail in Chapter 5.
72 Flesseman-van Leer, *Grace Abounding*, p. 16.

capacity for entering into fellowship with God and with others.[73] The real nature of humans is their 'Christ-nature' rather than 'Adam-nature,' for Christ is 'the true root of humanity' and 'the Head of the human race.'[74]

Maurice affirmed universal atonement on the basis of God's purpose in creation and redemption for humans to share Christ's nature.[75] The problem with limited atonement was that it did not accord with the reality of the Trinity as 'the ground on which all things stand, both things in heaven and things in earth.'[76] Maurice affirmed this foundation as more profound than all evil, and as the basis of the affirmation that Christ has taken away the '*sins of the world*.' Convinced of the unconditional nature of God's love, 'who desires all men to be saved and to come to the knowledge of the truth,'[77] Maurice could not conceive how one could declare 'that Christ came into the world not to save it, but to pronounce the condition of ninety-nine out of every hundred of its inhabitants hopeless.'[78] He believed that to deny the efficacy of the Cross for any person and to treat her as cut off from God was a denial of Christ's death and the full reality of the peace-offering which he had made in himself.[79] The Cross removed everything which gave one a sense of privilege or advantage over another. A great affront to 'the proud religionist,' God's love is absolute and universal, and the Sonship of Christ is the only basis for all communion between God and humanity.[80]

Because of his affirmation of universal atonement, Maurice was repeatedly accused of being a universalist. He adamantly denied this.[81] He did not perceive that salvation is automatic or without the need for repentance. Though all people may claim renewal and regeneration in Christ as their true condition, 'we shall only claim it when we believe that there is a Son of God and a Son of Man,' and when we receive 'the spirit of self-oblation, the spirit in which He offered Himself to God.'[82] He rejected as dangerous the idea of purgatory in which all people, regardless of how ungodly, would be saved through suffering enough pain for their sins,[83] yet he felt it was erroneous to claim that a person's eternal destiny is entirely determined within

---

73 Maurice, *The Life of F.D. Maurice*, Vol. II, ed. F. Maurice (London: 1884), p. 166, and *The Prophets and Kings of the Old Testament* (London and New York, 1904), p. 243, in Flesseman-van Leer, *Grace Abounding*, p. 16.

74 Maurice, *The Life of F.D. Maurice*, Vol. II, p. 408; *Theological Essays*, p. 148.

75 Scott argued for universal atonement on the basis of Christ's fulfillment of the whole law of God. Scott, as recorded by T. Erskine, 'Letter to Rachel Erskine' (6 September 1828), in *Letters*, Vol. I, p. 143, in Needham, *Thomas Erskine of Linlathen*, p. 224.

76 Maurice, *Doctrine of Sacrifice*, p. 194.

77 I Timothy 2:4 (RSV).

78 Maurice, *Word Eternal*, p. 28.

79 Maurice, *Doctrine of Sacrifice*, pp. 206–7.

80 Ibid., pp. 259, 268.

81 Maurice, *Word Eternal*, p. 14.

82 Maurice, *Doctrine of Sacrifice*, pp. 290–91.

83 Maurice, *Word Eternal*, note A, p. 31.

the limitations of this life.[84] He acknowledged the possibility of hell, not in terms of endless duration, but as separation from God and therefore from all possibility of continuance.[85]   But hell was seen as subservient to the love of God, who has pledged to destroy all that is unrighteous and evil.[86] MacDonald wrote a poem of thanksgiving for Maurice in one verse of which he summarized Maurice's teaching on hell. This verse was omitted for publication: 'He taught that hell itself is yet within/ The confines of Thy kingdom; and its fires / The endless conflict of thy love with sin, / That even by horror works its pure desires.'[87]

The utter vastness of God's goodness, that 'the abyss of love is deeper than the abyss of death,' is that which draws the sinner back with the hope of deliverance from the torment of his misery.[88] Maurice refused to make as a positive article of faith, 'that God's will, being what the Scripture says it is, shall *not* finally triumph.'[89] Neither would he claim as fact that every human would eventually conform to God's will, though he was utterly committed to a belief in 'a restitution of all things, which God who cannot lie has promised since the world began.'[90] It was a tension which he refused to resolve, choosing to trust God rather than his own speculations: 'There is such a darkness over the whole question of the possible resistance of the human will, that I must be silent, and tremble and adore.'[91]

Morality for Maurice was not based on a system of punishments or rewards, with fear or selfish pride as motivating forces.[92] It was based rather on loving surrender and trusting self-abandonment.[93] In the account of Abraham and Isaac, Abraham's obedience was in complete trust and surrender to offer back to God that which God had given to him. The '*real* victim' to be slain was Abraham, and when he had been slain, 'the ram caught in the thicket was all that was needed for the *symbolical* expression of that inward oblation.'[94] Abraham was able to learn in this way that 'You cannot trust God too much,' and that the offering of oneself is the root of one's being and freedom. [95] Self-sacrifice should never be ambitious, for it can only be accomplished in the context of the finished sacrifice of Christ, and only as it flows from him as its author and to him as its end.[96] Christ's perfect sacrifice has recreated

---

84 T. Christensen, *The Divine Order*, p. 290, from *Word Eternal*, p. 25; Maurice, *Theological Essays* (1853), p. 441.

85 Maurice viewed the idea of duration as a human projection of time onto the timeless concept of 'eternal'; *Word Eternal*, p. 9.

86 Maurice, *Doctrine of Sacrifice*, pp. 54–5.

87 MacDonald, in *GMAW*, p. 398.

88 Maurice, *Word Eternal*, p. 18.

89 Ibid., p. 16.

90 Maurice, *The Life The Life of F.D. Maurice*, Vol. II, pp. 19f.

91 Maurice, *Word Eternal*, p. 16.

92 Maurice, *Doctrine of Sacrifice*, pp. xli–xliii.

93 Ibid., pp. xliii–xliv, and Scott, 'On the Divine Will,' p. 22.

94 Maurice, *Doctrine of Sacrifice.*, pp. 43.

95 Ibid., p. 46.

96 Ibid., pp. 64–5.

humanity with the privilege and power to sacrifice themselves, redeeming them from the 'miserable death of independence and selfishness,' that they might live lives of freedom and harmony.[97] His Spirit is within them, offering the might of his own sacrifice, fueled by the gift of trust and belief.[98] All human relationships depend on this ability, for 'all right doing has its ground in Sacrifice.'[99] For Maurice, the Church is now God's means by which the revelation of God's true nature and true human nature may be made known to a dying world.

d. The Church and the World

Maurice saw individualism as an expression of the selfish orientation of humanity. He sought to distinguish between *personal* and *individual* for he felt that 'we shall have most sense and lively realization of our distinct personality when we cease to be individuals, and most delight to contemplate ourselves as members of one body in one Head.'[100] The Universal Church was seen as a family with Christ as its Universal head, standing in protest against a world of incoherent fragments in which each person is her own center.[101] It is of God's own making, not 'left to the faith and feelings and notions of men'[102] which result in exclusivism and fragmentation. The gift of belonging to the Communion of Saints is given to all through Christ, for 'by the righteousness of one, the free gift came upon all men unto justification of life.' Maurice, writing on this verse in the fifth chapter of Romans, wrote: 'We cannot enlarge the force or application of such a Gospel. God will confound us, if we dare, by any arrangement of ours, to narrow it.'[103]

   Thus the Church was affirmed as the normal state of human society, humanity with God, while the world evidenced the abnormality of society without allegiance to God.[104] The Church exists to witness to life as it is meant to be lived, and thus its distinctiveness is essential to maintain. To lose this uniqueness is to lose its meaning, its purpose, and paradoxically, its universality.[105] The unity of humankind in Christ shapes an identity for the Church which is 'inclusive, not exclusive, not inward-looking but outward-looking, and outward-looking because upward-looking.'[106] The

---

97   Ibid., p. 309.

98   Ibid., p. 290–93.

99   Ibid., p. 111.

100 Maurice, 'Letter to R. D. Trench' (1835), *Letters and Memorials of R.D. Trench (1888)* Vol. I, p. 190, in Vidler, *The Theology of F.D. Maurice*, p. 183.

101 Maurice, *Lincoln's Inn Sermons*, Vol. I, p. 251, in Vidler, *The Theology of F.D. Maurice*, p. 68.

102 Maurice, *The Kingdom of Christ* (Ev. ed.), Vol. II, p. 309, in Vidler, *The Theology of F.D. Maurice*, p. 219.

103 Maurice, *Doctrine of Sacrifice*, p. 160.

104 See *Theological Essays,* pp. 404f. and Vidler, *The Theology of F.D. Maurice*, p. 79.

105 Maurice, *The Kingdom of Christ* (Ev. ed.), Vol. I, pp. 260f., in Vidler, *The Theology of F.D. Maurice*, p. 70.

106 Ibid., p. 71.

Church invites the world to claim its gift of being in God's own family, an identity grounded on the very being of God, who in the Son has taken our nature to God's self. The Church is not a voluntary society grounded on the will and belief of individuals, but is an ontological reality emerging from the very will of God. Maurice asserted that there is no salvation outside the Church. This does not mean that 'no one can be saved beyond the limits of the visible Church, but that all salvation is within the Church and all who are saved will find when their eyes are opened that they belonged to the Church even though they knew it not.'[107]

In this ontological unity of humanity in Christ, Maurice saw a much 'broader meeting ground' for diversity than any human device for tolerance could ever fashion.[108] He called for ecumenism without any compromise of essential revealed truth, and for prayers to include all people:

> If they will not have a Common Prayer with us, we can make our prayers large enough to include them. Nay, to take in Jews, Turks, Infidels and Heretics, all whose nature Christ has borne. For He is theirs as well as ours. He has died for them as for us, He lives for them as for us. Our privilege and glory is to proclaim Him in this character; we forfeit our own right in Him when we fail to assert a right in Him for all mankind. The baptized Church is not set apart as a witness *for* exclusion but against it.[109]

However, in this call to unity he proclaimed the essential basis of the Trinity: 'no one shall persuade us, for the sake of Unity to part with this Name (of the Father, the Son and the Holy Ghost) or explain it away or substitute some other bond of union in the place of it.'[110] In this sense, the claim by some that Maurice was part of the 'Broad Churchmen' movement is erroneous and one which he himself denied. He accused Liberals of being anti-theological, who in their broadness were essentially narrow as they were based merely on all kinds of opinions: 'But what message have they for the people who do not live upon opinions or care for opinions.'[111] Similarly, in relationship to other religions, Maurice felt there is something to learn from each person's faith,[112] but in the end that all other religions are merely expressions of human systems. It is Christ who is the very Revelation of God.[113]

Because of his emphasis on unconditional grace and ontological union with Christ, Maurice's commitment to the society around him was as a commitment to extended family who had yet to become aware of their kinship. Thus the Christian

---

107 Ibid., p. 80.
108 Maurice, *The Conflict of Good and Evil in Our Day*, p. 182, in Vidler, *The Theology of F.D. Maurice*, p. 15
109 Maurice, *The Prayer Book and The Lord's Prayer* (London, 1880), p. 10.
110 Maurice, *Lincoln's Inn Sermons*, Vol. 2, p. 145, in Vidler, p. 226.
111 Maurice, *The Life of F.D. Maurice*, by F. Maurice, 1, pp. 183f., in Vidler, *The Theology of F.D. Maurice*, p. 218. Cf. Maurice, *Kingdom of Christ*, Vol. 2, pp. 15–16, in Torben Christensen, *The Divine Order: A Study in F.D. Maurice's Theology* (Leiden, 1973), p. 150n.
112 Maurice, *The Religions of the World* (London, 1877, orig. 1847).
113 Ibid., p. 241.

Socialist movement developed as an expression of solidarity with the world under the Fatherhood of God.[114] In response to the call they felt to witness to the true nature of and destiny of non-Christians, Maurice and Scott were both social activists. They were involved in beginning schools for women and working-class men, and because they believed Christ rejects no person, they felt an especially high call to care for the rejected, the poor, and the needy, and in this light to challenge the materialism of the age.

The ground for toleration of all people was to be found in the Church, not in the State, but both were necessary to provide a polar balance to the other. Just as a tyranny is likely if the Church professes to *be* the State, even so 'a State *without* a Church is bound to become a tyranny, for it is forced eventually to try and suppress whoever stands in judgment on it.'[115] Law administered by the society and love that draws all people to a spiritual awakening were both essential.

e. Creation and the Imagination

Knowledge of the Creator and God's redemption of creation in Jesus Christ led Maurice to emphasize the goodness of creation. The created order is caught up in the covenant of grace, and thus expresses meaning and purpose to humankind. As with Coleridge, the imagination perceives and conveys meaning in creation and thus is a vehicle for overcoming the dichotomy between the inner and outer worlds: 'The law of the imagination is a law of fellowship or intercommunion with nature; ... it creates only so far as it sees, and that it sees only so far as it has the faculty of creating ....'[116]

The bridging of polarities of the known and unknown, of the inner and outer worlds, is the gift of relationship accomplished most simply through metaphorical language, and most profoundly through the incarnation. Thus the imagination which accompanies and enables this bridging process is not artificial but integral. In this light, Maurice proclaimed: '... relationships are not artificial types of something divine, but are actually the means and the only means, through which man ascends to any knowledge of the divine.'[117] God has brought the Kingdom into the very midst of God's people, and therefore the world is rich in forms that are symbols of deeper meaning and substance. This can be most obviously grasped through the symbolism of the Bible, which Maurice felt must not be dissected and allegorized away: 'To some the language of symbols may seem unsatisfactory; some may even denounce it as idolatrous and profane. They may speak as they like; but if they will have the Bible, they must have symbols; they must be content to let God speak to

---

114 In 1850, Maurice accepted the designation of 'Christian Socialist' publicly; Reardon, *Religious Thought in the Victorian Age*, p. 208.

115 Prickett, *Romanticism and Religion*, p. 146.

116 Maurice, *Kingdom of Christ*, Vol. 1, p. 181, in Prickett, *Romanticism and Religion*, p. 140.

117 Maurice, *Kingdom of Christ*, p. 275, in Prickett, *Romanticism and Religion*, p. 141.

them through … His forms, and because no others could convey His meaning to the hearts … so well as they do.'[118] Creation and the imagination are gifts of God's grace and can be used by the Holy Spirit to communicate God's love and to draw people into deeper intimacy with God.

Prophetically, Maurice perceived the dangers of approaching creation without the illumination of God's Spirit, particularly in a technological age. He predicted increased fragmentation and alienation: '"Are we to live", he asked, in an age in which every mechanical facility for communication between man and man is multiplied ten-thousandfold", only that the inward isolation, the separation of those whom we meet continually, may be increased in a far greater measure?"'[119] Diminished sense of life's meaning and purpose was producing a combination of vacuity and frenetic activity: 'We feel sometimes as if we were born into a busy, and excited, and yet into an exhausted age … I do not mean that we pursue pleasure or profit less, but we pursue them without exhilaration. The appetite must be kept alive by continual excitements.'[120] In the midst of the increasing sense of hopelessness, he sounded forth the call to envision the Lord working toward the full restoration of creation:[121] 'And therefore, whatever holds the will in bondage, whatever makes these tongues incapable of praising their true King, must be swept away, that He may be known for what He is; that His heavenly glory may not be hid behind the clouds which have been drawn up from the earth.'[122]

3. Criticisms of Maurice and Contrasts with MacDonald

Maurice's conviction that Christ is the Head of every person who heralds the kingdom of God has been called 'unalloyed Romanticism.'[123] Furthermore, his belief that inner and outer worlds are harmonized and unified in Christ has also been attributed to the Romantic current of thinking. Even the idea that humanity was created for union with God, so basic to Maurice (et al.), has been labeled as Romantic. However, Maurice did not express subjectivism, escapism, or radical idealism. He worked very diligently to ground his thinking on the revelation of the Living Word of God as encountered in the Scriptures through the inspiration of the Spirit and in accordance with the early Church Fathers. If Romanticism is taken to mean the minority strand as discussed earlier, then this might possibly apply – that strand which urged uncompromising devotion to the discovery of Truth of Being in harmony with its Trinitarian foundations. Hindmarsh applied the label 'Romantic' to

---

118 Maurice, *Doctrine of Sacrifice*, p. 300.
119 Maurice, *Lincoln's Inn Sermons*, Vol. 5, p. 24, in Reardon, *Religious Thought in the Victorian Age*, p. 213.
120 See Maurice, *Doctrine of Sacrifice*, p. 296.
121 Ibid., p. 307.
122 Ibid., p. 311.
123 Hindmarsh, 'The Faith of George MacDonald,' pp. 116–18. Cf. Raeper, *George MacDonald*, p. 241.

Maurice and Scott pejoratively, however, as that which tempted MacDonald toward 'escaping into Idealism,' and into a deference for the aesthetic over the moral and for content over form.[124] If one studies the impact of Maurice (et al.) on MacDonald, one sees in reality a strong priority of realism and obedience in which attitudes toward the aesthetic and the ideal were informed and shaped by a desire to bring all into conformity with the will and revelation of God.

Though the full impact on MacDonald's theology will become apparent throughout the rest of this book, in which parallels to these thinkers abound, a few contrasting remarks on that which is distinctive in MacDonald will be made at this point. Greville MacDonald rightly perceives little difference between his father and Maurice in content, yet with some variance in emphasis. Greville identified the difference as primarily in their approaches to renewal. Whereas Maurice was 'concerned primarily with the Church's relation to God, my father's interest was with the individuals' such that 'the hope of one for the world's better living centred round Christian Socialism, and that of the other round a theocratic individualism.'[125] Thus he did not hold exactly the same socialist vision as Maurice, but advocated the priority of individual Christian responsibility in bringing hope and renewal to the needy over trying to effect change through legislation or organized societies. MacDonald writes of his hero, Robert Falconer: 'his conviction [was] that whatever good he sought to do ... aid must be effected entirely by individual influence. He had little faith in societies, regarding them chiefly as a wretched substitute ... for that help which the neighbour is to give to his neighbour ... Christians must be in the world as He was in the world ....'[126]

Along with this difference of emphasis, MacDonald's varied approach to theological communication is also pertinent. Whereas Maurice (et al.) conveyed beliefs through more traditional theological exposition, MacDonald communicated his theological perspectives primarily through imaginative literature. For this reason one biographer has commented that 'What A.J. Scott, McLeod Campbell, Thomas Erskine, and F.D. Maurice taught to the few, he has made plain and large to the many ....'[127]

MacDonald deeply respected Maurice, after whom he modeled Robert Falconer in *David Elginbrod.* He particularly delighted in his absolute trust in God, his utter relinquishment to God's will and his willingness to sacrifice all for his fellow human being.[128] Similarly, he greatly admired and learned much from Scott and Erskine. Raeper comments, however, that while acknowledging the deep influence of these and others, 'these men's writing should be seen acting on him rather as a dye on cloth – colours merge – echoes of other hues are visible – but the final mix, the

---

124 Hindmarsh, 'The Faith of George MacDonald,' pp. 48, 57.
125 *GMAW*, p. 401.
126 *RF*, pp. 365–6.
127 Johnson, *George MacDonald*, pp. 80–81.
128 *DE*, p. 333.

colour, is MacDonald's own.'[129] As MacDonald's own colors become evident, they will be shown to bear the same vividness of hope and confidence as these who would proclaim with Maurice:

> We shall not doubt that Christ is, and ever has been, the perfect Mediator between God and man, and that in Him all have access by one Spirit to the Father; but we shall ask ourselves with tenfold earnestness, how it comes to pass that we live so atheistically, so hopelessly, in the world, – how it comes to pass that we can bear to act as aliens and outcasts, when we have been made fellow-citizens with the Saints, and of the Household of God.[130]

4. Conclusion

> Let us understand it well, Brethren; we too are a people dedicated and sacrificed. To some power or other, good or evil, we must be devoted; there is no choice about that.[131]

MacDonald was a person dedicated to the pursuit of Truth that he might serve the Truth with his entire being. The influences on his life were manifold, cleansing the lenses of his theological perception and contributing various colors. From these influences MacDonald received encouragement to approach God more in light of God's self-revelation and to discern where human opinions obscured the vision of God's face in Christ. In their breadth they took him beyond his particular religious tradition, while freeing him to maintain and deepen those beliefs that were rooted in divine revelation. Logical straitjackets of mechanistic thinking could be dismissed, to reveal vibrant possibilities in life and creativity with God as the Lord of theology. When the logic of the Trinity became the central and ordering logic of theology, fences and boxes faded and all of creation and humanity were seen to participate in the meaning and purpose flowing from this Center.

As will be demonstrated, from this basis MacDonald offered theological responses which reflect greater creativity than many of those who influenced him, while also remaining more deeply rooted. This was possible because he managed to hold the thrusts of these influences in tension, anchored by his greater emphasis on obedience to the will of God than perhaps others had expressed, and yet soaring via the imagination in a way that by the Spirit of God enabled him fuller participation in God's own creativity. MacDonald's greater emphasis on obedience was important in ensuring that an acceptance of 'universal atonement' and God's unconditional love would not result in antinomianism and disregard for God's righteousness.

Desiring to serve more than to please, MacDonald was able to learn from a great variety of people, while giving allegiance to no particular party or group. Thus, he preached at Unitarian and Dissenting churches, though he was critical of their

---

129 Raeper, *George MacDonald*, p. 242.
130 Maurice, *Doctrine of Sacrifice*, p. 211.
131 Ibid., p. 63.

tendency toward popularism in order to enlarge the congregation and fill the coffers.[132] Too many were swayed by public opinion and thus kept what he called 'that huge slug, *The Commonplace*' carefully fed and cherished, an endeavor 'officered chiefly by divines and men of science.'[133] The antidote to letting this pervasive monster suck the life-blood from the somnolent soul was to let 'the word of God become as a fire in his bones.'[134] Of all the influences in MacDonald's life, love of God's Word, written and Living, and his desire for it to burn in him and transform him was the most profound. Thus a newspaper commented on MacDonald while in America: 'In others we have known the force of great minds, but in him the glow of a great soul.'[135] In the midst of 'hosts of thinking beings with endless myriads of thoughts' around, MacDonald rejoiced that 'God is nearest to us – *so* near that we cannot see him, but, far beyond seeing him, can know of him infinitely.'[136] The infinite treasure and source of all good influence was seen to abide in Christ: 'The Son of God *is* the Teacher of men, giving to them of His Spirit - that Spirit which manifests the deep things of God, being to a man the mind of Christ. The great heresy of the Church of the present day is unbelief in this Spirit.'[137]

Because MacDonald yearned above all to attend to God's Spirit, the truth he communicated expresses enduring wisdom. Chesterton likened his insights to a castle still standing in the mountains with the light inside burning bright, having survived the winds of an array of philosophies 'blowing through the world like the east wind.'[138] His communication of theology, influenced by those who have been mentioned, as well as others, enlivened what he received such that one may experience in reading MacDonald an awakening from the commonplace to experience more fully the reality of God's ways.

---

132 He consented to preach for the Unitarians, 'provided he was allowed to maintain his own doctrine of the Trinity'; Raeper, *George MacDonald*, pp. 256–7.
133 MacDonald, *The Marquis of Lossie*, pp. 110–11.
134 Ibid., p. 146.
135 Raeper, *George MacDonald*, p. 291.
136 MacDonald, *The Marquis of Lossie*, p. 345.
137 MacDonald, 'The Higher Faith,' *US*, 1, p. 54.
138 Chesterton, 'Introduction,' in *GMAW*, p. 11.

Chapter 4

MacDonald's Theology of the Imagination

MacDonald's reflections on the imagination are expressed throughout his writing, yet most concisely in two essays included in *A Dish of Orts*: 'The Imagination: Its Functions and its Culture' (1867) and 'The Fantastic Imagination' (1893). This chapter will focus on MacDonald's beliefs about the theological roots of the imagination, the work of the baptized imagination, the distinction between fancy and imagination, and his understanding of the relationship between the intellect, imagination, and faith. MacDonald viewed the intellect, imagination, and faith as gifts from God to be used harmoniously and in response to God's will and purpose.

1. Theological Roots of the Imagination

a. In the Nature of God

MacDonald expresses the influence of his Celtic Christian heritage in his reflections on the imagination. Affirmations of both the Triune and artistic nature of God offered a basis from which he was able to rehabilitate the imagination in the midst of traditions that often disparaged it. God's self-revelation as Father, Son, and Spirit was for him the epistemological key for all knowing: 'The secret of the whole story of humanity is the love between the Father and the Son. That is at the root of it all. Upon the love between the Son and the Father hangs the whole universe.'[1]

MacDonald's affirmation of the triune relations as the key to all knowing led him to seek understanding of the imagination and creativity in their light. God's creation is the outflow of divine grace which is at the heart of triune being: 'The love of God is the creating and redeeming, the forming and satisfying power of the universe.'[2] Understanding God as Trinity, with the Father and the Son bonded together in love and overflowing by the Holy Spirit in love and creativity in the universe, led MacDonald to a unique affirmation in the history of theology. He asserted that imagination is first and foremost an attribute of God, derivative of God's love.

Before seeking to understand human imagination in light of God's imagination, MacDonald was careful to acknowledge a radical difference between God and

---

1 George MacDonald, 'Knowing the Risen Lord,' *Proving the Unseen* (New York, 1989), p. 67.
2 'Browning's Christmas Eve,' *DO*, p. 213.

humanity. He held firmly to belief in God's sovereignty and freedom. In this way he averted the Romantic inclination toward pantheism. 'We must not forget, however, that between Creator and poet lies the one unpassable [*sic*] gulf which distinguishes ... all that is God's from all that is man's ... It is better to keep the word *creation* for that calling out of nothing which is the imagination of God ....'[3] God is for MacDonald the only true Creator, 'the first of artists.'[4]

MacDonald also affirmed an innate connection between God the Creator and human creatures, for humans are created in God's image. Rather than limiting the meaning of being created in the image of God to human rationality, MacDonald asserted that the 'prime operation of the power of God' was better understood as loving creativity.[5] This is a significant change of emphasis from the Calvinism of his youth, which correlated the power of God with sovereign will. MacDonald insisted that because: 'The imagination of man is made in the image of the imagination of God ... it will help much toward our understanding of the imagination and its functions in man if we first succeed in regarding aright the imagination of God, in which the imagination of man lives and moves and has its being.'[6]

In order to apprehend the imagination of God, MacDonald looked to God's self-revelation through Scripture and in Christ. He did not seek understanding of the imagination from a mere phenomenological or philosophical study of it. As with all things, MacDonald believed the meaning of the imagination was in its relationship to God: 'The whole of the universe was nothing to Jesus without His Father. The day will come when the whole universe will be nothing to us without the Father, but with the Father an endless glory of delight.'[7]

In identifying imagination as an attribute of God, MacDonald encouraged the idea of freedom and yet harmony within the interplay between divine thought and action, instead of mechanical necessity. As with Calvin, the universe could be approached as 'divine art' that evokes awe at the power and dynamic of Divine creativity.[8]

Here also MacDonald differentiated between the imagination of God and that of humanity. With God, imagination expresses a radical initiative, whereas with humanity it functions more responsively and derivatively. In both there is a putting of thought into form, but for MacDonald God was the creator of the meanings and the forms:

> But when we come to consider the acts embodying the Divine thought (if indeed thought and act be not with him one and the same), then we enter a region of large difference [from humans]. ... Would God give us a drama? He makes a Shakspere [*sic*]. Or would he construct a drama more immediately his own? He begins with the building of the stage

---

3   'The Imagination: Its Functions and Its Culture,' *DO*, pp. 2–3.
4   'Wordsworth's Poetry,' *DO*, p. 246.
5   'The Imagination,' *DO*, p. 2.
6   Ibid., p. 3.
7   MacDonald, 'Knowing the Risen Lord,' *Proving the Unseen*, p. 72.
8   John Calvin, *Institutes of the Christian Religion*, Vol. 1, trans. and ed. John T. McNeill and Ford Lewis Battles (Philadelphia, PA, 1960), Vol. 1, p. 53.

itself, and that stage is the world - a universe of worlds. He makes the actors, and they do not act, – they *are* their part.[9]

God's imagination is operative not only in creation, but also in God's penetration into human life with grace and guidance. Expounding on MacDonald's thought, John McIntyre connects the history of God's relationship to humanity, creation, incarnation, redemption, and sanctification with God's imaginative action.[10] Thus it becomes, according to McIntyre, the ground of God's immanence without loss of God's transcendence.

The Christ-figure in the *Princess* books, the great-great-grandmother Irene, exemplifies MacDonald's understanding of God's ongoing imaginative engagement with people.[11] MacDonald took seriously the biblical assertion that 'The Son is the radiance of God's glory, the exact representation of his being' (Hebrews 1:3). Thus, to represent characteristics in a Christ-figure for him was to convey aspects of God's nature.[12] One can see numerous echoes of biblical themes in MacDonald's stories, for he was steeped in Scripture and approached it as a well from which he drew images and ideas.

Grandmother Irene is a creative and compassionate presence, working with the Princess and Curdie to overcome the destructive forces around them.[13] She creates

---

9   MacDonald, 'The Imagination,' *DO*, pp. 3–4.

10 John McIntyre, *Faith, Theology and Imagination* (Edinburgh, 1987), pp. 48–60.

11 Clues to connect the great-grandmother with Christ are scattered throughout *The Princess and the Goblin* and *The Princess and Curdie*. These will be noted in subsequent paragraphs, but a few salient clues are: 'Irene' means peace; she is the source of light and is called 'the Mother of Light,' which correlates with MacDonald's name for God, which is the 'Father of Lights'; she is associated with the moon, which MacDonald used as an analogy for Christ in *Alec Forbes*; she is a great queen, but humbles herself to become a servant maid who is beaten yet brings about the defeat of evil; she is both judge and the one who is judged; she is described as the 'one centre of harmony and loveliness' in whom 'the whole of creation seemed gathered'; she baptizes with fire and suffers with those who are so baptized;she is recognized in the sharing of a meal and the pouring of the cup of red foaming wine; and she resembles the Rider on the horse in Revelation 19:11, 17, who 'called to all the birds' and executes judgment.

12 To depict God as maternal was consistent with MacDonald's theology and Celtic Christian heritage, as previously noted. Thus MacDonald wrote: 'There is no type so near the highest idea of relation to a God, as that of the child to his mother. Her face is God, her bosom Nature, her arms are Providence – all love – one love – to him an undivided bliss'; 'A Sketch of Individual Development,' *DO*, p. 44. For further reading in this area, see David Neuhouser, 'God as Mother in George MacDonald's "The Wise Woman,"' *Christianity and the Arts*, 4(4) (2000): 42–4.

13 According to Bonnie Lou Gaarden, female divine figures in the fantasies of George MacDonald indicate the traditionally feminine character of his ultimate values: emotion, intuition, instinct, nurture, interdependence, family orientation, cyclic models of development, and a vision of humanity as part of nature; Gaarden, 'The Goddess of George MacDonald,' unpublished thesis (University of New York at Buffalo, 1995), p.

ways of guiding them and sustaining them in the midst of their many trials. For the Princess, the grandmother weaves a ball of very fine thread, which she is to follow regardless of where it takes her. Serving as a rich metaphor for faith, the thread guides her many places where she must face her greatest fears. This includes the deep underground and walking past her gravest enemies, the Goblin King and Queen.

The grandmother creates ways to expand the Princess's capacity to trust, obey, and envision, that she might more fully participate with her in overcoming evil. The closer the Princess draws to her grandmother, the greater vision she has of the grandmother's beauty and compassionate creativity in the lives of the people around her. As the Princess's imagination expands in its ability to envision the grandmother's beautiful nature and realm, her character also grows to harmonize with her grandmother's self-giving and forgiving nature. The grandmother becomes a creative source of vitality both in the Princess's context and character.

Grandmother Irene's imaginative work is expressed also in the way she relates uniquely to each person in the kingdom. Whereas she had revealed herself to the Princess in the castle where she lived, it is in the mines where Curdie works with his father that he learns more of who she is. She is also with him in the thick of the battle and ultimately discloses herself most fully in a Eucharistic meal.[14]

With Curdie, she presents a different means of guidance and empowerment than she offered the Princess. Like Isaiah, whose lips needed the cleansing of burning coal before he could become God's prophet, Curdie must place his hands in the grandmother's purifying fire of roses before he can become her discerning servant.[15] MacDonald reveals her imagination's ability to identify so fully with Curdie when he has plunged his hands into the fire that she is able to bear the pain both with him and for him. Suffering does not mean God's absence, but rather God's long-suffering and creative presence. Initially Curdie was gifted with the ability to create poetry and songs to chase away the more obviously wicked goblins. Now Curdie has become equipped in his hands and heart to confront the deeper evil of insidious characters parading as creatures of beauty and nobility.

As with the princess, Grandmother Irene offers Curdie a mysterious and unexpected guide. His guide is an ugly creature, named Lina, whom he is initially loath to see, let alone to accompany. The development of Curdie's character depends on his ability to look beyond appearances, to have his imagination developed to see into the heart of things, the way the grandmother sees. As his vision of Lina's true

---

20. For a recent discussion of 'goddesses' in MacDonald's writing, see, for example, Fernando Soto, 'Chtonic Aspects of MacDonald's *Phantastes*: From the Rising of the Goddess to the Anodos of Anodos,' *North Wind*, 19 (2000), pp. 19–49.

14 MacDonald offers clear echoes here of the two disciples on the road to Emmaus who finally recognize Jesus in the breaking of the bread (Luke 24:13–35).

15 For an in-depth overview of the connections between Isaiah and *The Princess and Curdie*, see Kirsten J. Johnson, 'Isaiah/Curdie Correlations' (unpublished paper).

character develops, he grows to love her and work more creatively and effectively with her.

Effective service in the kingdom is linked to the strengthening of his imagination to harmonize more fully with Grandmother Irene's. Like her, he must grow to see beyond external ugliness to internal beauty, beyond the lowly status of people to noble character, beyond a sense of being alone and overwhelmed by the odds, to trust in One who is ever present and able to overcome all evil. MacDonald believed that God's creative Spirit enriches people's imaginations to 'live with the sense of the kingdom of heaven about them, and the expectation of something glorious at hand just outside that invisible door which lay between the worlds.'[16]

Curdie must learn that the grandmother creatively adapts to reveal her constant faithfulness in surprising ways, particularized to the needs of a situation or person. She is willing to appear in the stranger and in places one least expects (as the Celts had taught). Thus, as she sends him out she promises: 'But those who know me well, know me whatever new dress or shape or name I may be in; and by and by you will have learned to do so too.'[17] Thus, though she is a grand old lady, she humbles herself and becomes a maiden servant who is misunderstood, abused, and beaten, yet is able to achieve victory over those who are selfish and evil. She is able and willing to appear in that which is other and to employ imaginative measures to further justice and goodness.

Through her creative endeavors she is able to bring good out of evil, and healing out of pain. Curdie's thoughtless wounding of her precious dove had been used to draw him to her, to awaken awareness of his devolving character, and to call him to creative engagement with her kingdom purposes. Pain and suffering which come his way are transformed into deepened purpose and clarified direction, such that 'Curdie's hindrances were always his furtherance.'[18] Thus his prison becomes a route into the castle where he must venture to fulfill his calling.[19]

Included in MacDonald's portrayal of this divine figure is her deep compassion, her imagination's ability to see as if she were the other. Thus her expressions of judgment flow from love rather than stand in opposition to love. Though the grandmother wields judgment on the wicked ministers of the king, MacDonald reveals that she is aiming for restorative rather than retributive justice. Her goal is not annihilation of her enemies but their transformation. As MacDonald wrote in *Lilith*: 'Annihilation itself is no death to evil. Only good where evil was, is evil dead. An evil thing must live with its evil until it chooses to be good. That alone is the slaying of evil.'[20]

---

16 George MacDonald, *Annals of a Quiet Neighbourhood* (London, 1893, orig. 1867), p. 7
17 George MacDonald, *The Princess and Curdie* (Whitethorn, CA, 1997, orig. 1883), p. 78.
18 Ibid., p. 166.
19 This echoes Curdie's earlier imprisonment in the goblin's cave, from which Curdie is led out by the princess and her thread through the back of the cave. At that time he was not imaginative enough to conceive that his prison could be his very means of escape.
20 *Lilith*, p. 153.

To summarize, in the writing samples included above one can discern five key characteristics of God's imagination that MacDonald viewed as the roots out of which wise human imaginations may grow. First, divine imagination is part of God's loving nature, and thus it is wielded in creative self-giving. Second, to characterize God as imaginative is not to suggest a dichotomy between divine thought and actions, but rather to allow for freedom and interplay rather than mechanistic necessity. Third, God's imagination expresses radical initiative in creating a world filled with meaning and purpose. Divine creativity is rooted in love, meaning and purpose rather than in arbitrary will. Fourth, because God is imaginative and can enter into the perspective of the other, God is able to create particularized forms of self-revelation and guidance to honor the uniqueness of diversely created individuals. Through imaginative empathy, God is also able to enter into the pain and suffering of God's creatures and carry that with and for them.[21] Not only does this ease the suffering, it also deepens a sense of intimacy with God and helps the suffering to bear fruit. Thus God's imagination is transformative bringing good out of evil and life out of destruction. Fifth, God's engagement with people remains consistent with God's character, and thus judgment also is a creative expression of compassion and transforming power.

With the imagination rooted in the nature of God, MacDonald rejected the idea that the imagination should operate randomly, arbitrarily, or self-centeredly. MacDonald did not presume to know or to say much about the inner workings of God's imagination. However, in anchoring imagination as a Divine attribute, he sought to negate any Romantic notion that humanity could in an autonomous creativity reach the heights of Truth (like Icarus on wings of wax attempting to reach the Sun). The movement of the imagination is in grace from the Divine to the human. Creativity is a gift from God, because all of life finds it source in God. As artists we wait for 'the new life that is already throbbing in the eager heart of the master Musician – where all is vivid burning life.'[22]

MacDonald rejected notions that creativity derived from being ecstatically overwhelmed by some impersonal force. The ability to participate in God's creative purposes requires perception of meaning that can only be given by God. Thus he preached that one 'must be in the world as [Christ] was in the world, and then the world will blossom around him with all God's meanings, and not merely with men's sayings.'[23] In allowing humanity to participate in creativity there is a sense in which the movement is able to flow back to God, as imagination too is seen by MacDonald as a vehicle of service to and worship of God.

---

21 Similarly, Colin Manlove writes: 'MacDonald is different from all other writers we have so far considered ... [he] is much more incarnational in emphasis: his God has come down to us, made Himself part of our world'; Manlove, *Christian Fantasy* (Notre Dame, IN, 1992), p. 170.

22 'Letter to Mrs. William Cowper-Temple,' in *EC*, p. 274.

23 MacDonald, 'Growth in Grace and Knowledge,' *Proving the Unseen*, pp. 98–9.

Having depicted the imagination as integral to the nature of God, and overflowing into creation, MacDonald then described the imagination as that which puts thought into form, 'not necessarily uttered form, but form capable of being uttered in shape or in sound, or in any mode upon which the senses can lay hold ... the creative faculty.'[24] God's creation therefore is not merely three-dimensional, evidencing form alone, but hidden within it are aspects of divine meaning, thoughts, and purpose. *Creative* can be used only in the primary sense of God. The way in which humankind fulfils this aspect of being made in God's image relates to MacDonald's understanding of the nature of creation.

b. In the Nature of Creation

The relationship between creation and Creator has been controversial in the history of theology. It is beyond the scope of this book to deal exhaustively with this area, but a few preliminary remarks may be helpful in situating MacDonald's understanding

The idea of a sacramental universe, in which everything in creation mirrored some eternal truth, was prominent in the Middle Ages. Consistency and correspondence were seen between the eternal and heavenly patterns within God's mind, patterns within human thinking and the visible, physical universe. The objective rationality of the universe was seen as grounded in the rationality of God, such that 'the meaning of the universe ultimately lies in its sacramental reference beyond the temporal and visible to the eternity of God.'[25] Creation was harmonized and multi-layered in a hierarchical pattern by the hand of God, such that gothic cathedrals soaring heavenward were symbolic of this worldview. Everything was related analogously to God: 'Even a corpse, says Augustine, is like God to the extent that it still has some degree of order left in its decaying flesh and emerging skeleton. In such a universe, everything holds together, everything fits, everything is related.'[26]

This perspective of tight correspondence between God and creation was questioned during the Reformation. Creation's contingent rationality was affirmed, which cannot be applied *a priori*, but which must be worked out in response and openness to God and to the reality around: 'For Calvin, it was not God's mind which tied creation to himself in a relation of logical-causal necessity, but rather God's personal, loving act which bound him to the world.'[27] Fearing idolatry, lest the finite ever be imagined to be capable of the infinite, the Protestant tradition moved away from a more sacramental view to one that is metaphorical: 'One critical difference between symbolic and metaphorical statements is that the latter always contain the

---

24 MacDonald, 'The Imagination,' *DO*, p. 2.
25 Roger J. Newell, 'Participatory Knowledge: Theology as Art and Science in C.S. Lewis and T.F. Torrance,' unpublished Ph.D. thesis (University of Aberdeen, 1983), Vol. 1, p. 77.
26 Sallie McFague, *Metaphorical Theology* (Philadelphia, PA, 1982), p. 6.
27 Newell, 'Participatory Knowledge,' Vol. 1, p. 3.

whisper, "it is *and it is not*".'[28] Nature required greater transformation by grace than in Thomistic thought. From this basis, even the metaphorical aspect of creation came into question. A disparaging view of the natural and physical universe, now seemingly cut off from its role as that which reflects the glory of God was often the result of this shift even though Calvin himself affirmed this role: '[God] revealed himself and daily discloses himself in the whole workmanship of the universe ... this skilful ordering of the universe is for us a sort of mirror in which we can contemplate God who is otherwise invisible.' [29]

Overlooking this affirmation, but concurring with Calvin's insistence on the avoidance of confusion of the Creator with the creature and the sin of idolatry, Federal Calvinism leaned at times toward a radical schism between nature and grace, creation and Creator.[30] Because this harmonized with the philosophical dualism of the day, it gained acceptance as a more orthodox position.

MacDonald did not find this schism consistent with Scripture. It conflicted with his understanding of the nature of God, of creation, of the incarnation, and of redemption. MacDonald's thinking offers four challenges to a deistic separation of God from creation while avoiding a pantheistic merger of them. He advocated a limited form of sacramentalism and correspondence or continuity between God and creation.

First, with creation rather than the fall as the primary basis for his perspective on the world, MacDonald affirmed an intimate relationship between God and creation, with order and harmony built into the very nature of the universe. Humanity, created in God's image, was given the capacity to love and to create (in a contingent way). MacDonald did not ignore the destructive implications of the fall or of sin, but looked to Christ to see the original intent and *telos* of creation. Giving the dominant emphasis to creation over the fall was for MacDonald an affirmation of God's transcendence, that God is first and foremost over all, rather than anthropocentrically giving undue primacy to human sin and brokenness. Sin and evil are not the primary shaping forces of creation; God has been and will always be.

Second, MacDonald challenged the contemporary understanding of *creatio ex nihilo*. Though he accepted creation as 'God calling out of nothing,'[31] he disagreed with the interpretation that God created only according to God's will, and not as the overflow of God's love.[32] Rather, he asserted: 'This world is not merely a thing which God hath made, subjecting it to laws; but it is an expression of the thought,

---

28 McFague, *Metaphorical Theology*, p. 13.

29 Calvin, *Institutes of the Christian Religion*, 1.v. 1–2, pp. 52–3.

30 James Torrance, 'The Incarnation and 'Limited Atonement,' *Evangelical Quarterly*, 55 (1983): 83–94. See, for example, the works of Thomas Boston, S. Rutherford, Dickson, Durham, Witsius, 'The Sum of Saving Knowledge' in Scottish Theology; also C. Hodge's *Systematic Theology*, in North America.

31 MacDonald, 'The Imagination,' *DO*, pp. 2–3.

32 For MacDonald, 'The love of God is the soul of Christianity. Christ is the body of that truth. The love of God is the creating and redeeming, the forming and satisfying power of the universe ... Well does the poet ... say: "The loving worm within its clod / Were diviner

the feeling, the heart of God himself.'[33] As such, creation springs forth from God's self-giving love and is sustained by divine grace: 'Love only could have been able to create.'[34] Toward creation, God stands as a Father towards his own offspring.[35] This does not make matter co-eternal with God, which would limit God and divine freedom. Rather, it grounds matter in God's free gift of loving relationship, a far more dynamic and intimate connection than if creation were a mere extension of God's self, and also expressive of greater creativity. Here is immanence without pantheism, and harmony without loss of God's transcendence.

The third manner in which MacDonald overcame radical dichotomizing of God and creation was through refusing to separate God's creative acts from God's redemptive acts in Christ. Harmony, immanence, and unity were possible even with the fall, because for MacDonald creation cannot be seen in isolation from the incarnation and redemption. Certainly disorder and disunity had broken into the world through sin and evil, as powerfully portrayed by MacDonald in *Lilith*. But the incarnation and crucifixion were God's radical acts of both judgment and commitment to the recreation of God's broken world. Thus: 'at the heart of things and causing them to be ... is an absolute, perfect love; and ... in the man Christ Jesus this love is with us men to take us home. To nothing else do I for one owe any grasp upon life. In this I see the setting right of all things.'[36]

In Christ, the perceived barrier between the material and spiritual realms is broken down, without a loss of God's otherness. Humans share in the baptism of Christ's life and crucifixion, through which the dividing walls between God and humans, humans with one another, and humans with creation have been destroyed. Having shared in Christ's death, they now share in new life, and in Christ they are now 'a new creation' (2 Corinthians 5:17).[37] In Christ, nature and grace, Creator and creation have been brought together in redeeming and recreating love. The imagination also is baptized and participates in Christ's death and new life. Thus, unlike Calvin, MacDonald sought to understand creativity through knowledge of God the Redeemer rather than only through the knowledge of God the Creator.

Anchoring imaginative understanding in Christ makes it a dependent and not autonomous way of thinking, places relational demands on one who would seek to know and express truth imaginatively, places the source for imaginative ability outside of the individual artist, and requires that one acknowledge that the 'enlivener of the imagination' is Christ.[38] There is no separate principle of Beauty from which

---

than a loveless God'; 'Browning's Christmas Eve,' *DO*, p. 213. Cf. Eberhard Jüngel, *God as the Mystery of the World* (Grand Rapids, MI, p. 21.

33 'Wordsworth's Poetry,' *DO*, p. 246.

34 *RF*, p. 232.

35 MacDonald adopted the term 'offspring' from Acts 17:29.

36 'Individual Development,' *DO*, p. 75.

37 'The question is not at present, however, of removing mountains, a thing that will one day be simple to us, but of waking and rising from the dead now'; 'Creation in Christ,' *US*, 3, p. 21.

38 'Individual Development,' *DO*, p. 75.

to evaluate imaginative truth, for Christ is Truth, Goodness, and Beauty, who establishes and enlivens those truths which are in harmony with himself. God has made all things meaningful, and through God's redemptive power is transforming even the most painful and hideous of things into that which holds truth and meaning. However, the full meaning of creation remains hidden for those who resist the Creator. MacDonald saw the search for meaning as a cause for joy and greater intimacy with God.[39] Discovery of meaning is possible as one's heart becomes more and more like Christ's own heart: 'I am always finding out meaning which I did not see before, and which I now cannot see perfectly – for, of course, till my heart is like Christ's great heart, I cannot fully know what He meant.'[40]

MacDonald's emphasis on the Holy Spirit provides a fourth challenge to the idea of a dualistic chasm between God and creation. The Spirit of God is the one who now is actively at work enabling such a transformation in human hearts, that the meaning of God's creation might be more and more evident. The Spirit leads one to Christ that one might see the wisdom and depth in and behind all that God does, creates, and is in the process of redeeming: 'When the Soul is kindled or enlightened by the Holy Ghost, then it beholds what God its Father does, as a Son beholds what his Father does at Home in his own House.'[41] According to MacDonald, a wise imagination is the 'presence of the spirit of God.'[42] This was an acknowledgement of humanity's utter dependency on God for wisdom and truth, and not an attempt to diminish the uniqueness of God's creativity or to see human creativity as divine. Rather, human creativity is a gift of participation in God's creativity, for:

> Our hope lies … in the wisdom wherein we live and move and have our being. Thence we hope for endless forms of beauty informed of truth. If the dark portion of our own being were the origin of our imaginations, we might well fear the apparition of such monsters as would be generated in the sickness of a decay which could never feel - only declare - a slow return towards primeval chaos. But the Maker is our Light.[43]

c. In The Nature of the Imagination

With this view of creation, MacDonald was able to affirm meaning as integral to creation. The universe has an objective reality independent of humanity but intimately harmonized with it. The implications of this perspective for the imagination are fivefold.

1) God as the Source of Meaning and Imaginative Engagement

God, who establishes creation with meaning, is the source for proper imaginative engagement with that meaning. MacDonald was very clear that God's thoughts and

---

39 Ibid., p. 41.
40 'Letter to His Father' (Arundel, 20 May 1853), in *GMAW*, p. 184.
41 Jacob Behmen, *Aurora*, trans. Law, in *DE*, p. 40. See also 'The Imagination,' *DO*, p. 25.
42 'The Imagination,' *DO*, p. 28.
43 Ibid., p. 25 (see 2 Corinthians 4:6).

ways are far beyond humanity's. Thus he distinguished human thought processes from God's, acknowledging that for God thought and Word are prior to things, whereas with humanity, for thought to be valid it must be derivative. Rather than seeking truth in subjective probing or in abstractions, one's thoughts are best informed by the reality of the things around.[44] The imagination cannot wield the sword of truth if it does not correspond with reality as God has created it. Therefore, MacDonald sought to 'keep in front of the things, and look through them to the thoughts behind them. I want to understand! If a thing were not a thought first, it would not be worth anything! Could a thought be worth anything that God had never cared to think?'[45]

MacDonald rejoiced over the vastness of God's thoughts and imaginings. Thus he urged his readers to allow their imaginations to climb and soar as high as possible in the context of their relationship with God: 'Shall God's thoughts be surpassed by man's thoughts? ... God's creation by man's imagination? No. Let us climb to the height of our Alpine desires; let us leave them behind us and ascend the spear-pointed Himmalays [*sic*] of our aspirations; ... still shall we find the heavens higher than the earth, and his thoughts and his ways higher than our thoughts and our ways.'[46]

MacDonald was concerned that many people had been trapped in the confines of their own thoughts and abstractions for too long. They had lost the power of wonder and awe, the power to be so inspired by the work of the Master's hands that they could begin to envision God's greatness and glory. This is not to suggest that God may be truly known outside of Christ, for such inspiration and insight are dependent on being in him and on being indwelt by him.[47] MacDonald concurred with Coleridge, who wrote: 'I more than fear the prevailing taste for Books of natural theology, demonstrations of God from nature, etc ... Evidences of Christianity! I am weary of the word ... remembering only the express declaration of Christ himself: No man comes to me, unless the Father leadeth him!'[48]

2) The Incarnation's Validation of Created Form
The incarnation of the Son of God strengthens the validation of the created order, for the 'Word became flesh and dwelt among us.' Jesus Christ is the 'image of the invisible God, the exact representation of God's being,' God-with-us in the material world. The realm that hosts God's presence is one that the imagination may take seriously. Thus MacDonald's understanding of creation did not call forth an approach of escapism from the world as was common in the Romantic approach to the imagination. Though MacDonald did not view this world as his true home and resting place, still it had been granted authenticity by God. God had created it, the

---

44   See Manlove, *Christian Fantasy*, p. 165.

45   *HA*, p. 28.

46   'The Higher Faith,' *US*, 1, pp. 63–4.

47   'Whatever springs from any other source than the spirit of Jesus, is of sin, and works to thwart the divine will'; *Malcolm*, p. 335. MacDonald did not conceive of this in any narrowing kind of way, but because he held such a glorious vision of Christ, this was an expression of greater freedom and inclusiveness.

48   Coleridge, *Aids to Reflection*, p. 309.

Son had indwelt and redeemed it, and the Spirit is in the process of transforming and bringing creation to ultimate fulfillment. The ideal for him was not an abstraction, but the most real, and was manifest in Jesus Christ, who was 'at home with every form of life, because one with the Heart of all life.'[49] Thus, Greville wrote: '… the more surely George MacDonald realized his Christ, the more surely did he behold God in primrose and lark and child ….'[50]

Thus creation for MacDonald was 'the signature of God's immanence,' and humanity, sharing in '*substantial* unity' with the natural world, can discern personal meaning in it.[51] As Manlove points out, a single thing for MacDonald 'would seem to be and mean many things,' such that language is at times incapable of describing it clearly.[52] Yet, one may imitate Jesus' use of images from the world to communicate truth:

> Where does He find symbols whereby to speak of what goes on in the mind and before the face of His Father in heaven? Not in the temple; not in its rites; not on its altars; not in its holy of holies; He finds them in the world and its lovely-lowly facts; on the roadside, in the field, in the vineyard, in the garden, in the house; in the family, and the commonest of its affairs - the light of the lamp, the leavening of the meal, the neighbour's borrowing, the losing of the coin, the straying of the sheep.[53]

3) Inherent Rather than Projected Meaning

MacDonald was careful to avoid subjectivism, which would stress that meaning was a projection onto creation rather than inherent in it: 'There must be truth in the scent of that pinewood: someone must mean it. There must be a glory in those heavens that depends not upon our imagination: some power greater than they must dwell in them.'[54] This is in contrast to Raeper's assertion that MacDonald embraced the Romantic pattern for art in which 'The primary source and subject matter of a poem, therefore, are the attributes and actions of the poet's own mind.'[55] Rather, MacDonald declared, 'To tell him as comfort, that in his own thought lives the meaning if nowhere else, is mockery worst of all; for if there be no truth in them, if these things be no embodiment, to make them serve as such is to put a candle in a death's-head to light the dying through the place of tombs.'[56] Such a perspective for him was an expression of narcissism, wearing the blinders of pride.[57]

---

49   'Letter to Mrs. Russell Gurney' (1 September 1878), in *EC*, p. 287.

50   *GMAW*, p. 404.

51   Ibid., p. 482.

52   Manlove, *Christian Fantasy*, p. 177.

53   MacDonald, *Life Essential: The Hope of the Gospel*, ed. Rolland Hein (Wheaton, IL, 1974), p. 30; hereafter cited as *HG*.

54   *RF*, p. 123.

55   M.H. Abrams, *The Mirror and the Lamp* (Oxford, 1953), p. 22, cited in Raeper, *George MacDonald*, p. 110.

56   'Individual Development,' *DO*, p. 61.

57   Ibid., p. 60.

Thus when he wrote that the 'world is … the human being turned inside out,'[58] he was not claiming that the world exists only in the mind of the observer. He was asserting that because of harmony between humanity and the world, the world can help one to better understand oneself. It is from the world that forms and ideas surface which clarify what is innate to humanity: 'the world is … an inexhaustible wardrobe for the clothing of human thought. … take the word *emotion* itself – and you will find that its primary meaning is of the outer world. In the swaying of the woods, in the unrest of the "wavy plain," the imagination saw the picture of a well-known condition of the human mind.'[59]

The imagination's function was not to invent new life, but rather to be a bridge by which the wondrous life of God may be discovered, conveyed, and experienced. Any life that humans would invent would fall far short of that which God would share with us: 'The Lord did not die to provide a man with the wretched heaven he may invent for himself, or accept invented for him by others; he died to give him life, and bring him to the heaven of the Father's peace; the children must share in the essential bliss of the Father and the Son.'[60]

4) Multi-dimensional Nature of Life

To see the world with the eyes of science alone, as facts without value except such as can be exploited by humankind, was for MacDonald a flattening of the universe and a squeezing of it into boxes as limited as human reason itself: 'Those who put their faith in Science are trying to live in the scaffold of the house invisible.'[61] MacDonald lived at a time when scientific discovery unhinged many Victorians' faith that had been connected to belief in six-day creation. With Darwinian thought and the discoveries of a world far older than accounted for in six-day creation, many had turned to science for security to hold at bay the possibility of anarchy and chaos as the essential character of the universe. MacDonald was not threatened by such scientific discoveries, because he was convinced that God was still the Creator and had ordered the universe in ways that naturally surpassed human comprehension. He affirmed the imagination guided by the Spirit of this Creative God, as that which opens one's eyes and rescues the world from the reductionism of mundane utilitarianism. Thus, in *Phantastes*, Anodos realized that:

> art rescues nature from the weary and sated regards of our senses, and the degrading injustice of our anxious everyday life, and appealing to the imagination, which dwells apart, reveals Nature in some degree as she really is, and as she represents herself to the eye of the child, whose everyday life, fearless and unambiguous, meets the true import of the wonder-teeming world around him, and rejoices therein without questioning.[62]

---

58 Ibid., p. 9.
59 Ibid., pp. 9–10.
60 'The Truth in Jesus,' *US*, 2, p. 261.
61 'Individual Development,' *DO*, p. 58.
62 *Phantastes*, pp. 89–90.

It is the dull and unchildlike who are unable to see the miracle of the interrelatedness of the universe: 'They are blessed to whom a wonder is not a fable, to whom a mystery is not a mockery, to whom a glory is not an unreality – who are content to ask, "Is it like Him?"'[63]

Creation by the Word of God meant for MacDonald a universe filled with song and meaning, with God having 'put beauty into nature, knowing how it will affect us, and intending that it should so affect us; that he has embodied his own thoughts thus that we might see them and be glad.'[64] Thus, for example, MacDonald found in the reality of the moon and the sun a metaphor for the Son and the Father, 'But the mune ... maun be like the face o' Christ, for it gies licht and ye can luik at it notwithstandin.'[65]

> ... of all material things the sun is likest to God ... If God did not shine into our hearts, they would be dead lumps of cold ... You can't shine of yourself, you can't be good of yourself ... If you turn your face to the sun, my boy, your soul will, when you come to die, feel like an autumn with all the golden fruits of the earth hanging in rich clusters, ready to be gathered ... You will die in peace, hoping for the spring - and such a spring.[66]

Other examples are the fire which spoke of purity and purification, the rose which bespoke freedom, and the snowdrop, humility. One sees especially in *Phantastes*, *Lilith*, and the *Princess and Curdie* harmonious, multi-level ordering of relations, rather than a flat-leveled and simple causal system. John Pridmore describes *Phantastes* as including 'many realms which overlap or interpenetrate, and multiplicity of worlds eliding with each other.'[67]

5) Inspiration of the Spirit

The inherent pattern and meaning become accessible to humankind as the light of God illumines one's imagination. Thus the imagination could function as a mirror of the truth of God. However, it was not a passive way of thinking, but rather a mode of inquiry as well as receptivity: '... To inquire into what God has made is the main function of the imagination. It is aroused by facts, is nourished by facts, seeks for higher and yet higher laws in those facts; but refuses to regard science as the sole interpreter of nature, or the laws of science as the only region of discovery.'[68] For MacDonald, therefore, just as God's imagination expresses meaning and purpose through created forms and reality, human imagination searches out that meaning and purpose to enable understanding and creative expressions that harmonize with God's.

---

63 'The Higher Faith,' *US*, 1, p. 63.
64 'Wordsworth's Poetry,' *DO*, pp. 246–7.
65 *AF*, p. 251.
66 MacDonald, *Ranald Bannerman's Boyhood*, pp. 281, 283 (Ranald's father speaking).
67 John Pridmore, 'George MacDonald's Transfiguring Fantasy,' in *Seven: An Anglo-American Literary Review*, 20 (2003): 57.
68 'The Imagination,' *DO*, p. 2.

The imagination is the faculty for 'those infinite lands of uncertainty lying all about the sphere hollowed out of the dark by the glimmering lamp of our knowledge.'[69] The light which is given to and through the baptized imagination expresses, but always stands *under*, the Truth, which shines with radiance so far beyond the imagination that the latter is always in the role of a handmaiden or a servant. It is never to be seen as that which can itself hold or master the Truth.

The imagination must 'tune its instrument … to the divine harmonies within' creation, 'for the end of imagination is *harmony*.'[70] As a gift for discerning and revealing where there is concord and dissonance with God's design and purposes, the imagination may serve the truth. And such a revelation may awaken awareness and remorse for departure from that harmony along with increasing effort at resonance with it. Thus it is a way of self-transcendence, rather than self-aggrandizement, of God-centeredness rather than self-centeredness, of receiving with gratitude rather than of grasping with fear.

d. The Nature of the Artist in the Context of the Baptized Imagination

It is not surprising that for MacDonald the closer one is to Christ the Creator, the more faithful and vibrant the imagination will be. Closeness to Christ, in character and in relationship, is a gift from God. New creation in Christ for people is an ontological reality through his incarnation, crucifixion, and resurrection, which means that the image of Christ's character can be on all people. However, the full realization and growth of that character only happens in the context of a deepening relationship with him. To see beyond and behind visible reality with imaginative perceptiveness and depth requires: (1) humility, (2) renewal, and (3) love.

1) Childlike Humility
Childlike humility was a continual theme for MacDonald, who saw it as a vital attitude for artists. As MacDonald readily admitted: 'Lord, pity us; we have no making power.'[71] He asserted that the artist was less a *Maker* than a '*Trouvère*, [or] *Finder*.'[72] This entails the recognition that 'No man is capable of seeing for himself the whole of any truth; he needs it echoed back to him from every soul in the universe; and still its centre is hid in the Father of Lights.'[73] It requires openness to reality as it is in itself, including an attitude of trusting awe that reality has meaning and order granted to it and sustained by God.

Imaginative understanding involves ongoing awareness of mystery and pursuit of the wonders of life. Thus the artist does not aim falsely at complete conceptual grasp of the truth, nor become self-satisfied about what is known. MacDonald compared

---

69 Ibid., p. 29.
70 Ibid., p. 35.
71 *DOS* (23 March), p. 61.
72 'The Imagination,' *DO*, p. 20.
73 Ibid., p. 22.

people who are intellectually complacent with horses that prefer the dull twilight of their stables to the exhilarating air and loveliness of the countryside.[74] The artist's role is not to impose a body of information, but rather to awaken a sense of wonder and desire, 'not to give him things to think about, but to wake things up that are in him; or say, to make him think things for himself.'[75] The process might begin by awakening a person to 'a sense of indwelling poverty' and yearning for the dull ember within to 'burn – and give light and heat.'[76]

One sees humble yearning not only in MacDonald's writing about the imagination, but in his own use of it. He expressed a childlike wonder about all of life. He was deeply tied to the earth and the reality around him, such that even his fantasies are rich with images of the earth – homely cottages, simple meals of bread and milk, old women with spinning wheels, cozy fires, and so on. He used these earthly images to awaken people to the sacramental reality of all things, believing that even the simplest things can open windows to greater meaning and life.

The childlike is at the heart of truth for MacDonald. Thus, in 'The Golden Key,' the Oldest man of all is a naked child, and the sage in 'The Wise Woman' reveals that 'hers was the old age of everlasting youth.'[77] As Pridmore has noted, the open-ended nature of many of MacDonald's stories reflects the belief that one must continually seek that which is beyond the story and beyond our lives:[78] 'If you think that it is not finished – I never knew a story that was.'[79] One must continually seek with hope and confidence that 'a great good is coming.'[80]

For the artist, that good might look something like the image of a child which MacDonald conveys in 'The Wise Woman.' In an open glade in the forest, 'on the root of a great oak, sat the loveliest little girl, with her lap full of flowers of all colours, but of such kinds as Rosamond had never before seen.' The girl's eyes express the 'liquid shining' of 'the laughter of the spirit.' Though she delights in the flowers she has gathered, she is yet willing to cast them away. And each flower she casts does not wither, but becomes rooted and grow into fullness of life.[81]

2) Renewal
The need for a second birth is also essential to the artist who would embrace and aptly use the redeemed imagination:

---

74 'The Butcher's Bills,' in *GCC*, p. 55.
75 'The Fantastic Imagination,' *DO*, p. 319.
76 'The Butcher's Bills,' *GCC*, pp. 50–51.
77 'The Golden Key' and 'The Wise Woman or the Lost Princess,' *GCC*, pp. 278–9, 365.
78 Pridmore, 'George MacDonald's Transfiguring Fantasy,' pp. 49–65.
79 'The Wise Woman,' *GCC*, p. 376.
80 *Phantastes*, p. 185.
81 'The Wise Woman,' *GCC*, p. 360.

That thou art nowhere to be found, agree
Wise men, whose eyes are but for surfaces;
Men with eyes opened by the second birth,
To whom the seen, husk of the unseen is,
Descry thee soul of everything on earth.
Who know thy ends, thy means and motions see;
Eyes made for glory soon discover thee.[82]

An artist is not only able to see the earth with new eyes but also in Christ is made a participant with God's creativity. As one draws near to the Father in Christ, God's Spirit enables new forms and thoughts to bubble up in the artist which are part of God's own creative process.[83] One may experience Jesus in the heart's chamber, 'tending the fire, and making it burn with the words of the eternal love and tenderness and patience.'[84] This participation requires not only the cleansing wrought by Christ's redemption, but also an ongoing purity, for 'It is God who gives thee thy mirror of imagination, and if thou keep it clean, it will give thee back no shadow but of the truth.'[85]

In addition, MacDonald emphasized the vital need for obedience in order to share in God's own creativity, for 'he that will do the will of THE POET, shall behold the Beautiful … We believe, therefore, that nothing will do so much for the intellect or the imagination as *being good* - we do not mean after any formula or any creed, but simply after the faith of Him who did the will of his Father in heaven.'[86]

Order and obedience for the artist who embraces the gift of a baptized imagination are not confining and restrictive. Rather, they are like keys which open to the artist greater and greater realms of mystery, granting an ever-expanding vision which is founded on the Truth of reality. For MacDonald, doors and windows are recurring images: 'For his is the realm of openness, of light and space, of sun, stars, and storm – the realm of the falcon. To know this realm you cannot be "cabined, cribbed, and confined" in dark houses, dark religions, or dark egos.'[87]

3) Love
Along with humility and a commitment to have one's life renewed and ordered by God, MacDonald affirmed the need for an artist to be filled with the love of God. It is God's own love as revealed in Jesus Christ which propels one into deep sympathy with the object of one's contemplation, and which enables true engagement with it. Love can uncover the poetic element even in 'the most common pug-faced man

---

82 *DOS* (6 February), p. 31.
83 'The Imagination,' *DO*, p. 24.
84 'Letter to Mrs William-Cowper Temple' (November 1877), in *EC*, p. 270.
85 George MacDonald, *Salted with Fire* (London, 1897), p. 47.
86 'The Imagination,' *DO*, p. 36.
87 Ann Boaden, 'Falcons and Falconers: Vision in the Novels of George MacDonald,' *Christianity and Literature*, 31(1) (1981): 10.

in creation.'[88] Love seeks to find order and meaning in the beloved, and to act in accordance with that order. This is not to restrict art to mere imitation, but rather to see that love opens up one's perspective to new relationships and interconnections which in turn increase one's love and appreciation for the object.

This is most obviously evidenced by MacDonald in his novel *At the Back of the North Wind*. The North Wind, which was for MacDonald very closely tied to his own physical suffering and lung disease, became for him an object of love and appreciation, as expressed through the boy Diamond. The greater his love, the more Diamond is able to approach the North Wind with gratitude and understanding, which in turn illuminates his (and the reader's) perspective on suffering and death. With his enriched imagination, Diamond's suffering becomes the fertile ground from which he can enter into the suffering of others and bring healing and renewal. His imagination is cleansed from fear, with its gripping and crippling nature. Rather, it becomes a source of love, empathy, and freedom, even in the face of death.

It is love which also helps the artist make the connection between doing and being, such that imaginative activity is not divorced from life but as actively engaged with it. Thus the heroes and heroines in MacDonald's books are often also artists whose very art equips and enables others.[89] The purposes of art and of life are one, such that in *Phantastes*, art and life exist on interchangeable terms.[90] Furthermore, the role of the artist is not seen as marginal in a society, but very integral to the ongoing vitality and vision of the society. The artist's prophetic voice harkens people back to reality as it was meant to be perceived and lived.

2. The Baptized Imagination's Role in Overcoming Dualist Thought

MacDonald's Trinitarian approach to the imagination provides significant insights into overcoming dualist thought. Though he did not write explicitly about this subject, the influence of Maurice and Coleridge's extensive writing is visible in his writing. As noted previously, Coleridge believed that the basis of all truth was the doctrine of the Trinity. He perceived in the Trinity clues to understanding creation which overcame both dualism and paradox, which he described through the concept of polarity. Polarity is evident in the Trinity, with God as both Father and Son, both Creator and creature (Jesus Christ), bound together in love by the Holy Spirit. Otherness need not threaten mutual indwelling and uplifting, but rather may enhance and include such mutuality.

Without a Trinitarian basis of reality, the self stands either in utter alienation from reality or totally lost in it. With dichotomy and dualism between humanity and God, either the self is illusion, for God alone is true Being, or the self is engulfed

---

88 *AF*, p. 271.

89 For example, Annie (in *Alec Forbes*) contributes to the building of the boat by being a bard and reciting poetry. Anodos's (*Phantastes*) artistic expression helps the brothers as they prepare for war against evil enemies.

90 See David S. Robb, *George MacDonald* (Edinburgh, 1987), pp. 89–90.

in the Being of God, or the self asserts itself as god.[91] With a Trinitarian basis, polar opposites become agents of transformation in a dynamic interplay, and the relationship itself becomes critical as an aspect of the two entities. The imagination offers a bridge that holds the tension in a polarity and equips one to discern, as in a metaphor, both where there is difference and commonality. It is the imagination's capacity to 'see as if' one were the Other that facilitates the bridge. And it is the imagination's power to retain the mystery of unresolved differences which sustains the polar tension.

For MacDonald, the cleansing and recreation of the imagination in Christ made it an apt relational bridge between polarities. The ability to 'see as if' one were the Other and to hold fast regardless of the differences requires the 'death' of the broken self and of the dull or distorted imagination. It requires a baptism of the imagination. MacDonald viewed the baptized imagination as a cleansing of conscience and an awakening to consciousness which radically confronts dualistic walls. This is a process which one sees in Anodos's development, the main character of *Phantastes*, and which MacDonald hoped to catalyze in the reader as well (as indeed occurred with C.S. Lewis).[92]

As *Phantastes* opens, Anodos is shown to be alienated from nature, from himself, and from others, living dualistically in opposition to everything which is other than himself. The other (whether it is, for example, his great-grandmother, the marble lady, or nature, in the form of the trees) is something he either strives to control, use, and absorb or to fight and to keep at a distance. Even his relationship with himself is a dualism of 'self' and 'shadow-self.' The logic of utilitarianism pervades his understanding initially. His journey through *fairie* land seems to have no ostensible purpose, which mirrors the meaning of his own name, 'pathless,' for he is led out of the realm of utilitarianism and into the imaginative realm. Though there is continuity between both worlds, one aspect of his normal world which becomes obviously problematic in the land of *fairie* (or imagination) is self-centered, non-relational thinking. When he tries to approach life in *fairie* through this filter, the results are often very destructive.

For Anodos to become more whole and to learn to love, he must be willing to die to himself and to his self-referent dualistic ways of thinking. MacDonald represents these deaths or baptisms in numerous ways often connected to water and/or the word. Anodos is called to leave the familiarity of this world and enter into fairie by his great-grandmother, whose voice recalls 'reedy river banks.'[93] He is urged on in this process of dying and rising by the transformation of his bedroom into a place

---

91 Owen Barfield, 'Either: Or,' in *Imagination and the Spirit*, ed. Charles A. Huttar (Grand Rapids, MI, 1971), pp. 32–8.

92 R. McGillis describes MacDonald's contribution to nineteenth-century narrative as his ability to break out of the 'binary framework' and to 'posit the possibility of thinking beyond such opposites'; Roderick McGillis, 'Phantastes and Lilith: Femininity and Freedom,' in William Raeper, *The Gold Thread* (Edinburgh, 1990), pp. 32–4.

93 *Phantastes*, p. 7.

of running waters, a spring overflowing from his basin and a stream of clear water running over his carpet with its patterns 'forsaking their fixed forms and become fluent as the waters.'[94] Likewise, fairie will challenge Anodos to forsake his fixed patterns of thought that cause alienation from, rather than relationship with, others.

Throughout *Phantastes*, Anodos's personal engagement with the written word is evident as a means of cleansing, baptism, and renewal. Early on, he discovers 'wondrous tales of Fairy Land, and olden times, and the Knights of King Arthur's table' in a book that offers protection in a cottage window from the evil ash tree.[95] The book offers protection for him also, through the story of Sir Percivale, who has fallen when seduced by a 'demon lady.'[96] Anodos is enrapt by the story, but his imagination is not yet cleansed and renewed enough for him to see as if he were Sir Percivale and to be wary lest he also succumb to such a lady's wiles. Many more 'deaths' must follow. It is not until much later that he will be able to transcend himself and enter fully into the text. One such example is with the story of Cosmo, who falls in love and must choose between possessing his beloved and letting her go free through his own death: 'Who lives, he dies, who dies, he is alive.'[97] Anodos enters fully into this story and becomes one with the protagonist: 'I was Cosmo, and his history was mine.'[98]

Many failures and many baptisms are required for Anodos to gain understanding of the interrelatedness of all of creation, which MacDonald describes as 'an interradiating connection and dependence of the parts.'[99] He acknowledges having been 'a man beside myself.'[100] After he had violated a girl by breaking her pure crystal globe, his grief and guilt had opened him to refreshment and renewal from a 'cheerful little stream' as a much-needed rebirth. Anodos had followed the stream and climbed into a boat on the stream where he was able to 'lose himself' and be cradled to sleep:[101] 'I felt as if I had died in a dream and should never more awake.'[102]

Another failure, death, and water rebirth sequence is evident in his relationship to the marble lady. Though warned not to touch her, Anodos grasps for her after his song has unveiled her and freed her to move. His refusal to heed this warning means she is lost to him once more. In desolation and depression he wanders, finally welcoming death by plunging 'headlong into the mounting wave below. A blessing, like the kiss of a mother, seemed to alight on my soul, a calm, deeper than that which accompanies a hope deferred, bathed my spirit.'[103] Again, Anodos feels embraced

---

94   Ibid., p. 9.
95   Ibid., p. 15.
96   Ibid., p. 16.
97   Ibid., p. 95.
98   Ibid., p. 84.
99   Ibid., p. 77.
100 Ibid., p. 72.
101 Ibid., p. 66.
102 Ibid., p. 67.
103 Ibid., p. 126.

and soothed, 'like a little sick child, that I should be better to-morrow.'[104] Whether through being reborn in water or, like Sir Percivale, 'plunging into the torrent of mighty deeds,'[105] Anodos's imagination becomes more and more a tool of love and relationship than of fear and distortion.

As Anodos begins to overcome his dualistic approach to life, he begins to live more fully and more freely. In his love for the marble woman and his imaginative song, he had freed her physically from her marble imprisonment, but it is not until he has overcome his compulsion to possess her that he becomes dynamically responsive to who she is. Anodos has moved from an 'either/or' orientation to life,[106] which destroys creativity (depicted, for example, in his destructive grasp of the child's crystal globe), to an ability to see his own interconnectedness with all of life.

Through greater imaginative identification with himself (his own past and present) and with others, Anodos's conscience is enlivened. This means he is able simultaneously to feel surer of who he truly is, while also being able to give himself to another. It is the song of the girl whose globe he had broken which calls him out of the prison (literally portrayed as a prison) of pride and self-satisfaction, another aspect of his 'either/or' thinking (either I am nothing, or I am supremely noble).[107] She sings to him: 'From the narrow desert, O man of pride, / Come into the house, so high and wide.'[108] Though he had felt trapped there, the song calls him beyond himself, making it possible for him simply to open the door and walk out. Then he is able to give his life for others, and in so doing to become truly himself.

MacDonald demonstrates the imagination's power to dissolve the many walls erected for self-preservation and control. As Anodos gains the vision that the world is many-layered and undergirded by a loving presence, he is able to begin to let down his guard, to identify with others, to draw wisdom from the intermingling realms of text, fantasy, and daily life.[109] He is able to die that he might also live.

MacDonald used stories like this to draw readers in that they also might die to themselves and experience the renewal possible by discovering their truer selves. In this way he demonstrated the heart of the gospel: the 'Son came to us – died for the slaying of our selfishness, the destruction of our mean hollow pride, the waking of our childhood.'[110] One must be on guard lest 'the old man, dead through Christ, shall not, vampire-like, creep from his grave and suck the blood of the saints ...,'[111] as Lilith attempted with Vane in *Lilith*. The goal was the expansion of the imagination, empathy with the other, and a sense of interconnection with all of life. MacDonald

---

104 Ibid.

105 Ibid., p. 60.

106 For example, 'Either I must possess and master, or I have no part in that which I desire.'

107 *Phantastes*, pp. 160–63.

108 Ibid., p. 164.

109 Cf. Pridmore, 'George MacDonald's Transfiguring Fantasy,' p. 55, and Rebecca Ankeny, *The Story, the Teller and the Audience in George MacDonald's Fiction* (Lewiston, NY, 2000).

110 'The Voice of Job,' *US*, 2, p. 187.

111 *PF*, p. 166.

described the process in a sermon entitled 'Life': 'Our souls shall be vessels ever growing, and ever as they grow, filled with the more and more life proceeding from the Father and the Son ... what the abundance of the life he came that we might have, we can never know until we have it ... as if we must die of very life ... and be filled with a wine which our souls were heretofore too weak to hold!'[112]

Finally, a very obvious treatment of the movement from dichotomy to polarity through the imagination can be found in MacDonald's short story 'The History of Photogen and Nycteris.' A dualism which becomes a rich polarity is obvious in the development of the boy and girl in the story. Watho is a queen who values knowledge for power, and tries to establish utter separation between the boy (Photogen), who is permitted to see only the day, and the girl (Nycteris) who is allowed to experience only the night. With her determination to maintain rigid dualities and acquire power through knowledge, she epitomizes MacDonald's sense of the destructiveness of intellect without imagination. The *other* for her is an object of manipulation and control, never of empathy or identification. When she loses control of the other, she seeks its destruction. Watho, in her effort to control and master, tries to hold fast to the radical separation of things, and cannot grasp any greater reality than these things in isolation from each other. There is no room for mystery, no room for love. She is an extreme form of Mr. Greatorex in 'Gifts of the Christ Child,' who 'had been indulging his intellect at the expense of his heart.'[113]

In contrast, through their hunger for more, Photogen and Nycteris meet and seek to come to terms with that which is fundamentally *other*. Nycteris, who has lived entirely in the night and darkness, has a more developed imagination and readily sees a kinship in Photogen. She assumes he is a girl like her, which greatly offends him. Nycteris extends herself to care for him with his terror of the night, and is patient and forgiving when he fails to reciprocate that care for her in the daytime. They, like Anodos, must each die to their own myopic ways of thinking and acting. Their life and their freedom depend on being able to enter into the perspective of the other, to gain a sense of their commonality and appreciation of their differences. As their sense of interconnectedness develops, that which had been divided becomes that which enhances and fulfils the other, both in terms of the boy and the girl, and day and night. The central image is of light, and the movement of increased understanding and harmony with reality is reflected in the story's flow from the lamp, to the moon, to the sun, and finally to the Kingdom which needs no other light than the Son of God.

MacDonald's embrace of the imagination as that which overcomes dualistic thinking did not extend like the Romantics to its idolization, to seeing *it* as the place of salvation. Christ alone can assume that role, for he is the Word made flesh, the One who is The Mediator, who breaks down the walls of separation.[114] It is the Trinity that establishes all basis of relationship and meaning, for in God's breaking

---

112 'Life,' *US*, 2, pp. 154–5.
113 *GCC*, p. 14.
114 Ephesians 2:14.

through humanly erected barriers between the sensible and the intelligible, the phenomenal and the noumenal, it is no longer possible to see anything or anyone in utter isolation. Still it is the gift of the imagination which helps the meaning of what God has done and is doing to penetrate, to surface, and to bear fruit. The imagination offers a bridge over which a relationship and even love may travel, for it is able with love to move one beyond oneself into the realm of identification or sympathetic indwelling with the other.

3. Distortions of the Imagination: Distinguishing between Imagination and Fancy

MacDonald was well aware of the danger of distortion in the use of the imagination, and therefore was careful to distinguish between *fancy* and *imagination*. He based his distinction on whether new forms were 'mere inventions' or 'embodiments of old truths.'[115] Critical to its being validated as an embodiment of an old truth is the imagination's relationship to moral law, to the ways and will of God: 'Obeying law, the maker works like his creator; not obeying law, he is such a fool as heaps a pile of stones and calls it a church.'[116] Fancy was associated with unharnessed and whimsical thinking which meddles 'with the relations of live souls … in moral things he must obey – and take their laws with him into his invented world as well.'[117] The imagination must be harnessed to the mind of Christ, the will of God. The result of unharnessed thinking can be seen in three areas: overemphasis on emotional impact, viewing imaginative thought and work merely as ornamentation, and using the imagination to create objects of illusion and superstition.

a. Fancy as Overemphasis on Emotional Impact

MacDonald reacted against the Romantic impulse to evaluate art on the basis of the strength of the emotion evoked by it. A passionate response can be the result of fanciful thinking and writing and have no real connection with Truth. He confronted this issue specifically in dealing with the work of Byron:

> The Byron-fever is in fact a disease belonging to youth, as the hooping-cough to childhood, – working some occult good no doubt in the end. It has its origin, perhaps, in the fact that the poet makes no demand either on the intellect or the conscience, but confines himself to friendly intercourse with those passions whose birth long precedes that of choice in their objects – whence a wealth of emotion is squandered.[118]

---

115 'Essays on Some of the Forms of Literature,' *DO*, p. 231.
116 'The Fantastic Imagination,' *DO*, p. 315.
117 Ibid., p. 316.
118 *AF*, pp. 207–8.

He conceded that there was in Byron 'a magic of that physical force of words,' but was concerned that an emphasis on mere forcefulness could divert attention from character development.[119] The imagination is not a tool for manipulation of the emotions, but rather to align the emotions with reality and with Truth.

b. Imagination as More than Ornamentation

In an age of growing cynicism about the nature of meaning and of Truth, the imagination was granted the task of providing ornamentation. MacDonald saw this as a fanciful reduction of the imagination's purpose. He demonstrated through a character in *Alec Forbes of Howglen* named Cupples that cynicism inhibits true creativity.[120] Mr. Cupples sought to find 'color' outside of a relationship with God, and not finding it, submitted to a grayness about all of life which led to despair and alcoholism. His creativity became totally blocked until he could begin to open up to the meaningfulness of life in relationship to others, to nature, and finally to God. If the imagination is closed to its Life's source, the 'ornamentation' it provides will tend to assume the grayness of the cynicism it attempts to color. In this way it will be an echo of meaninglessness or triviality. Furthermore, because MacDonald believed that the imagination contributed substantially in providing cognitive content, he did not accept an ornamentalist view of metaphorical language.[121]

c. Fancy as the Source of Illusion and Superstition

Similarly, fancy rather than imagination was seen as that which created illusions. MacDonald held that the imagination must run 'upon the rails of truth,'[122] which was summed up for him as the Will of God. The freedom to dream and to imagine was greatly encouraged, but it was always to be in the context of movement toward increasing intimacy with God: 'When a man comes to trust in God thoroughly, he shrinks from castle-building, lest his faintest fancy should run counter to that loveliest Will; but a boy's dreams are nevertheless a part of his education. And the true heart will not leave the blessed conscience out even of its dreams.'[123]

Outside of the context of worship, fancy would take over and create great distortions. This was especially obvious for MacDonald in the area of the 'spiritualism.' To approach the Unknown in this way was 'to creep through the sewers of it to get in. I would not encounter its lovers of garbage, its thieves, impostors, liars, plagiaries, and canaille of all sorts, except I could serve them.'[124] Thus he felt that 'the most killing poison to the imagination must be a strong course

---

119 Ibid., p. 208.
120 Ibid., p. 332.
121 Cf. Janet Martin Soskice, *Metaphor and Religious Language* (Oxford, 1987), pp. 1, 24–5.
122 *HA*, p. 49.
123 *CW*, p. 35.
124 Ibid., p. 47.

of "spiritualism."'[125] Rather than submitting to the servant role of the imagination, fancy becomes with the occult a tool of control and manipulation. True use of the imagination would not bow to the allure of illusion or evil, but would actually cast such bewitchment aside. This is portrayed in *The Princess and the Goblins* through Curdie's repeated defeat and repulsion of the goblins by the use of song and poetry. It is also evident in the quotation of Luther's which MacDonald cited in *Rampolli*: 'An evil spirit cannot dwell / where companions are singing well ....'[126]

For MacDonald, the distinction between *fancy* and *imagination* could be seen as parallel to the distinction between license and a liberty of love: 'Licence is not what we claim when we assert the duty of the imagination to be that of following and finding out the work that God maketh ... It is only the ill-bred, that is, the uncultivated imagination that will amuse itself where it ought to worship and work.'[127] Thus, to negate the imagination because of its abuse in the realm of fancy resembles speaking 'of religion as the mother of cruelty because religion has given more occasion of cruelty, as of all dishonesty and devilry, than any other object of human interest.'[128] Whereas fancy is that which takes people far from their home, from reality as known and experienced, the imagination embodies truth in such a way that one feels as if one is coming *home* – home to a deeper understanding, such that it unveils within the very stable of the mundane an epiphany of meaning.

4. The Relationship between Reason, Imagination, and Faith

> The universe is infinitely wide,
> And conquering Reason, if self-glorified,
> Can nowhere move uncrossed by some new wall
> Or gulf of mystery, which thou alone,
> Imaginative Faith! canst overleap,
> In progress towards the fount of love.[129]

In addition to being demeaned by association with fanciful thinking, the imagination had also been devalued because of its seeming inferiority to reason.[130] It was considered an embarrassment to faith which might by association with imagination be condemned as fanciful. MacDonald addressed this confusion and clarified both the harmony and distinctiveness of reason, imagination, and faith. He avoided the dualistic 'either/or' approach which has often been applied through analyses,

125 Ibid.
126 MacDonald, *Rampolli*, p. 115, citing from Luther's *Song Book*.
127 'The Imagination,' *DO*, p. 12.
128 Ibid., p. 26.
129 Wordsworth (1833), *DO*, p. 30.
130 For example, Hobbes specified the use of metaphors, tropes, and other rhetorical figures as one of the main causes of 'absurd conclusions,' especially in theology; cited in T.R. Wright, *Theology and Literature* (Oxford, 1988), p. 22. See also J. Locke, *Essay Concerning Human Understanding* (Oxford, 1894), Vol. 2, pp. 146–7.

which tends to force people to cling to reason, imagination, or faith at the expense of the others. MacDonald had trained as a scientist, so he was not disparaging of analytic thought, but wanted to clarify reason's limitations in the light of faith and imagination.

a. Reason and Imagination

To discuss analytic thinking, MacDonald used the terms 'reason' or 'intellect.' He asserted that the imagination 'is aroused by facts, is nourished by facts, seeks for higher and yet higher laws in those facts; but refuses to regard science as the sole interpreter of nature or the laws of science as the only region of discovery.'[131] Both imagination and reason require an objective basis in order that the truth of being might be honored: 'There were no imagination without intellect, however much it may appear that intellect can exist without imagination.'[132] The difference emerges in how empirical understanding is gleaned and how it is interpreted and used.

Because the main function of the imagination is 'to inquire into what God has made,'[133] to seek God's meaning in creation, the imagination seeks understanding from within. God's Spirit is the guide in both penetration and interpretation. This is an understanding through integration with the object rather than through dissection from a position of being removed from it: 'To *think* a thing is only to look at it in a glass [mirror]; to know it as God would have us know it, and as we must know it to live, is to see it as we see love in a friend's eyes – to have it as the love the friend sees in ours.'[134] Thus 'science may pull the snowdrop to shreds, but cannot find out' the purpose and meaning for which it was created.[135] Having achieved this harmony with the object, the imagination perceives bridges between it and other aspects of creation. The intellect uses the bridges of the imagination as well, for the discovery of the laws governing objects and for the derivation of models by which analyses of those objects may be understood and described.

MacDonald said to the person of science: 'We yield you your facts. The laws we claim for the prophetic imagination. "He hath set the world *in* man's heart," not in his understanding. And the heart must open the door to the understanding.'[136] Thus he compared the relationship of the intellect to the imagination with that of the laborer to the architect: 'What we mean to insist upon is, that in finding out the works of God, the Intellect must labour, workman-like, under the direction of the architect, Imagination.'[137] Images were seen as prior to concepts, and it was the imagination which was able to extend the 'straitened' (*sic*) region belonging to the pure intellect.[138] The imagination 'sweeps across the borders, searching out new lands into which

---

131 Ibid., p. 2.
132 'The Imagination,' *DO*, p. 11.
133 Ibid., p. 2.
134 MacDonald, *DG*, p. 7.
135 'The Imagination: Its Functions and its Culture,' *DO*, p. 10.
136 Ibid., p. 12.
137 Ibid., p. 11.
138 Ibid., p. 14.

she may guide her plodding brother.'[139] The imagination's discoveries were more important, 'only, wherever Pegasus has shown the way through a bog, the pack-horse which followed has got the praise of the discovery ....'[140] The imagination and intellect were meant to work together, each with its own role yet in harmony with the other.

The limitations of an exclusively intellectual approach were often portrayed in MacDonald's writing. People in his novels, who were bent on amassing knowledge, were incapacitated in relationships and creative processes, and were abstracted in thought and being from the rest of life.[141] Efforts to understand life in this way often led to conclusions that were mere constructs of the mind and distortions of truth. MacDonald especially reacted against this approach theologically, for it resulted in human theories about God, about Christ and his benefits rather than a transforming relationship with Christ. These theories 'will as certainly breed worms as any omer of hoarded manna.'[142] Thus he exclaimed: 'although there is no dividing of the one from the other, the heart can do far more for the intellect than the intellect can do for the heart.'[143] 'A little wonder is worth tons of knowledge.'[144]

b. Faith and Imagination

MacDonald affirmed Bacon's idea that 'Imagination is much akin to miracle-working faith.'[145] Faith, like imagination, moves one beyond mere facts, for reason cannot compass the infinite mysteries of the Godhead. He 'always claimed that faith transcends mind and fact; that its domain is the Kingdom of Love, Imagination and Creative Law – the verities which Science was then so busily and fussily discounting.'[146]

MacDonald in no way asserted equality between faith and imagination, however. Imagination was seen as 'an endless help towards faith, but it is no more faith than a dream of food will make us strong for the next day's work.'[147] It is knowing God 'as the beginning and end, the root and cause, the giver, the enabler, the love and joy ... [that] is life; and faith, in its simplest truest, mightiest form is – to do his will.'[148] The

---

139 Ibid., p. 14.

140 *CW*, p. 46.

141 See Watho in 'The Day Boy and the Night Girl,' Lufa and Walter in *Home Again*, and Harry in *David Elginbrod*.

142 MacDonald, *England's Antiphon*, p. 6.

143 Ibid., p. 4.

144 *HA*, p. 42.

145 'The Imagination,' *DO*, p. 14. Though Bacon denigrated both faith and imagination in the name of science, MacDonald in his ecumenical way received truth from him, in this case the relationship between faith and imagination. He did not agree with Bacon that facts exist in an autonomous, value-free sphere.

146 *GMAW*, p. 336.

147 *DG*, p. 7.

148 Ibid.

imagination depends on faith lest it become like fancy and 'go forth in building airy castles of vain ambition, of boundless riches, of unearned admiration.'[149]

In the context of faith, both imagination and intellect may be transformed and renewed toward increasing alignment with Truth and obedience. For MacDonald, religion cannot 'rise up into her own calm home' when one of these wings is 'broken or paralyzed.'[150] Thus in *Sir Gibbie*, after Janet introduces Gibbie to the story of Jesus, MacDonald goes on to narrate the holistic demands of such truth: 'thus had Gibbie his first lesson in the only thing worth learning, in that which, to be learned at all, demands the united energy of heart and soul and strength and mind ....'[151] Because one is given not just faith in Christ, but also his very faith, Christ works from within to heal, harmonize, and integrate faith, imagination, and reason. It is Christ's Spirit which can keep them on the rails of Truth, which is their liberation and not their slavery.

---

149 'Imagination,' *DO*, p. 30.
150 Ibid.
151 *SG*, p. 141.

Chapter 5

Imagination and Theological Transformation

MacDonald's central theological affirmation was: 'The Word became flesh and dwelt among us.' For MacDonald, Jesus Christ is the source of all truth, beauty and goodness: 'The one originating, living, visible truth, embracing all truths in all relations, is Jesus Christ.'[1] Relationship with Jesus includes personal, theological, and social transformation. The incarnation was the means of complete cleansing through Christ's life, death, and resurrection, yet each person and each generation is called to appropriate afresh its gifts of cleansing, healing, and renewal. Such an appropriation includes openness to transformation of one's thoughts about God and God's realm. This chapter will explore MacDonald's central use of the imagination to inform and transform theology.

Theology, in MacDonald's experience, had been used to marginalize the Word made flesh and to recreate abstractions of God after the image of broken humankind. A remote god puffed up with concern about his own glory, playing with the eternal destiny of humans as if they were pawns in a game of self-exultation, seemed more like people MacDonald knew than the God of Jesus Christ. MacDonald worked his entire life to call people back to the reality of the incarnation: 'For a man to theorize theologically in any form, while he has not so apprehended Christ, or to neglect the gazing on him for the attempt to substantiate to himself any form of belief respecting him, is to bring on himself … errors.'[2]

Initially, MacDonald ushered forth the call to consider Christ through more direct sermons and pastoral work in Arundel. MacDonald preached the love of God for all people, and Christ's life, death, and resurrection as an expression of God's love and power. He took seriously Christ's claim to all authority, and thus challenged people to obey his teachings. He was willing, for example, to preach Jesus' call to trust more in God than in possessions or wealth. These and other frontal assaults on their theology became a catalyst among the congregation to find a new pastor rather than alter their priorities.[3]

---

1   'The Truth,' *US*, 3, p. 79.
2   'Browning's "Christmas Eve,"' *DO*, pp. 206–7.
3   Cf. Rolland Hein, who writes: 'MacDonald's emphasis upon obeying Christ's teachings in everyday life seemed quite removed from the exposition of Calvinist doctrines which they wanted to hear'; Hein, *The Harmony Within: The Spiritual Vision of George MacDonald* (Chicago, IL, 1999), p. 22.

As a rejected pastor who felt called to keep preaching, MacDonald refined the way he approached theological transformation. Jesus' teaching was richly imaginative and transformative, working to dissolve false notions, to construct new visions of reality, and to catalyze people to act on those visions.[4] Such an imaginative approach reached the intellect through the heart, which MacDonald realized is the best way to facilitate theological transformation: 'But it would be of no use to try to get it out of his head by any argument ... To get people's hearts right is of much more importance than convincing their judgments. Right judgment will follow.'[5]

MacDonald had experienced what Malcolm Guite describes as a certain kind of abstract theology. Because it 'used words in such a way as to alienate people from the incarnate Word, so now it falls to the artist to redeem language, to use imaginative language to restore what a language devoid of imagination has destroyed.'[6] MacDonald relied on the Bible and its imagery when developing a more imaginative approach to theology. In fact, as he grew older he wrote to a dear friend that his experience was of 'more and more delight in my New Testament.'[7]

However, MacDonald believed one should not approach the Bible as a proof text, as one would approach 'a proposition of Euclid or a chemical experiment.'[8] Rather, MacDonald saw it as 'the most precious thing in the world because it tells me his story. ... It is Jesus who is the Revelation of God, not the Bible' though it 'is indeed sent us by God.'[9] MacDonald understood the Bible as analogical, not because it falls short of the standards of truth, but precisely because the truth to which it witnesses can only be expressed in such language. Since the main actor of the biblical story is God, appropriate language is necessary. Jesus' main mode of teaching as parabolical exemplifies proper language about God and God's kingdom.

MacDonald believed that the Bible and theology are to equip people to see Jesus, to trust him as Master and Savior, and to follow him in all aspects of their lives. The one 'who will order his way by the word of the Master shall partake of his peace, and shall have in himself a growing conviction that in him are hid all the treasure of wisdom and knowledge ....'[10] In fact, for MacDonald, Jesus is literally *theology*, the logos of God. Thus, he wrote: 'Gibbie's ideas of God he got all from the mouth of Theology himself, the Word of God,' whom he encountered as Janet Grant read to him from the New Testament.[11] Good theology reflects Jesus, and therefore conveys truth that is personal and dynamic.

---

4   I am indebted to James Fowler for this tri-partite description of the work of the imagination; James Fowler, 'Future Christians and Church Education,' in Theodore Runyon (trans. and ed.), *Hope for the Church* (Nashville, TN, 1979), pp. 103–4.

5   *SP*, pp. 470–71.

6   M. Guite, 'Christ and the Redemption of Language,' in Jeremy Begbie (ed.), *Beholding the Glory* (Grand Rapids, MI, 2000), p. 28.

7   'Letter to Mrs. William Cowper-Temple' (20 March 1879), in *EC*, p. 292.

8   'Letter to an Unknown Lady' (1866), in *EC*, p 154.

9   Ibid., p. 154.

10 Ibid.

11 SG, p. 141.

MacDonald demonstrated that a biblically infused imagination is vital for discipleship toward Christ-likeness. The rest of this chapter will focus on the ways in which, for MacDonald, the imagination serves theology by nourishing a more Christ-centered vision of God. First, in theological transformation the imagination operates as a solvent on encrusted and deadening concepts to open a new way to deep and abiding faith in God.[12] Second, the imagination can nourish visions of God's nature and kingdom that fill the heart with hope for this life and for life hereafter. Third, this chapter will introduce the imagination's ability to catalyze obedience, which is essential to transforming theology. Chapter 6 will include a more thorough exploration of MacDonald's vision of humanity liberated for obedience in holistic theological transformation.

1. Subversive Solvent toward Faith

> But thou art making me, I thank thee, sire.
> What thou hast done and doest thou know'st well,
> And I will help thee: gently in thy fire
> I will lie burning; on thy potter's-wheel
> I will whirl patient, though my brain should reel.
> Thy grace shall be enough the grief to quell,
> And growing strength perfect through weakness dire.[13]

MacDonald experienced the painful cost of theological transformation in his own life. He knew that deepened faith and trust were essential to enable openness to such a process. Before the seed of faith could grow, the ground of the hardened heart and intellect had to be softened. The baptized imagination works as a solvent on human presumptions of control. In this way it can cleanse and open up the heart to redirect it toward the Living God: 'Wherever the water of life is received, it sinks and softens and hollows, until it reaches, far down … and thenceforth there is in that soul a well of water springing up into everlasting life.'[14]

MacDonald expresses at least two dynamics to make way for faith and trust to flourish: awakening the imagination, and confronting distorted images of God. In some ways theology in MacDonald's era had become parasitic, draining Christian confidence in God. As Lilith had to face her own brokenness and become willing to lose her clenched hand to save her life, even so MacDonald created narratives to help people face the implications of their espoused theology. His stories demonstrate the destructiveness of trying to attain theological mastery in lieu of serving the Master.

---

12 Robert Trexler writes: 'His very best stories operate within a new space, a borderland in which old certitudes must be dismantled before they can be reinvigorated'; Trexler, 'George MacDonald: Merging Myth and Method,' *Bulletin of the NY C.S. Lewis Society*, 34(4) (July/August 2003): 1–13.

13 MacDonald, *DOS* (2 October), p. 201.

14 Ibid., p 143.

In order for the imagination to work as a solvent, MacDonald endeavors to engage readers and reactivate their imaginations. The deadening spell of the Enlightenment had to be cast off in order to awaken people to the dynamic life of faith.

> For repose is not the end of education; its end is a noble unrest, an ever renewed awaking from the dead, a ceaseless questioning of the past for the interpretation of the future, an urging on of the motions of life, which had better far be accelerated into fever, than retarded into lethargy. By those who consider a balanced repose the end of culture, the imagination must necessarily be regarded as the one faculty before all others to be suppressed.[15]

MacDonald's description of the power of the imagination to awaken and educate is relevant to our own era. 'The key pathology of our time,' according to Walter Brueggemann, 'is the reduction of our imagination so that we are too numbed, satiated, and co-opted to do serious imaginative work.'[16] Much of MacDonald's approach was to awaken readers to the desolation which results from dulled imaginations by depicting it through various narratives. Along with awakening the imagination, MacDonald used the imagination to expose the theological perspectives which he considered distorted and inconsistent with God's revelation in Jesus Christ. The heart of his critique was directed at concepts which weaken trust and obedience through their depictions of God.

a. Reawakening the Imagination

MacDonald worked to stimulate imaginative growth and development in people. One key approach was to portray the protagonists of his stories on a journey in which they are confronted with mysteries and wonders that expose the limits of their own ways of thinking and living. MacDonald's readers are invited to enter into the journeys vicariously to awaken their deeper desires, which were often dulled by egocentric and mechanistic ways of thinking. He reveals that God's creativity in nature and human creativity in the arts provide sources of renewal along the journey if one will be open to them. The imagination challenges the deadening tendency to want to contain truth in controlled boxes and convenient systems.

MacDonald believed that theological theories which were developed into water-tight systems actually militated against their truth claims in allowing no room for mystery: 'If I knew of a theory in which was never an uncompleted arch or turret, in whose circling wall was never a ragged breach, that theory I should know but to avoid: such gaps are the eternal windows through which the dawn shall look in. A complete theory is a vault of stone around the theorist - whose very being yet depends on room to grow.'[17] Closed theological systems were not grounded in the Eternal, but in the transitory, and therefore were full of distortion, for the Eternal can

---

15 'The Imagination,' *DO*, pp. 1–2.

16 Walter Brueggemann, *Interpretation and Obedience* (Minneapolis, MN, 1991), p. 185.

17 *Malcolm*, p. 296.

never be contained in any human theoretical structure: 'The greatest forces lie in the region of the uncomprehended.'[18]

The imagination with its embrace of mystery is able to challenge what MacDonald calls 'intellectual greed' which would seek to explain everything. Intellectual greed is a problem of the 'self,' and the self, not the intellect, is the real enemy of both discipleship and creativity.[19] The self finds it offensive to encounter that which cannot be mastered, to admit utter dependence and need. However, even the self is a mystery and must not be diminished by abstraction and analysis, but rather seen in the context which offers it health – a context of relationships and integration with life.

MacDonald imaginatively portrayed the struggle of the self for power and the need for it to be cast out and to 'die.'[20] It is a frequent theme in his work, but most vividly portrayed in the pilgrimages of his protagonists in *Phantastes* and in *Lilith*. It is noteworthy that he wrote *Lilith* at a point of great concern about his son Greville's struggles. MacDonald awakens readers to the cost of intellectual greed in *Lilith*, through Vane's encounter with a radiant creature he calls a bird-butterfly. This creature is eager to share its light and to guide him. Overwhelmed by its beauty and glory, Vane seeks to hold it in his hand rather than to follow it. He grabs it, and in so doing extinguishes its light and discovers he is left only with a 'dead book with boards outspread [which] lay cold and heavy in my hand.'[21]

In addition to pilgrimage narratives, examples of MacDonald's use of the imagination to awaken the imagination abound. He uses humorous imagery to convey dullness of imagination in 'The Light Princess' and *The Princess and the Goblin*.

The 'light princess' has been cursed from birth with an absence of gravity. She is too 'light-headed' to be able to fall in love.[22] She lacks all imaginative capacity to enter into the experience of others, and thus is utterly self-absorbed: 'She cares for nothing here. There is no relation between her and this world.'[23] Her imagination is initially enlivened when by accident she finds herself in a lake. Water, she discovers, is the one place where she experiences gravity, and it awakens passion in her to be immersed in water as much as possible. It causes her to yearn for something beyond herself.

A prince falls in love with her and sacrifices himself to ensure she will have as much water as that to which she has grown accustomed. She is still so imaginatively dull that she understands nothing of his sacrifice or impending death. The prince sings a love song to awaken her which includes: 'Let, I pray, one thought of me / Spring, a

---

18 'The Fantastic Imagination,' *DO*, p. 319.
19 David Holbrook, 'George MacDonald and Dreams of the Other World,' *Seven: An Anglo-American Literary Review*, 4 (1983): 27–37.
20 MacDonald, *St. George and St. Michael* (London, 1886), Vol. 3, p. 129.
21 *Lilith*, p. 47.
22 'The Light Princess,' *GCC*, pp. 121, 128–9.
23 Ibid., p. 127.

little well, in thee; / Lest thy loveless soul be found / Like a dry and thirsty ground.'[24]
Her imagination ultimately only awakens when in the prince's dying moment she
feels both grief and love. In this story, MacDonald dispels the common notion that a
strong imagination can be equated with 'light-headedness,' and awakens the reader
to the essential role it plays in the deepest of human experiences.

In *The Princess and the Goblin*, MacDonald reveals that imaginative dullness is
connected also with thick-headedness. The goblins have very hard heads filled with
knowledge, yet are extremely vulnerable in their tender feet (weak soles/souls?).
They are very proud of their technological skills and ability to create lamps which
they feel are vastly superior to the sun, freeing them to live subterranean lives. Their
dull-wittedness means they appreciate only the utility of a thing, not the wonder
of something beyond their control. Thus they congratulate themselves: 'What a
distinction it is, to provide our own light, instead of being dependent on a thing hung
up in the air … Quite glaring and vulgar, I call it, though no doubt useful to poor
creatures who haven't the wit to make light for themselves!'[25]

The goblins 'hated verse of any kind,' but valued deviousness and cleverness.
They use their knowledge to torment those who live above ground.[26] Their purpose is
to expand their area of control, not to grow in character or creativity. Destructiveness
naturally results, ultimately the destructiveness of their own lives and realm.

A third story of imaginative awakening deals with intellectual naiveté. Photogen,
in 'The History of Photogen and Nycteris,' parallels the many characters in
MacDonald's stories who begin as rather unimaginative but who are awakened
to their own limitations and the wonder of life beyond their control. MacDonald
exposes in Photogen's character the common illusion that with enough hard work
and determination, humans can bring all things under their rule. Before Photogen
can develop faith in something greater than himself, he needs a liminal experience
in which he is confronted with the absurdity of his egocentric illusions. As a person
raised only in the light, he is confident of his mastery of all things, with little
imagination or sense of mystery.

MacDonald believed that 'the influences of reviving nature' were instrumental
in awakening people to larger truths.[27] Nature offers a terrifying awakening for
Photogen to an utterly new experience of reality – that of darkness and night. He
is faced with his own fear and finitude. Such a humiliation is initially hard for him
to bear, but it becomes a doorway out of his isolation and imaginative dullness. He
develops the capacity to see as if he were the other, in this case Nycteris, the girl
raised only in darkness. And he learns to value things for their beauty and mystery
rather than simply as objects of conquest. As with Margaret in *David Elginbrod*,
mystery opens up a way to the sacred, and to communion with the other.[28] It also

---

24 Ibid., p 151.
25 MacDonald, *The Princess and the Goblin* (Oxford, 1990 edn.), p. 45.
26 Ibid., pp. 37, 6.
27 *DE*, p. 22.
28 Ibid., pp. 32–3.

expands Photogen's character and identity such that he discovers that his very being exists in communion. MacDonald conveys the theologically rich perspective articulated more recently by Eastern Orthodox theologians such as John Zizioulas: 'True being comes only from the free person, from the person who loves freely – that is, who freely affirms his being, his identity, by means of an event of communion with other persons.'[29]

MacDonald offers what Tolkien described as 'recovery': 'We need, in any case, to clean our windows; so that the things seen clearly may be freed from the drab blur of triteness or familiarity – from possessiveness.'[30] It requires an awakening to the larger realities of life and growth in humility, whether by seeing ourselves mirrored in the selfishness of the princess, the ludicrous lives of the goblins, going on a journey with a character like Photogen into nature and relationship, or by discovering the gift of poetry, music, or the arts like numerous other characters of MacDonald's.[31]

In these ways, MacDonald awakens the reader to the possibility of self-transcendence, first in the lives of his characters, and second in their own lives. He alerts them to the dangers of illusion and alienation, and offers possible means of escape. As C.S. Lewis wrote: 'Literary experience heals the wound, without undermining the privilege of individuality ... Here, as in worship, in love, in moral action, and in knowing, I transcend myself; and am never more myself than when I do.'[32]

b. Confronting Distorted Images of God

It is the heart that is not yet sure of its God, that is afraid to laugh in his presence.[33]

They shut up God's precious light in the horn lantern of human theory, and the lantern casts such shadows on the path to the kingdom as seem to dim eyes insurmountable obstructions. Instead of God's truth they offer man's theory, and accuse of rebellion against God such as cannot live on the husks they call food.[34]

In working to deepen faith, MacDonald offered subversive images which both critiqued perspectives of God that he thought were untrue to Jesus' revelation, and opened people up to visions which seemed more harmonious with Jesus' character. MacDonald developed images reflecting harsh and punitive characteristics, such as a harsh schoolmaster or a cruel pastor, as well as images to portray a more tender view of God's loving nature, such as feminine images, images from nature, and wise

---

29 John D. Zizioulas, *Being as Communion* (London, 1985), p. 18.

30 J.R.R. Tolkien, 'On Fairy-stories,' *in Tree and Leaf* (London, 1992, orig. 1964), p. 53.

31 A few examples are Hugh and Margaret reading Coleridge and Wordsworth in *David Elginbrod*, Robert Falconer and his violin in *Robert Falconer*, and Malcolm and the poetry of Novalis in *Malcolm*.

32 C.S. Lewis, *Experiment in Criticism* (Cambridge, 1961), pp. 140–41.

33 *SG*, p. 141.

34 *WMM*, p. 106.

fathers or mentors. In order to clarify MacDonald's critique, a summary of those beliefs he disputed will be interspersed with his iconoclastic imagery. Because the Federal Calvinist view of the atonement was so integral to beliefs about God, it will also be a significant focus of this section.

1) Legal and Vindictive Rather than Relational and Restorative
MacDonald grieved that the understanding of God presented to him early on bore greater similarity to his cruel schoolmasters than to the God and Father of Jesus Christ. MacDonald used parodies of his teachers to reflect back to his culture what Federal Calvinist ideas about God's character were actually suggesting. He took ideas of God out of the sanitizing air of the abstract and earthed them to reveal their implications. MacDonald revealed that common portrayals of God would be repugnant if attributed to normal human beings:[35]

> There is not to be found a more thorough impersonation of his own theology than a Scotch schoolmaster of the rough old-fashioned type. His pleasure was law, irrespective of right or wrong, and the reward of submission to law was immunity from punishment. He had his favourites in various degrees, whom he chose according to inexplicable directions of feeling ratified by 'the freedom of his own will.' These found it easy to please him, while those with whom he was not primarily pleased, found it impossible to please him ... one cannot help thinking it must have been for his own glory rather than their good that he treated them thus.[36]

Through the teacher in *Alec Forbes of Howglen*, MacDonald fleshed out the assumptions and implications of using primarily legal terms for framing God's relationship with humankind. The legal framework meant that God was depicted as Judge often to the exclusion of being Father. Such a depiction emerged from a process which began with philosophical theories of God as impassible, immovable, and omnipotent. It also derived from separating nature and grace, and from elevating the fall of humankind (seen as the breaking of the Law) to be the framework of humankind's relationship with God, rather than creation and redemption.[37] God was supremely the Lawgiver and Judge: 'They think of the father of souls as if he had abdicated his fatherhood for their sins, and assumed the judge. If he put off his fatherhood, which he cannot do, for it is an eternal fact, he puts off with it all relation to us.'[38]

Relationship with God was seen by the Federal Calvinists of whom MacDonald wrote as being established on more of a contractual than a covenantal basis. God's encounter with Abraham initiated the contract, which MacDonald described as being

---

35 Cf. 'A God who cannot suffer cannot love either. A God who cannot love is a dead God. He is poorer than any man or woman'; Moltmann, *The Trinity and the Kingdom of God*, trans. Margaret Kohl (London, 1981), p. 38.

36 *AF*, p. 117.

37 See the following section for further development.

38 'Justice,' *US*, 3, p. 160.

for them: 'such a legal document constituting the only reliable protection against the character, inclinations, and duties of the Almighty, whose uncovenanted mercies are of a very doubtful nature ....'[39] With humanity's relationship to God reduced to legal terms, and with humanity's consistent failure to fulfill the requirements of those terms, God in his holiness became unapproachable: '... unable to believe in the forgiveness of their father in heaven, they invented a way to be forgiven that should not demand of him so much; which might make it right for him to forgive; which should save them from having to believe downright in the tenderness of his father-heart, for that they found impossible.'[40]

MacDonald did not want to diminish the idea of God as Lawgiver. However, the distortions produced by isolating this as the one great attribute of God emptied God's 'Fatherhood' of true and eternal meaning. In order to convey this, MacDonald's depicts a schoolmaster who with his harsh blows reflects the nature of a god emptied of parental love and motivated by raw 'justice.'

> ... theology had come in and taught him that they were in their own nature bad-with a badness for which the only set-off he knew or could introduce was blows ... these blows were an embodiment of justice; for 'every sin,' as the catechism teaches,' deserveth God's wrath and curse both in this life and that which is to come.' The master therefore was only a co-worker with God in every pandy he inflicted on his pupils.[41]

It was as if the fall had obliterated completely any vestige of the *imago dei* from humans, along with God's fatherly care for any but the elect: 'For [human] nature was hell, being not born *in* sin and brought forth in iniquity, but born sin and brought forth iniquity.'[42]

In order to convey the impact of giving such central focus to the fall, MacDonald revealed the rather dour personalities of those who most adamantly espoused this view. The kind of legal view which MacDonald confronted seemed to rob people of joy, as evident, for example, in the grandmother in *Robert Falconer* and mother in *What's Mine's Mine*. Sin was elevated above grace in terms of the relative impact on humanity both now and eternally, such that the fallen condition, hell, and destruction became the theological framework through which life was perceived. God may act as Father only to the very few arbitrarily chosen, but as one is never certain of being among the elect, the relational possibilities remain uncertain. Without such emphasis on the fall, it was claimed, the seriousness of sin would be underestimated and the Cross diminished of its power to re-establish the elect in a proper legal relationship to God.

MacDonald, in emphasizing God's nature as loving Father, did not deny the seriousness of sin, however. It is because of God's parental love that nothing will

---

39 *AF*, p. 162.

40 'Justice,' *US*, pp. 140–41.

41 *AF*, pp. 132–3.

42 *RF*, pp. 76–8. See Maurice, *The Prayer Book and the Lord's Prayer* (London, 1880), p. 118.

be held back in freeing sons and daughters from the corruption and devastation of sin. The theme of God as a consuming fire was recurrent in his writing, for he believed: 'All sin is unpardonable. There is no compromise to be made with it.'[43] Yet for MacDonald the normative state was not fallenness, but righteousness evident through the overarching metanarrative of Scripture: the goodness of creation, humanity created in God's image, Christ's redemptive recreation of humanity in that image, the presence of the Holy Spirit in God's children, and the eschatological reconciliation of all things in Christ. And for MacDonald, God's Fatherly/Motherly character is central to Christ's revelation.

When viewed through a forensic framework, law and justice became abstract entities separate from God, rather than understood in the context of divine reconciling love. Law was treated as resolute and supreme even over God, whose glory and grace depended on submitting to its demands. This idea is somewhat evident in Lewis's portrayal of the atonement in *The Lion, The Witch, and The Wardrobe*, which would have concerned MacDonald, his 'mentor.'

In contrast to resolute law, God was conceived as arbitrary and untrustworthy, offering 'terms worthy of an old Roman father, half law-circumventing lawyer, half heartless tyrant.'[44] Justice was identified as the application of penalties for sin, and salvation as the freedom from the consequences of the just punishment. God seemed more concerned with vindictive punishment than with the restoration of sons and daughters. These views seemed not only dishonoring to God, but highly illogical:

> They say first, God must punish the sinner, for justice requires it; then they say he does not punish the sinner, but punishes a perfectly righteous man instead, attributes his righteousness to the sinner, and so continues just … Justice *could not* treat a righteous man as an unrighteous; neither, if justice required the punishment of sin, *could* justice let the sinner go unpunished … Pray God I have no righteousness imputed to me … nothing will serve my need but to be made a righteous man, one that will no more sin.[45]

MacDonald rejected the idea of imputed righteousness. It seemed to be more a theory *about* the biblical perspective than one derived *from* it: 'We have the word *imputed* just once in the New Testament.'[46] He explained that it is used with regard to Abraham's faith which was imputed to him for righteousness.[47] To conceive of God the Father of Jesus Christ being satisfied in clothing sons and daughters with a veneer of righteousness was not MacDonald's idea of biblical law or justice: 'There is no clothing in a robe of imputed righteousness, that poorest of legal cobwebs spun by spiritual spiders.'[48] In a humorous portrayal of a mother questioning her son about the robe of righteousness Christ had given, she asked, '"An' what called he them,

---

43 'It Shall Not Be Forgiven,' *US*, 1, p. 88.
44 *WMM*, p. 98.
45 'Righteousness,' *US*, 3, p. 212.
46 Ibid.
47 Ibid., pp. 213–14.
48 'The Last Farthing,' *US*, 2, p. 104.

Johnnie, that put on the robe?" ... "Whited sepulchres," answered Johnnie, indebted for his wit to his wool-gathering.'[49] Without a Trinitarian sense of Christ, the God-human, coming in the Spirit to mediate God to humanity, one was left with only a veneer or show of righteousness, rather than 'life essential.'[50]

MacDonald depicted the distant and self-preoccupied image of God that results from rejecting Christ's full mediatory role. Though the Patristic fathers taught that Christ had assumed our full humanity in order to transform it from within, Federal Calvinists maintained an extrinsic view, Christ paying a debt rather than participating in our humanity. It was as if God would not draw near to filthy sinners. MacDonald's hero David Elginbrod characterizes the issue in this way: 'An' that'll no be dune by pittin' a robe o' richteousness upo' him, afore he's gotten a clean skin aneath't. As gin a father cudna bide to see the puir scabbit skin o' his ain wee bit bairnie, ay, or o' his prodigal son either, but bude to hap it a' up afore he cud lat it come near him!'[51] The extrinsic salvation taught by Federal Calvinists was, according to MacDonald, a 'sort of legal fiction, Jesus was treated as what he was not, in order that we might be treated as what we are not.'[52] MacDonald was adamant that '... Christ is our righteousness, not that we should escape punishment, still less escape being righteous, but as the live potent creator of righteousness in us ... He *is* our righteousness, and that righteousness is no fiction, no pretence, no imputation.'[53]

MacDonald observed that an extrinsic view of the atonement actually promoted lawlessness and a sense of impunity from any punishment for one's sins. This was antithetical to the import of true theology. Hogg's parody, *Confessions of a Justified Sinner*, referenced in MacDonald's work, portrays the idea of hollow righteousness rather dramatically when the very 'righteous' wife of the laird, assured by her minister that certainly she was among the elect, exclaims: 'How delightful to think that a justified person can do no wrong! Who would not envy the liberty wherewith we are made free?'[54] The minister and the laird's wife proceed together to conceive two illegitimate children. The laird insightfully comments to Mr. Wringhim, the minister: 'You are one, Sir, whose righteousness consists in splitting the doctrines of Calvin into thousands of undistinguishable films, and in setting up a system of justifying-grace against all breaches of all laws, moral or divine.'[55]

It is this particular working out of human ideas of legality which MacDonald rejected, not the idea of God's wrath against sin or the need for the satisfaction of God's justice. MacDonald argued: 'They invented a satisfaction for sin which was an insult to God. He sought no satisfaction, but an obedient return to the Father.

---

49 *DE*, p. 39.
50 'Life,' in *US*, 2, p. 152
51 *DE*, p. 37.
52 'Righteousness,' *US*, 3, p. 210.
53 'The Last Farthing,' *US*, 2, p. 104.
54 Hogg, *Confessions*, p. 24.
55 Ibid., p. 26.

What satisfaction was needed he made himself in what he did to cause them to turn from evil and go back to him.'[56]

MacDonald opposed views of the atonement that reduced the idea of justice to the punishment of sin. The idea that God is bent on destroying both sin and sinner rather than on transforming the sinner into one who is just was also parodied in Hogg's *Confessions*. The man who ascribes to this theory feels called to partner with God in destroying all sinners that the saints may inherit the earth.[57]

MacDonald also believed the Federal Calvinist opposition of justice to mercy was unfounded: 'There is *no opposition, no* strife whatever, between mercy and justice. Those who say justice means the punishing of sin, and mercy the not punishing of sin, and attribute both to God, would make a schism in the very idea of God.'[58] For MacDonald, justice is administered because of God's merciful desire to restore, rather than a vengeful anger to destroy. MacDonald wrote: 'Nothing can satisfy the justice of God but justice in his creature. The justice of God is the love of what is right, and the doing of what is right. Eternal misery in the name of justice could satisfy none but a demon whose bad laws had been broken.'[59] Punishment is executed 'in order to deliver his creature.'[60] Thus justice for MacDonald is the destruction of sin in God's creation to bring creatures into right relationships with the Father and with one another.

Because MacDonald viewed God's nature as Love, he rejected the idea of suffering as a satisfaction for sin. Only human hate and human revenge would find such satisfaction in the suffering of the guilty one.[61] To attribute to God satisfaction in the suffering of One who is innocent seemed unthinkable:

> If there be no satisfaction to justice in the mere punishment of the wrong-doer, what shall we say of the notion of satisfying justice by causing one to suffer who is not the wrong-doer? And what, moreover, shall we say to the notion that, just because he is not the person who deserves to be punished, but is absolutely innocent, his suffering gives perfect satisfaction to the perfect justice?[62]

MacDonald parodied this kind of attitude in *Alec Forbes of Howglen*, through the schoolmaster who feels it is just to inflict punishment on any and all students based on their natural depravity and on the idea that vindictive punishment is the right arm of justice. When Annie is found to be guilty of a misdemeanor, Alec, though innocent, willingly takes the brutal punishment in her place. It is obvious that though

---

56 'Justice,' *US*, 3, p. 141. Cf. John McLeod Campbell, *The Nature of Atonement* (6th edn., London, 1915), p. 134.

57 James Hogg, *The Private Memoirs and Confessions of a Justified Sinner* (London, 1926), p. 143.

58 'Justice,' *US*, 3, pp. 114, 119.

59 *WMM*, p. 109.

60 'Justice,' *US*, 3, p. 127.

61 Ibid., p. 125.

62 Ibid., p. 136.

Alec's response is noble, Murdoch Malison is anything but just in his approach, and it is only his pride that is satisfied. The idea that God could be satisfied by brutally punishing Christ, making it possible for him to be merciful to the few while still applying punishment to the multitudes of the unregenerate, is proclaimed by a young minister in *Malcolm*. In his sermon he delights in comparing the punishment of the lost to the dogs outside Jerusalem, 'condemned to rush howling for ever about the walls of the New Jerusalem, haunting the gates they durst not enter.'[63]

MacDonald longed to enable people to look deeper into the truth of God's self-revelation, and as Michael Phillips comments, to look 'into the inexhaustible depths of God's loving plan.'[64] According to MacDonald, Christ suffered not to placate God and to meet God's penal demands, but as God with us, laboring to transform humanity and to effect deep reconciliation. The atonement offered cleansing from the pollution of sin, not merely the punishment, enabling not a legal outcome, but one of fellowship.[65] God's goal for creation and the fulfilling of the Law was for MacDonald best summarized by Jesus, both in his life and his words: 'Thou shall love the Lord your God with all your heart, soul, strength and mind, and your neighbor as yourself.' The Law serves the purpose of relationship, 'That you will be my people and I will be your God,' rather than emptying it of any true relational content. To focus on the atonement as God's vindictive punishment changes the 'Christian' message into a paganism of external rituals: 'The use of form where love is not is killing ... It is life that awakes life.'[66]

2) Fearsome Rather than Loving

> There was no escaping her. She was the all-seeing eye personified - the eye of the God of the theologians of his country, always searching out the evil, and refusing to acknowledge the good![67]

> He leaned over the world, a dark care, an immovable fate, bearing down with the weight of his presence all aspiration, all budding delights of children and young persons: all must crouch before him, and uphold his glory with the sacrificial death of every impulse, every admiration, every lightness of heart, every bubble of laughter.[68]

What astounded and angered MacDonald more than any other aspect of Federal Calvinism was what he considered its misrepresentation of God as more fearsome than loving. The image of a vindictive judge searching to crush any opposition or breach of the law evoked the desire to flee rather than to draw near in faith. MacDonald offered an analogical depiction of this perspective through the miners'

---

63 *Malcolm*, p. 303.

64 Phillips, *George MacDonald*, p. 200.

65 Campbell, *The Nature of Atonement*, p. 194.

66 George MacDonald, *The Elect Lady* (London, 1888), p. 82.

67 *RF*, p. 152.

68 Ibid, p. 156.

approach to the divine figure, the great-great-grandmother, in *The Princess and Curdie*. The miners misjudge her to be untrustworthy and cruel. They resolve to avoid her and run from her, thus determining never to examine their prejudices about her. They project onto her their own deviousness and selfishness, and read all of her attempts to aid them in that light. For some, it is easier to believe that she does not exist at all than to be willing to grant any measure of goodness in her. In *The Elect Lady*, MacDonald describes this tendency as slander of God: 'They talk about the glory of God, but they make it consist in pure selfishness! According to them, he seeks everything for himself; which is dead against the truth of God, a diabolic slander of God. It does not trouble them to believe such things about God; they do not even desire that God should not be like that; they only want to escape him.'[69]

MacDonald saw such notions of God as pagan rather than Christian. They were 'the Moloch which men have set up to represent him,' which distorts both the nature of God and the nature of the atoning sacrifice of Christ's life and death.[70] MacDonald believed that pagan notions of sacrifice reflect human offerings to avoid punishment and the wrath of God. Such sacrifices are offered to deflect the consequences of sin, easing guilt and suffering while avoiding the need for transformation. Thus the event of sacrifice is viewed as central and as temporarily or partially erecting a shield for the guilty as protection from the righteous, angry Deity. As Maurice wrote, the idea 'that He stepped in, as their Advocate to shield them from their Father's indignation; that He offered His blood which was an adequate purchase-money or ransom from it' goes contrary to all biblical notions of sacrifice of which God is the source.[71] The goal of human-based sacrifice is not at-one-ment with God, but self-preservation and protection. MacDonald challenged the Federal Calvinist view of the atonement because it reinforced pagan tendencies to depict God as one whose bloodthirsty nature demands appeasement.

Because God evokes more fear than love in this context, sacrifice which offers protection from God becomes primary. MacDonald's characters frequently argue about what is most central to faith. For many, the atoning act is the object of faith rather than One who offered atonement. Those of the Federal Calvinist orientation often try to persuade the hero or the heroine to put their trust in the atonement, which is seen as exclusively the work of Christ on the cross, and the merits he gained for humanity thereby. These depictions were obviously taken from his life experiences, for as MacDonald's son, Greville, commented: 'My Aunt Angela remembered one such guest declaring, *à propos* of the atonement, that if Jesus Christ had been born one day and crucified the next, His work for the world had been accomplished.'[72]

The life of Christ was seen as rather secondary, or at least as distinct from his work. Because he was seen as having come to perform a legal function, the moment of accomplishing this was the all-important event. The incarnation, God becoming

---

69 MacDonald, *The Elect Lady*, pp. 311–12.

70 *RF*, p. 156.

71 Maurice, *Doctrine of Sacrifice*, p. 133.

72 *GMAW*, p. 105.

one with us in Christ, and Christ's teaching faded into the shadows of the crucifixion. With a weakened idea of the incarnation and little emphasis on Jesus as the revelation of the Father, the suffering of Christ was not tied to the eternal loving nature of God, but only to this moment on the cross. The window which opened at Calvary revealed primarily God's anger and wrath for Federal Calvinists.

If God is seen as only sending Jesus to effect an external and legal transaction, then God remains aloof, distant, and somewhat unknowable. One can know God partially in an economic sense, but not an immanent sense. Thus MacDonald characterized the people of his day as clinging more to the merits of Christ than to God, being unable to trust a God whose character was unknown and whose act on the cross demonstrated power without real presence, and forgiveness for the few without real cleansing of even those few. How could one trust a God who was more concerned to obtain glory than to express love?

MacDonald perceived that according to some believers, God could not wait to vent his righteous anger on unredeemed humanity, with Jesus being able only just to hold this at bay for a short duration. He characterizes this view through a sermon preached by a young minister in *Malcolm*:

> Fellow sinners … haste ye and flee from the wrath to come. Now is God waiting to be gracious – but only so long as his Son holds back the indignation ready to burst forth and devour you … Yet even *he* could not prevail for ever against such righteous anger; and it is but for a season he will thus entreat; the day will come when he will stand aside and let the fiery furnace break forth and slay you … But do as ye will, ye cannot thwart his decrees, for to whom he will he showeth mercy, and whom he will he hardeneth.[73]

MacDonald parodied the idea of God's appetite for sacrifice in *Robert Falconer*, through Grannie, who discovers that Robert has found and is using his grandfather's violin, a sure route to evil and sin: 'His violin lay on its back on the fire, and a yellow tongue of flame was licking the red lips of a hole in its belly. All its strings were shrivelled up save one, which burst as he gazed. And beside, stern as a Druidess, sat his grandmother in her chair, feeding her eyes with grim satisfaction on the detestable sacrifice.'[74]

To believe that God could find satisfaction and glory in the sacrifice of the Son merely because God's wrath was appeased and the sin of a few children was covered was to portray God as a god of the 'pagans,' one who cared more for external show than for the effecting of deep renewal. For MacDonald, such a theology of God was inconsistent with Jesus' life and teaching. Worship of God would often be out of dread and fear, not because one desired to know and experience God's presence, but because in distrust, one wanted to do what one could to keep God at a distance.

That God could take pleasure in the suffering of any creature was to MacDonald a defiling thought: 'It is no pleasure to God, as it so often is to us, to see the wicked suffer. To regard any suffering with satisfaction, save it be sympathetically with

---

73 *Malcolm*, p. 187 (a young minister speaking).
74 *RF*, p. 151.

its curative quality, comes of evil, is inhuman because undivine, is a thing God is incapable of.'[75] Yet this view was justified as guarding the glory of the Lord.

God was not only portrayed as taking pleasure in the suffering of the Son and in unregenerate creatures, but also as taking little pleasure in anything other than that which would directly preserve God's sovereignty and glory. Thus it was taught that on the Sabbath, laughter, play, walking anywhere but to and from church, reading, or discussing anything but religion would be an offence to God. MacDonald saw this as a denial of the God who created the world, and who formed his soul, heart, and brain. It seemed to represent more closely an image of a capricious demon or a proud bailiff.[76]

Rather than believe in such a god, he asserted that it would be better and more honoring to God for one to be an agnostic until such a time as God revealed God's self truly: 'Of all teachings that which presents a far distant God is the nearest to absurdity. Either there is none, or he is nearer to every one of us than our nearest consciousness of self. An unapproachable divinity is the veriest of monsters, the most horrible of human imaginations.'[77] MacDonald grieved that people were willing even to grant to dogs more of the divine nature than some were willing to acknowledge as essential to God.[78]

MacDonald's burden regarding the consequences of such an inadequate view of the atonement was pastoral as well as theological. He mourned to see the impact on people of believing in only a legal and external relationship with God. His writing exposes the oppressiveness which was experienced from such dread of God. One author writes: 'No critic of Calvinism ever did so effectually expose the demoralizing tendencies of the system as George MacDonald did in [*Robert Falconer*].'[79] The grandmother in *Robert Falconer* feels hopeless at times for her wayward son who does not seem to have a share in the merits of Christ as one of the elect. She lives in fear of a God who will certainly let him burn in hell for eternity as a result of God's rejection of him:

> Not one smile broke over the face of the old lady as she received them … I think it was rather that there was no smile in her religion, which, while it developed the power of a darkened conscience, overlaid and half-smothered all the lovelier impulses of her grand nature. How could she smile? Did not the world lie under the wrath and curse of God? Was not her own son in hell for ever? Had not the blood of the Son of God been shed for him in vain? Had not God meant that it should be in vain? For by the gift of his Spirit could he not have enabled him to accept the offered pardon? … How could she smile?[80]

---

75 'Justice,' *US*, 3, p. 131.

76 *RF*, p. 78.

77 George MacDonald, *Sir Gibbie* (London, 1914), p. 166; hereafter cited as *SG*.

78 *RF*, p. 232.

79 Alexander Webster, 'George MacDonald's Influence on Scottish Religion,' in *Wingfold*, 52 (Fall 2005), p. 30.

80 *RF*, p. 232.

Fear was the obvious result – fear of God, fear of not being chosen, fear of being cast into the outer darkness both in this life and in the next, and fear that loved ones will also be cast out. This religion was more evocative of the idea of escape from than of refuge in God. MacDonald saw the congregational quick escape after church services as symptomatic of this theology: 'When the service was over, almost before the words of the benediction had left the minister's lips, the people, according to Scotch habit, hurried out of the chapel, as if they could not possibly endure one word more.'[81]

If Robert's righteous grandmother herself would grieve over her lost son, would not God, his maker, also grieve and endeavor somehow to save him as well? Erskine saw that the only cure for this malaise of 'religion' was '… something which will rekindle love towards God, by taking away fear and inspiring confidence.'[82] MacDonald concurred that the problem is human blindness about the reality of God: 'Our minds are small because they are faithless … If we had faith in God, as our Lord tells us, our hearts would share in His greatness and peace. For we should not then be shut up in ourselves, but would walk abroad in Him.'[83] The inability of his Calvinist contemporaries truly to call God Father left them ill-equipped to experience or to express the goodness and the grace so evident in the New Testament, or to persevere in a radical kind of obedience which MacDonald saw as integral to the teaching of Christ: 'We are and remain such creeping Christians, because we look at ourselves and not at Christ.'[84]

2. Creatively Constructive toward Trust, Hope, and Faith

> We thank thee for thyself. Be what thou art - our root and life, our beginning and end, our all in all … Thou livest; therefore we live. In thy light we see. Thou art – that is all our song.[85]

Not only is imagination helpful in critiquing theology, it is also vital in nourishing visions of God's nature and kingdom that fill the heart with trust, hope and faith:

> In very truth, a wise imagination, which is the presence of the spirit of God, is the best guide that man or woman can have; for it is not the things we see the most clearly that influence us the most powerfully; undefined, yet vivid visions of something beyond, something which eye has not seen nor ear heard, have far more influence than any logical sequences whereby the same things may be demonstrated by the intellect.[86]

---

81 Ibid., p. 168.

82 Thomas Erskine, *The Unconditional Freeness of the Gospel* (Edinburgh, 1870), p. 8.

83 George MacDonald, *Annals of a Quiet Neighbourhood* (London, 1893), p. 476

84 'The Eloi,' *US*, 1, p. 170.

85 'The Castle: A Parable,' *GCC*, p. 198. Cf. Brian J. Walsh and Sylvia C. Keesmaat, *Colossians Remixed: Subverting the Empire* (Downers Grove, IL, 2004), p. 144.

86 'The Imagination,' *DO*, p. 28.

Theological transformation both evokes and emerges from holistic responses to truth. Faith was meaningless in MacDonald's estimate unless it was lived. As Rolland Hein states, MacDonald 'felt the raw intellect was simply unable to comprehend Christianity apart from the response of full obedience.'[87] And he believed the life of faith is fueled by an imagination burning with hope and trust.

MacDonald demonstrates that the imagination is vital to theology for it is a tool of conversion by which narrow definitions of reality are cracked open that hope-filled visions might emerge. In ways that sharpen the vision and hearing of his readers, MacDonald employed the imagination not only as a solvent to deconstruct false views of God, but as a creative tool to construct analogs of God's character more harmonious with Jesus' revelation. He sought to encourage people to hope in a God who was utterly trustworthy, to relinquish all lesser hopes, and to gain a hunger and thirst for the goodness of God and God's kingdom alone: 'If it is true that we are made in the image of God, then the paramount, absorbing business of our existence it to know that image of God in which we are made and to know it in the living Son of God ... But alas, most of us like to pare away the words of Christ instead of looking at them until they fill heaven and earth.'[88] The imagination can serve theology through honoring the words and revelation of Christ and thus lead to heightened consciousness and indestructible hope in God: 'Perhaps Life is most conscious to itself in the form of Hope ... No questioning can destroy our Hope. Everywhere and at every time, there is something at the door.'[89]

a. 'Renewed' Analogs of God

> For surely the only refuge from the heathenish representations of God under Christian forms, the only refuge from man's blinding and paralysing theories, from the dead wooden shapes substituted for the living forms of human love and hope and aspiration, from the interpretations which render scripture as dry as a speech in Chancery – surely the one refuge from all these awful evils is the Son of man; for no misrepresentations and no misconception can destroy the beauty of that face which the marring of sorrow has elevated into the region of reality, beyond the marring of irreverent speculation and scholastic definition. From the God of man's painting, we turn to the man of God's being, and he leads us to the true God, the radiation of whose glory we first see in him.[90]

MacDonald developed images of divine love and forgiveness which could generate in his readers hope that was consistent with biblical revelation. Two key images evident throughout his writing are of God as Father and as Mother (or Grandmother). He incorporated these images of God to reassure readers of God's faithfulness and good intentions for all creatures. In fact, one writer commends MacDonald with 'one

---

87 Hein, *The Harmony Within* (1999), p. 44.

88 MacDonald, 'The Family of Jesus,' *Proving the Unseen*, p. 12.

89 MacDonald, 'Hope,' *Broadlands* (1887), from Barbara Amell (ed.), *Wingfold*. See *Wingfold* (Summer 2005) and (Fall 2003).

90 *DE*, p. 328.

specific honour … that of being the first instinctively Scottish writer to popularize the idea of God's Fatherhood.'[91] Rather than fearfully hoping to escape from God, readers were encouraged to draw near in intimate relationship with God. In this way he was able to communicate his core belief about the nature of God and life essential for humans: 'This life, this eternal life, consists … in absolute oneness with God … It consists in a love that is as deep as it is universal, as conscious as it is unspeakable; a love that can no more be reasoned about than life itself.'[92]

1) God as Father

MacDonald's favourite parable was of the prodigal son, and it formed a core theme in a number of his books.[93] He wanted his readers to receive hope in God who is tender and forgiving. Like Robert Falconer, who goes into the 'far country' to seek out his lost father, MacDonald sought to restore to people's imagination the fatherhood of God which had fallen into disrepute. Robert, as a Christ-figure, demonstrates the nature of one who seeks out the lost to restore them to fullness of life.

MacDonald was convinced that what was done on earth in Christ's saving life and work is a reflection of what the Father does eternally, because the Father and the Son are one.[94] A God less than Jesus Christ, unconcerned with the suffering of humankind, with some vague unknowable character, was seen by him as 'but an idol of the heathen, modified with a few Christian qualities.'[95] Jesus is the true elder brother who leads repentant prodigals home to a Father who is utterly trustworthy. Thus the vicar in *Annals of a Quiet Neighbourhood* proclaimed: 'So you see God is tender – just like the prodigal son's father – only with this difference, that God has millions of prodigals, and never gets tired of going out to meet them and welcome them back, every one as if he were the only prodigal son He had ever had. There's a father indeed!'[96]

Home Again is a novel about such a prodigal, and of his father who grants the son the freedom of living outside of his will while eagerly praying and waiting for his wayward son's return. In this way MacDonald endeavored to demonstrate the gentle but persistent self-giving love of the Father. Furthermore, this parable is the Scripture read in *Robert Falconer* to the repentant but fearful *soutar* on his deathbed,

---

91 Alexander Webster, 'George MacDonald's Influence on Scottish Religion,' in *Wingfold* (Fall 2005), p. 31.

92 'Life,' *US*, 2, p. 152.

93 The parable of the prodigal son is mentioned in *David Elginbrod*, *Adela Cathcart*, *Unspoken Sermons* Series One, *Annals of a Quiet Neighbourhood*, *England's Antiphon*, *Robert Falconer*, *Ranald Bannerman's Boyhood*, *Sir Gibbie*, and *The Vicar's Daughter*, to name just a few. In at least twenty-five of his books there is an explicit reference to this parable at a key moment in the narrative, poem, or sermon. Hein notes that the parable of the prodigal son is for MacDonald 'the central parable of Christianity, offering the basic pattern of spiritual experience for all people'; Hein, *The Harmony Within* (1999), p. 50.

94 'Life,' *US*, 2, p. 143.

95 *RF*, p. 459.

96 *Annals of a Quiet Neighbourhood*, p. 203.

in which he finds great hope knowing that the Father makes no mention of all the repentant prodigal's sins, but rather brings out the best of everything to celebrate his homecoming.[97]

2) God as Motherly

Not only did MacDonald work to increase hope and trust by rehabilitating images of God as Father, he also offered images of God's Motherly nature.[98] Feminine images that encourage one to draw near to be embraced, renewed, refreshed, and healed abound in MacDonald's narratives. The protective nurturing care of the womanly Beech Tree dispels Anodos' fear of the Ash, revives his heart and offers guidance for his journey. The motherly sea offers him a baptism of love and renewal. Wise women throughout MacDonald's books demonstrate love that is both comforting as well as empowering. The way in which he uses such imagery to offer theological transformation will be demonstrated through MacDonald's depictions of a great-great-grandmother. As Kathy Triggs points out, MacDonald refers to the great-grandmother as the 'Mother of lights,' which parallels his recurring title for God as the 'Father of lights,' such that 'it suggests he is visualising the Princess as a feminine aspect of God.'[99]

In *The Princess and the Goblin*, MacDonald offers rich contrasts to Federal Calvinist images of God who will not draw near to filthy sinners, because they would only tarnish God's glory. The grandmother warns the princess of an imminent trial of her faith and urges her to come directly to her in the time of testing. When the trial is upon her, however, the princess fails to run immediately to her grandmother, and instead panics. She runs out of the castle, up the hill, and proceeds to fall down and cover herself with mud.

Upon seeing the light from Grandmother Irene's lamp, she comes to her senses and follows the light back to the castle and into the grandmother's presence. Seeing the glory and beauty of her queenly grandmother, she feels 'dirty and uncomfortable.'[100] Though the grandmother's arms are outstretched and inviting, the princess hesitates to draw near. Yet the grandmother 'sprung from her chair' and 'caught the child to her bosom, and, kissing the tear-stained face over and over, sat down with her in her lap.'[101] The grandmother's response reveals MacDonald's deep conviction that God's glory and God's love are one, and that in Christ, God has drawn near to sinners with a healing and cleansing embrace. The princess protests: '"But, grandmother, you're so beautiful and grand with your crown on; and I am so dirty with mud and rain! I

---

97 *RF*, p. 115.
98 As David Neuhouser writes: 'Perhaps the theme MacDonald emphasized most in his writings was that of God as a loving father. However, in his fairy tales God is portrayed as a loving mother'; Neuhouser, 'God as Mother in George MacDonald's "The Wise Woman,"' *Christianity and the Arts*, 4(4) (2000): 42–4.
99 Kathy Triggs, *The Stars and the Stillness: A Portrait of George MacDonald* (Cambridge, 1986), p. 108.
100 MacDonald, *The Princess and the Goblin*, p. 79.
101 Ibid., p. 80.

should quite spoil your beautiful blue dress."' Unselfish love, more appropriately associated with God's glory, is evident in the grandmother's reassurance: 'You darling! do you think I care more for my dress than for my little girl?' [102]

MacDonald communicates hope in a God whose glory is not contaminated by contact with fallen creatures, but is thus expressed. In this way he conveys the orthodox belief that Christ assumed our fallen humanity in order to cleanse and redeem it from within. He reveals that cleansing does not happen at a distance from God, but through nearness to God. Christ is truly *God with us*.

Thus he challenges the idea that one must first become clean, and only then can draw near to God, as if it were humanly possible to do this in any case. It is only the great-grandmother who can take the burning rose and cleanse away the mud. When the princess sees the stains removed from the grandmother's dress, she begs her to apply such cleansing to all of her, even as Peter had relinquished his initial hesitation to have Jesus wash his feet and begged for a complete cleansing instead.[103] Complete cleansing for the princess comes later in the form of a baptismal bath, because as yet she is unable to bear the consuming fire of the burning roses. It is humans who are too frail to endure the full glory of God's presence. God's glory needs no more protection from diminishment and defilement in human presence than Jesus Christ needed to protect himself from the defilement of tax collectors, lepers, or prostitutes.

All of this is too much for the princess to understand. She tries to comprehend what is happening and how the grandmother's light could shine through the walls in the way it shone to lead her back home. But the grandmother explains: 'Ah! that you would not understand if I were to try ever so much to make you – not yet – not yet.'[104] Her hope does lie not in understanding such things, but in obeying as much as she is given to follow and to understand. So the grandmother proceeds to give her something she has been spinning for her, a fine thread that will always connect the princess at her end to the great-grandmother at the other end. The princess is called to follow the thread and to trust that wherever it may lead, her grandmother will be holding the other end. Obedience is the way to greater understanding.

To summarize, MacDonald's image-rich portrayals of God communicate at least six transforming understandings of God's nature, which were particularly challenging in his own context. First, MacDonald believed that it is in Jesus that the glory of God may be rightly understood, the glory of self-giving love first expressed within the Trinity and then in creation. The glory of the Father is not that he was made gracious by the atonement, but that he offers atonement in Jesus because he is gracious. Christ did not earn God's love for humankind, but expressed it: 'For in self-giving, if anywhere, we touch a rhythm not only of all creation but of all being. For the Eternal Word also gives Himself in sacrifice; and that not only on Calvary. For when He was

---

102 Ibid.
103 John 13:6–9.
104 MacDonald, *The Princess and the Goblin*, p. 81.

crucified He 'did that in the wild weather of His outlying provinces in the torture of the body of his revelation, which He had done at home in glory and gladness.'[105]

Second, MacDonald understood the inner-trinitarian relationships as primary, and the relationship between God and humanity as derivatory. He wrote that the bond of the universe is the devotion of the Son to the Father, and the life of the universe is the love of the Son to the Father and the Father to the Son. It is out of this primary unity between Father and Son that our unity with God, our at-one-ment, emerges.[106] 'I and the Father are one' is the center-truth of the universe; and the circumfering truth is 'that they also may be one in us.'[107]

Third, understanding God as Father/Mother carried with it the sense of God as a provider. With humanity as utterly dependent, God provides all that is necessary for salvation, including the ability of the individual to respond with repentance, faith, and obedience:

> A grace I had no grace to win
> Knocks now at my half open door:
> Ah, Lord of glory, come thou in! –
> Thy grace divine is all, and more.[108]

Fourth, as mentioned before, God's Fatherhood/Motherhood implied for MacDonald that the essence of the atonement is relational and personal, rather than an external transaction. MacDonald believed that God's *hypostasis* is lived out in *ekstasis*, and the relational nature of God's Being shapes what is essential to the atonement. Thus, contrary to Calvinist criticism, believing in the universality of the atonement does not logically necessitate an automatic salvation in which heaven has been *purchased* by the blood of Jesus, buying each person's way into eternal life. Drawing near to the Father through knowing Christ was for MacDonald the only true good for humankind: 'I believe that there is nothing good for me or for any man but God, and more and more of God, and that alone through knowing Christ can we come nigh to him.'[109]

A fifth implication for MacDonald, of knowing in Christ that God is Father/Mother, is the realization that God's love precedes divine forgiveness and is unconditionally extended to all.[110] Reparation for sin was essential, but in accordance with God as Father, it is a propitiation for the sins of all, communicating that 'Forgiveness is love toward the unlovely.'[111] This view is portrayed in 'The Wise Woman' when in response to Rosamond's question 'How could you love such an ugly, ill-tempered,

---

105 'The Creation in Christ,' *US*, 3, pp. 11–12.
106 Ibid., pp. 18–19.
107 'Freedom,' *US*, pp. 96–7.
108 Excerpt from 'The Grace of Grace,' *PW*, 1, p. 312.
109 'Justice,' *US*, 3, p. 154.
110 'It Shall Not Be Forgiven,' *US*, 1, p. 80.
111 'Ibid., p. 78.

rude, hateful, little wretch?' the Wise Woman responds: 'I saw, through it all, what you were gong to be.'[112]

As Father/Mother, the grace God gives is of God's self. Thus, with the Reformers, MacDonald would maintain the identity between the content of God's self-communication in Jesus Christ and God's eternal nature. He affirmed that all is complete in Christ, such that though faith is necessary, it does not in a sense *add* anything to the salvation provided. Because of this, MacDonald called for preachers to begin with the good news of salvation rather than an attempt to convict of sin: 'The clergyman has the message of salvation, not of sin, to give … Salvation alone can rouse in us a sense of our sinfulness.'[113]

Finally, the Fatherhood/Motherhood of God means that what God desires for his children is both their freedom and their unity with God and one another. To experience this freedom and unity, one must be a disciple of Christ, the One who offers in himself the atonement. It is this for which Christ gave himself, this which is the only true goal of human life, and this which comprised MacDonald's purpose in writing and teaching: 'I believe that to be the disciple of Christ is the end of being; that to persuade men to be his disciples is the end of teaching.'[114]

b. New Visions of Obedience

> A man who has not the mind of Christ - and no man has the mind of Christ except him who makes it his business to obey him – cannot have correct opinions concerning him …
> Our business is not to think correctly, but to live truly; then first will there be a possibility of our thinking correctly.[115]

Another way in which MacDonald worked to foster hope was to offer narratives of human life moving from struggles and brokenness to increasing likeness to Jesus Christ: 'The human God … is … for the joy of deliverance, for the glory of real creation, for the partakings of the divine nature, for the gaining of a faith that shall remove mountains, and for deliverance from all the crushing commonplaces of would-be teachers of religion ….'[116] MacDonald attempted to enlarge the human heart and inspire vision of God's highest calling so that people would be encouraged to go beyond their brokenness and their narrow religiosity and morality. He sought 'to *show* excellence rather than talk about it, giving the thing itself, that it may grow into the mind.'[117]

MacDonald endeavored through 'living' examples to communicate that Jesus was more than the instrument of atonement earning certain merits for the few. Hope did

---

112 'The Wise Woman,' *GCC*, p. 366.
113 *RF*, pp. 461–2.
114 'Justice,' *US*, 3, p. 156.
115 Ibid., p. 135.
116 'Letter to a lady with whom he had stayed' (1886), cited in Hein, 'George MacDonald: A Portrait from His Letters,' *Seven: An Anglo-American Literary Review*, 7 (1986): 5–19.
117 'The Imagination,' *DO*, p. 38.

not lie in salvation mechanistically applied, but in the gift of participation in the life of Christ. His understanding of the inclusive love of God was not a depersonalized, cheap, universal grace, but the personal gift of God's self, who demands and empowers response: 'It seems to me that the only merit that could live before God is the merit of Jesus … In the same spirit he gave himself afterward to his father's children, and merited the power to transfuse the life-redeeming energy of his spirit into theirs: made perfect, he became the author of eternal salvation unto all them that obey him.'[118]

In aiming for visions of transformed lives through the power of Christ working within, MacDonald did not underestimate human struggle and brokenness. *Sir Gibbie* begins with a barefoot mute urchin living in urban poverty with an alcoholic father who continually drinks himself into a stupor and must be sought out and dragged home by his wee son. The son, Gibbie, witnesses the brutal, racist murder of his only friend, is forced into homelessness, and wandering the countryside, is falsely accused, brutally beaten, and is caught up in a devastating flood and earthquake. *Alec Forbes of Howglen* depicts Alec confronted with all the temptations of a young man who leaves home for the city and for university. *Thomas Wingfold, Curate* conveys the challenges of a minister who has no real faith. *What's Mine's Mine* deals with the historic calamity to Scottish crofters who are forced off of their land, yet struggle to remain faithful to their clan to the very end. MacDonald suffered too much in his own life to skim over the surface of life's difficulties in his narratives.

Yet his hope in God was too great to wallow in the struggle and pain. One would not be induced to live a hope-filled life unless one had a vision toward which one was moving. Diamond's inspiring vision is compared with the vision of Dante (called 'Durante') in *At the Back of the North Wind*. Often MacDonald's protagonists demonstrate the power of God to transform those who will learn from and follow Christ. This is similar to Eastern Orthodox thought, for, as Grano explains, 'the entire life of piety in the Eastern Church is based upon striving for the ideal or goal, which is to be like Christ.'[119] MacDonald seeks to lift up what is possible in Christ, to enflesh what Christ-likeness would look like in current contexts, and to inspire people to hope for more than merely getting by. According to Grano, 'All pious Orthodox people read the lives of the saints, and in these and other characters in MacDonald's novels they would find something very similar, a piety with the same flavour.' In this way, the lives of his heroes and heroines could themselves become 'living sermons.'[120]

Living toward Christ-likeness equips one to move beyond fearful self-preservation, and to love as Christ loved. But MacDonald was realistic about how common this ideal would be. Thus he writes in *Sir Gibbie*, when Gibbie himself expresses saint-like character:

---

118 MacDonald, *HG*, p. 88.
119 Robert W. Grano, 'An Orthodox Appreciation of George MacDonald,' *Touchstone* 12(2) (July/August 1999): 16.
120 Ibid.

One believing like him in the perfect Love and perfect Will of a Father of men, as the fact of facts, fears nothing. Fear is faithlessness. But there is so little that is worthy the name of faith, that such a confidence will appear to most not merely incredible but heartless. The Lord himself seems not to have been very hopeful about us, for he said, When the Son of man cometh, shall he find faith on the earth? A perfect faith would lift us absolutely above fear. It is in the cracks, crannies, and gulfy faults of our belief, the gaps that are not faith, that the snow of apprehension settles, and the ice of unkindness forms.[121]

MacDonald acknowledged that for each person there was 'a worm [which] lay among the very roots of his life.'[122] This worm, which MacDonald most often depicted as self-in-opposition-to-God, must be destroyed for one to be free. Sin is like this worm which eats away at one's own true life and becomes parasitic on the lives of others, like the snake which drains the water from the land in 'The Light Princess.' Self must be conquered and die, for 'Self is a quicksand; God is the only rock.'[123] Thus MacDonald acknowledged evil and portrayed characters who are truly evil and spiritual forces which are adversarial to God, in order to empower people to act with conviction and courage in the face of evil. To picture, for example, unforgiveness as a 'cold smile deep in my heart like a moth-eaten hole' is both clarifying and catalyzing.[124]

He also conveyed these ideas in the midst of loving relationships and the sufficiency of God to offer encouragement for those feeling defeated by evil: 'We have done much that is evil, yea, evil is very deep in us, but we are not all evil, for we love righteousness; and art not thou thyself, in thy Son, the sacrifice for our sins, the atonement of our breach?'[125]

MacDonald worked to inspire people with the empowering vision that God desires true sons and daughters, 'children of his soul, of his spirit and of his love – not merely in the sense that he loves them, or even that they love him, but in the sense that they love like him, love as he loves.'[126] Becoming true sons and daughters, they will begin to seek God's Kingdom first, to be one with God's will, to be at home with God. Thus humankind participates in being God's children by virtue of both coming forth from God's heart and returning to God, that they might share in divine being and nature.

The costs and challenges his protagonists face enflesh his belief that this second birth is not automatic: 'He does not *make* them the sons of God, but he gives them power to become the sons of God: in choosing and obeying the truth, man becomes the true son of the Father of lights.'[127] MacDonald reveals that this is more than mere obedience of the law, for this filial obedience comes from knowledge of the heart of

---

121 *SG*, p. 203.
122 MacDonald, *Flight of the Shadow* (London, 1891), p. 12.
123 *HA*, p. 242 (Walter to Lufa).
124 'Letter to his Wife,' in *EC*, p. 83.
125 'The Voice of Job,' *US*, 2, p. 191.
126 'Abba Father,' *US*, 2, p. 123.
127 Ibid., p. 127.

the Father, whence the law comes, that '*Abba Father!*' might be central in all we do or think.

Though all are children of God, this second birth of becoming true sons and daughters is only possible because of the unique Son of the Father: 'Never could we have known the heart of the Father, never felt it possible to love him as sons, but for him who cast himself into the gulf that yawned between us. In and through him we were foreordained to the sonship: sonship, even had we never sinned, never could we reach without him.'[128]

MacDonald worked to inspire people toward the freedom of obedience. Without the imagination and encouragement to dream dreams, life can easily be reduced to survival and attempts to avoid or numb the pain, as in MacDonald's portrayal Gibbie's father, whose poetic spirit had been crushed: 'The time had been when now and then he read a good book and dreamed noble dreams.'[129] He stopped reading, gave up his noble dreams, and lived only with hope for the next drink till he eventually drank himself to death.

For MacDonald, 'It is life that awakes life. All form of persuasion is empty except in vital association with regnant obedience. Talking and not doing is dry rot.'[130] In order to honor the Life that is the source of all life, MacDonald patterned his theology after the 'Word made flesh,' showing forth the truth of Christ through the frailty of lives and stories. He sought to resist docetic approaches which exalted abstract human theories and marginalized Jesus' life, teaching, and personality. In his commitment to follow Jesus, he worked to make apparent the presence and love of the transcendent God in all aspects of life, and so to offer 'real vision: for instead of making common things look commonplace, as a false vision would have done, it had made common things disclose the wonderful that was in them.'[131]

The imagination's ability to express truth relationally, personally, and with mystery is critical for theology. Rather than providing a safe escape from personal struggle and growth, it calls one to awaken, to arise, and to go forth in pilgrimage with the One who transforms, heals, and redeems.

---

128 Ibid., p. 129.
129 *SG*, p. 10.
130 MacDonald, *The Elect Lady*, p. 82.
131 MacDonald, 'The Shadows,' *GCC*, p. 168.

Chapter 6

Renewed Vision of Humanity

As previously demonstrated, MacDonald desired to receive and communicate truth utterly informed by and conformed to Christ. This rooted him in orthodoxy and freed him to break out of molds that shaped some of his contemporaries' views. Thus, as we have seen, he challenged both conventional theories of the atonement and attitudes toward the use of the imagination in theology. Furthermore, his robust Christology freed him to welcome influences from varied sources and prophetically to offer nourishment appropriate to people across time and culture. MacDonald had a profound sense of both the nature of human hungers and the nature of that which would satisfy those hungers. He characterized the dilemma of humanity in many ways. One which stands out as a continual and relevant theme centers on the condition identified in Daniel's prayer, that of 'confusion of face,' or loss of identity:[1] 'To us, O Lord, belongs confusion of face, to our kings, to our princes, and to our fathers, because we have sinned against thee.'[2]

This condition is depicted most graphically in *Lilith*, in which Vane sees a dimly lit hall filled with dancers, 'gorgeously dressed and gracefully robed,' many with beautiful, flowing locks of hair, but none of whom have a human face. Instead they have only skull fronts, with lidless living eyes, and are unable to speak or to smile. Thus Vane inquires: 'Had they used their faces, not for communication, not to utter thought and feeling, not to share existence with their neighbours, but to appear what they wished to appear, and conceal what they were? and, having made their faces masks, were they therefore deprived of those masks, and condemned to go without faces until they repented?'[3]

MacDonald believed that true identity was not created by seeking the right image or persona to project. Rather, identity is a gift discovered in relationship with Jesus Christ: 'All that the creature needs to see or know, all that the creature can see or know, is the face of Him from whom he came. Not seeing and knowing it, he will never be at rest; seeing and knowing it, his existence will yet indeed be a mystery to him and an awe, but no more a dismay.'[4] It is only in knowing Christ by his Spirit,

---

1 MacDonald wrote of the gospel: 'the time will come when its truth shall be apparent, to some in confusion of face, to others in joy unspeakable'; 'Individual Development,' *DO,* pp. 68–9.
2 Daniel 9:8 (RSV).
3 *Lilith*, pp. 85–6.
4 MacDonald, 'God's Family,' *HG*, p. 56.

and through him the Father, that individuals and theology itself can return to their true face: 'The true self is that which can look Jesus in the face, and say, *My Lord*.'[5]

It is from this perspective that MacDonald offers relevant insights for today. He repeatedly revealed his purpose to be centered around three endeavors: (1) to show forth the face of God, (2) to draw all people to God, and (3) to reveal the high calling and purpose for which humanity was created, that each might develop a face of childlike trust, freedom, and obedience, like the very face of Jesus. Chapter 5 revealed MacDonald's imaginative efforts to show forth the face of God as revealed in Christ in order to encourage people to draw near to God. This chapter will focus on MacDonald's perspective on the identity and high calling of humanity which flows from one's relationship with God.

MacDonald's affirmed that 'when we understand Him, then only do we understand our life and ourselves. Never can we know the majesty of the will of God concerning us except by understanding Jesus and the work the Father gave Him to do.'[6] MacDonald's relationship with Jesus transformed his vision of humans as primarily depraved and of forgiveness as merely covering over sin. Instead, he envisioned humans as new creations in Christ.

To live out one's identity as a new creation means to know and follow Jesus Christ. MacDonald felt it was a foolish reversal to exalt self-knowledge and self-preoccupation as the means by which one 'finds oneself.' Such a distortion lies at the heart of the evil of Gwyntystorm in *The Princess and Curdie*. Ironically, MacDonald depicts the source of this perspective as a number of the clergy, who are 'always glad to seize on any passing event to give interest to the dull and monotonic grind of their intellectual machines ....' One of the preachers on 'Religion Day' gives expression to this self-referent view by explaining the 'first fundamental principle ... was that every One should take care of that One. This was the first duty of Man.'[7] MacDonald reveals through his story 'The Wise Woman' the insidiousness of a worldview that revolves around the self as *Somebody* and as the primary *Somebody* in one's world.[8]

For MacDonald, 'The mind that delights in that which is lofty and great, which feels there is something higher than self, will undoubtedly be drawn towards Christ ....'[9] Thus he argued that 'Man is not made to contemplate himself, but to behold in others the beauty of the Father.'[10] Identity is not found in isolation, and it is not something that is an end in itself. Thus he affirmed via Malcolm: 'I would spend my best efforts to make them follow him,' that they might 'grow as beautiful as God meant [them] to be when he thought of [them] first ....'[11]

---

5   'The Eloi,' *US*, 1, p. 171.

6   *ML*, p. 77.

7   MacDonald, *The Princess and Curdie*, p. 315.

8   'The Wise Woman,' *GCC*, p. 285.

9   'Browning's Christmas Eve,' *DO*, p. 198.

10 *HA*, p. 93.

11 *ML*, pp. 76, 80.

God's thought in creating humankind is what MacDonald identified as 'their substance, their *hypostasis*.'[12] This thought or purpose of God for humankind is seen reflected in the very nature of Jesus Christ, 'who is the root and crown of our being, and whom to know is freedom and bliss.'[13] To be fully human is to know this One who is our Alpha and Omega – the One in whose image we were created in the beginning and who is the *telos* of our existence as new creations in Christ. MacDonald took seriously the promise that 'When he appears, we shall be like him.'[14] Yet, how does one develop a face that reflects the radiance, beauty, and goodness of Jesus' own face?

MacDonald emphasizes at least three important dynamics in nurturing a relationship with Christ through which new life and identity may flow: (1) in worship, (2) in the work of obedience, and (3) in community. Like three movements of a concerto, MacDonald interweaves these themes throughout his writing. Through them he conveys harmonies which can address the dissonance arising from contemporary fears of silence and solitude, disillusionment with the meaninglessness of work that is severed from faith, and loneliness in alienation from others and God. They are like the music that Tolkien's Ilúvatar offers to harmonize the cacophonous discord of Melkor, who refused to find his source in the imperishable flame.[15]

1. Worship and Embracing Silence to Hear the Word

> He began first to become aware of a certain stillness pervading the universe like a law; a stillness ever being broken by the cries of eager men, yet ever closing and returning with gentleness not to be repelled, seeking to infold and penetrate with its own healing the minds of the noisy children of the earth.[16]

a. Entering into Solitude

Confusion about existence and identity MacDonald saw as the only possibility where there was no openness to the mind of Christ or to the movement of God's Spirit. Without the wisdom of God, the meaning and order which God created in all things is beyond human comprehension. To describe this lack of perception, MacDonald adopted Goethe's analogy of standing outside a cathedral's stain glass windows and judging it as merely 'dusk and dimness.' It is only by entering into the sanctuary

---

12 Ibid., p. 76.

13 Ibid., p. 332.

14 1 John 3:2 (RSV). MacDonald depicts the way in which Tangle and Mossy through their pilgrimage of life grow to reflect the beauty of the 'divine' figures in *The Golden Key* and yet remain distinctively themselves: 'You are like them all. And yet you are my own old Mossy!'; *GCC*, p. 282.

15 J.R.R. Tolkien, *The Silmarillion*, ed. Christopher Tolkien (Boston, MA, 1977).

16 *AF*, p. 140.

that one can envision 'glorious splendour truth.'[17] Similarly, when in disbelief one 'stands outside and not within, he sees an entangled maze of forces, where there is in truth an intertwining dance of harmony.'[18] The call to stand 'within' is a call to solitude which comes from the heart of God, who yearns to give rest and peace to God's children.

MacDonald pictured each person with a door of escape from the outside, which leads inside to the place of 'profound repose of perfect love.'[19] This door is 'haunted with the knockings of the hand of Love' who beckons one into a realm of 'infinite quiet, not the solitude the wounded spirit imagines. Least of all a waste, for there the silence itself is God.'[20] When God's creatures enter or even look into 'these regions of silent being where God is ... the fountain of their life springs aloft with tenfold vigour and beauty.'[21]

Entering into silence and solitude with God is like Tangle's bath in 'The Golden Key': '... she began to feel as if the water were sinking into her, and she were receiving all the good of sleep without undergoing its forgetfulness. She felt the good coming all the time ... All the fatigue and aching of her long journey had vanished. She was as whole, and strong, and well as if she had slept for seven days.'[22] Similarly, God's presence offers cleansing, healing, and Sabbath rest. MacDonald continues: 'After being in that bath, people's eyes always give out a light they can see by.'[23] Unlike the haunting 'living lidless eyes' of the faceless dancers, here are eyes that shine forth to illumine the way. When Mossy emerges from the same bath later, the Old Man of the Sea explains that he has now tasted death. Times of solitude and silence include elements that correlate with baptism, dying, and rising. One relinquishes the illusion that one must always be in charge and in control.

It is in solitude and silence that one gives over all cares to the all-caring One. Learning through times of silence to entrust all to God was fundamental for MacDonald in deepening one's identity as a child of God: 'There are those who say that care for the morrow is what distinguishes man from the beast; certainly it is one of the many things that distinguish the slave of Nature from the child of God.'[24]

---

17 'Browning's Christmas Eve,' *DO*, pp. 198. He went on to say: 'This is true concerning every form in which truth is embodied, whether it be sight or sound, geometric diagram or scientific formula. Unintelligible, it may be dismal enough, regarded from the outside; prismatic in its revelation of truth from within. Such is the world itself, as beheld by the speculative eye; a thing of disorder, obscurity, and sadness: only the child-like heart, to which the door into the divine idea is thrown open, can understand somewhat the secret of the Almighty.' MacDonald also used Goethe's poem in *Adela Cathcart* (London, 1882, orig. 1864), pp. 180–81.

18 'Browning's Christmas Eve,' *DO*, p. 215.

19 *CW*, p. 233.

20 Ibid.

21 *AF*, p. 151.

22 'The Golden Key,' *GCC*, p. 275

23 Ibid., p. 276.

24 *CW*, p. 175.

Drawing near to God is the chief concern of humankind, and the highest privilege. MacDonald recoiled from seeing it as some sort of duty and thus turning it into a grievous burden. Rather, it is 'the simplest blessedest thing in the human world.'[25] In another sense it is also the most natural, for he saw the essential dynamic in both the spiritual and physical world as a 'turning again to the source.'[26]

In this movement to the 'inside,' one increasingly becomes aware that 'all vision is in the light of the Father.'[27] It is light which God freely gives continually, though humankind would block it with 'thousands of difficulties,' for 'God must reveal or nothing is known.'[28] It is only in this light that it becomes vividly apparent that God is at the center, and the self is not. Here one begins to know God and to discover a rightful place for oneself.

In the silence of solitude with God, one learns that God is 'nearer to us than the air we breathe, nearer to us than the heart of wife or child, nearer to us than our own consciousness of ourselves, nearer to us than the words in which we speak to him, nearer than the burning of our hearts at the story of his perfect Son ....'[29]

b. Encountering God as Thou

No longer is God merely an abstraction, but a Thou, who breaks out of human conceptions and discloses God's character through Jesus Christ. Along with images of God as Father and Mother, MacDonald also emphasized the childlikeness of God. His portrayal of the 'oldest man of all' in *The Golden Key* was as a child whose face expressed 'an awfulness of absolute repose.'[30] This emphasis was based on Jesus' teaching about becoming as children to enter the Kingdom of God, from which MacDonald understood that Jesus, who is the true image of humans, must himself be as a child: 'In the face of the Lord himself, the childhood will be triumphant – all this wisdom, all this truth upholding the radiant serenity of faith in his father.'[31]

MacDonald is remarkable in this context for seeing and affirming tender and approachable characteristics of God, without diminishing God's greatness. Theologically, he had been raised with a harsh, more masculine picture of God. Thus it is striking that he associated God with qualities normally attributed to children and women, whose social status was considerably lower than men. His insights in this regard speak to those who question Christ's revelation, because he was a male and because the Church has often emphasized certain masculine qualities of God. They also encourage greater receptivity to God's presence which may be experienced in many unexpected places and people, like the many revelations of the Wise Woman

---

25 'The Hands of the Father,' *US*, 1, p. 183.
26 Ibid., p. 182.
27 *SP*, p. 174.
28 'A Sermon,' *DO*, p. 287.
29 *CW*, p. 191.
30 'The Golden Key,' *GCC*, p. 278.
31 'The Child in the Midst,' *US*, 1, p. 17. Cf. *Adela Cathcart*, pp. 20–21.

or the Great-great-grandmother. As the children in these stories grow into this heightened awareness, they become increasingly true themselves, and thus learn to be more attentive in their seeking.

In order to recognize the surprising nature of God, one needs help in rethinking what is worthy and unworthy in life. Not only does such rethinking encourage greater openness to God, it offers a corrective to false ambition which distorts identity. MacDonald's divine characters reshape one's expectations about God and about oneself in God's image.

The wise woman in *The Lost Princess* reveals the patience, wisdom, and persevering love of God, who guides and yet who is often absent from view. Yet her last words to the princess are: 'My child ... I shall never be far from you.'[32] Similarly, in *Phantastes* the old woman of the cottage provides refuge and renewal for Anodos, as well as wise guidance. She herself suffers to rescue him from danger, and in tenderness nurtures him back to health.[33] Lona is the Christ-like figure in *Lilith*, who gives herself entirely in love and service, and who sacrifices her life to redeem her mother and to save her people. The timeless grandmother in *The Princess and Curdie* books is able to heal the sick and weakened king through the purification of her fire of roses which causes her more pain than the king. At the last battle, she is the one who brings about final victory, but she only reveals her true identity as she is pouring the wine for Curdie. Leaving the room, she returns in a royal purple robe and all kneel at her feet. Her delight remains to serve, and though the king offers her his throne, she makes them all sit down, and 'in ruby crown and royal purple she served them all.'[34]

MacDonald wrote of the 'womanhood' which dwells in God, and called God 'Him who is Father and Mother both in one,' as well as 'father and mother and home.'[35] Motherhood represented for MacDonald the idea of constancy and the embodiment of the homeward call which he also saw in the portrayal of the father in Jesus' parable of the prodigal son. If God was associated primarily with wrath, punishment, and power, one dare not draw near. If we are in the image of that God, then what kind of creatures are we? MacDonald worked to transform people's image of God, and so to validate character qualities which might otherwise be demeaned rather than received joyfully as a gift of identity from God: 'You can imagine the tenderness of a mother's heart who takes her child even from its beloved nurse to soothe and to minister to it, and that is like God; that is God.'[36] One may draw near to God, see the face of God in these ways, and discover the joy of participating in the divine nature.

---

32 'The Wise Woman,' *GCC*, p. 375.
33 *Phantastes*, pp. 128–44.
34 *The Princess and Curdie*, p. 217.
35 *Adela Cathcart*, p. 142
36 'True Christian Ministering,' *DO,* p. 301.

c. Discovering a Place for Oneself

In returning to God in Jesus Christ, one's own reality becomes clarified. It is there that one is free to be a child again and to realize how utterly dependent one is upon God. One must come empty-handed into the presence of God, recognizing that there is nothing one can 'bring unto thee, until thou enrich us with that same.'[37] There is no good one can do without God, nor is there any existence possible separate from God. The reality of human dependence is not a crippling discovery, as many would believe, but rather the basis of real freedom. For as MacDonald believed and as Erskine wrote: 'it is this very Spirit of dependence which keeps open all the sluices and avenues of their souls to admit the fulness of God ... [it] is the open door by which God enters the heart.'[38]

MacDonald saw Christ's acceptance of dependence or humility, as 'essential greatness, the inside of grandeur,' 'But the humble men of heart alone can believe in the high – they alone can perceive, they alone can embrace grandeur.'[39] Humility is the attitude which reflects truth, whereas independence is an illusion.

As it is pride and the illusion of self-sufficiency which denote weakness, MacDonald portrays Anodos in *Phantastes* growing in strength and wisdom as he gains awareness of his inability and his need. Thus he is finally able to admit: 'I learned that it is better, a thousand-fold, for a proud man to fall and be humbled, than to hold up his head in his pride and fancied innocence.'[40] Freedom gained in this fall does not emerge through wallowing or even glorying in the degradation, as Anodos realized, but through no longer focusing on oneself at all. This is the great uplifting which MacDonald claims for Christianity, which uplifts 'to a table-land accessible only to humility. He alone who is humble can rise - and rising he lifts with him.'[41]

In contrast, to believe that the self is at the center, to embrace only that which seems personally efficacious and appealing, is to betray what was intended for oneself and for one's neighbors. Commenting on Polonius's speech to Laertes in *Hamlet*, MacDonald argues: 'if a man make himself the centre for the birth of action, it will follow, "*as the night the day*", that he will be true neither to himself nor to any other man.'[42] Because the worship of self has nothing in it to raise one to a higher standard, MacDonald pictured it as producing a reverse moral devolution in which a person becomes more and more like a beast, and less and less like the image of God.[43] Furthermore, self-centeredness produces a kind of blindness to the gifts of

---

37 *DE*, p. 4.
38 Thomas Erskine, *The Unconditional Forgiveness of the Gospel* (Edinburgh, 1870), pp. 11–12.
39 'Individual Development,' *DO,* p. 70.
40 *Phantastes*, p. 166.
41 *CW,* p. 365.
42 MacDonald, *The Tragedie of Hamlet*, p. 39.
43 See, for example, *The Princess and Curdie.*

God around, because 'we are so filled with foolish desires and evil cares, that we cannot see or hear, cannot even smell or taste the pleasant things round about us.'[44]

The dissatisfaction inevitable even when the foolish desires are all granted was portrayed by MacDonald in 'The Carasoyn.' Having everything she wants, the fairie queen yearns for the supreme prize, a special potion called Carasoyn. The Carasoyn, which is helpful for those who are good, brings decrepitude and old age to the fairies, who are afterward 'punished by being made very rich.'[45] This is similar to MacDonald's conjectures about hell, which is 'just a place where God gives everybody everything she wants, and lets everybody do whatever she likes, without once coming nigh to interfere!'[46]

In truth, a view of the self as central and independent produces not freedom, but slavery. The people who live by their own relativistic standards, who have willingly relinquished their children and are materialistically thriving in the town of Bulika in *Lilith* are those driven by fear and suspicion of others. Lilith, who most fiercely claims her independence and her own way, reveals a bondage to that which is destroying her. She is unable to receive or give love to anyone, but instead operates parasitically on others. One who is unwilling to rise above oneself becomes a captive to one's instincts and basic drives. Thus MacDonald asserted: 'The world might be divided into those who let things go, and those who do not … those who are always doing something on God's creative lines, and those that are always grumbling and striving against them.'[47]

Freedom lies in who God is, and not in one's ability to rescue oneself. One's life is hid with Christ, and not to be found in any other pursuit but that of union with him.[48] To that end, MacDonald urged: 'Life is at work in us – the sacred Spirit of God travailing in us.'[49] The Spirit's influence can gain root as one is brought to a point of seeking the help God has been offering all along. In contrast to contemporary movements centered on positive self-esteem and self-contentment, MacDonald believed spiritual and psychological health begin with discontentment and dis-illusionment with the self. This 'dislocation and relocation' of the self corresponds to a restoration of what Erskine calls true gravity, such that the soul in need is brought into its proper orbit around God.[50]

In it only through this proper reorientation of the self toward God that one can discover that this is a dependency of freedom and love. As the earth only exists because it orbits the sun and thus receives continual life-giving nourishment, even so in lives orbiting around the Son, God would continue to love and nourish God's children. Life so oriented toward God increases the heart's openness to God's

44 MacDonald, cited in Raeper, *George MacDonald*, p. 257.

45 MacDonald, 'The Carasoyn,' in *GCC*, p. 220.

46 MacDonald, *Mary Marston*, Vol. 2, p. 336, in Raeper, *George MacDonald*, note 46, p. 408.

47 *HA*, p. 26.

48 'A Sermon,' *DO*, p. 287.

49 'On Polish,' *DO*, p. 194.

50 Erskine, *The Unconditional Forgiveness of the Gospel*, p. 58.

ongoing self-disclosure and loving nature. God does not force divine self-revelation on people: 'To him who has not ears to hear, God will not reveal himself; any other revealing would be death by terror.'[51] Thus, even God's revelation in Christ is veiled and only accessible to those who trust and respond.

It is in worship and adoration that the weight of one's sense of self-importance and self-preoccupation is lifted. This 'victory over the self is the victory of God in the man, not of the man alone ... In whatever man does without God, he must fail miserably – or succeed more miserably.'[52] Here one may look up to Christ, and in the light of his glory receive the gift of a growing humility. This growth weakens one's temptation 'to think himself the centre around which the universe revolves,' and one is able then 'leave it to the pismire to be angry, to the earwig to be conceited, and to the spider to insist on his own importance.'[53] Here, in communion with God, one finds that for which one has been searching all along. And here alone, one is brought to be with God at the true center of all things.[54]

From this experience of solitude and worship, MacDonald saw naturally flowing a worship of bowing one's entire life in homage to God. He described such a movement in *The Marquis of Lossie*: '... then the soul of Clementina rose and worshipped the soul of the universe; her spirit clave to the Life of her life, the Thought of her thought, the Heart of her heart; her will bowed itself to the Creator of will, worshipping the supreme, original, only Freedom – the Father of her love, the Father of Jesus Christ.'[55] Thus MacDonald exhorted: 'the way to worship God while the daylight lasts is to work,' and this means the need to conform one's will to the will of the Father, and so to live in harmony with God's ways and God's purposes.[56]

2. Embracing the Work of Obedience in Response to the Word

> Is thy strait horizon dreary?
> Is thy foolish fancy chill?
> Change the feet that have grown weary,
> For the wings that never will.[57]

Just as MacDonald's call to solitude was a call to worship and to 'speechless adoration,' so his call to work was a call to soar in the freedom of obedience to God. He offers refreshing insight to contemporary struggles over the gap between orthodoxy and orthopraxis, the loss of the value of goodness as a worthy pursuit,

---

51 *CW*, p. 313.
52 'Self-denial,' *US*, 2, p. 212.
53 'St. George's Day, 1564,' *DO*, pp. 128–9.
54 'Browning's Christmas Eve,' *DO*, p. 214.
55 *ML*, p. 340.
56 'The Hands of the Father,' *US*, 1, p. 183.
57 'Forms of Literature,' *DO*, p. 234.

confusion about the basis of freedom, and fearful preoccupation with security which has driven many to a sense of boredom and meaningless in their work.

a. Reclaiming Orthopraxis as Essential for Orthodoxy

MacDonald perceived in his own age the travesty of faith which was claimed but which was not followed:

> It is little wonder so many reject Christianity while so many would-be champions of it hold [it] from them at arms' length ... They do not brood on it in their hearts on their beds in the stillness; it is not their comfort in the night-watches; it is not the strength of their days, the joy of their conscious being. For them it is a separable thing, not the essential of their life! The unbelievers might well rejoice in the loss of such a God as many Christians would make of him. But if he be indeed the Father of our Lord Christ, of that Jew who lived and died doing the will of his Father, and nothing but that will, then the one prayer worth offering is, 'Let thy will be done, O God, and nothing but thy will!'[58]

He saw a lack of faith appropriation evident not only in individual's lives, but also in the way the Church was often run. The orientation toward money and deference to the rich, such that gain was seen as primary, security and comfort as secondary, and the will of God as *immaterial* (inconsequential because it seemed nonmaterial), was described by MacDonald as a conducting 'of the affairs of the church on the principles of Hell.'[59] So abominable did he find this presentation of Christianity that he saw it as 'enough to drive the world to a preferable infidelity.'[60] In the midst of the doubts raised about the existence of God, MacDonald felt it was worse to claim faith in a God who was not worthy of being heeded or obeyed than to admit to no faith at all: 'If God be not worth minding, what great ruin can it be to imagine his non-existence?'[61]

MacDonald also attributed this gap between faith and practice as emerging from confusion about doctrine: 'The word *doctrine*, as used in the Bible, means *teaching of duty*, not *theory*.'[62] Simple obedience to the will of God for MacDonald was not to be overshadowed by a preoccupation with intellectual doctrinal issues. Neither could orthopraxis be delayed until one's orthodoxy was adequately refined. He likened such a postponement to setting aside essential medicine known to help one's ailment, in order to dabble in the study of various schools of treatment:[63] 'Oh the folly of any mind that would explain God before obeying him!'[64] Rather, 'Your faith is your obedience,' in which one obeys 'every word of the Master.'[65]

---

58 *CW*, p. 191.
59 *ML*, p. 244.
60 Ibid., p. 244.
61 *HA*, p. 77.
62 'Letter to His Father' (Arundel, 15 April 1851), in *EC*, p. 151.
63 'Justice,' *US*, 3, p. 152.
64 Ibid., p. 115.
65 Ibid., p. 151.

MacDonald saw obedience as the 'soul of knowledge.'[66] Thus, 'until a man begins to obey, the light that is in him is darkness.'[67] In such darkness, it was not surprising to him that there was a problem of 'gloomy doubts and terrible depression.' The remedy was to 'Go and do God's will,' which included exerting the will to rejoice and rejecting the 'Tempting Voice to despair.'[68] MacDonald was very clear that obedience in itself was not the issue, but obedience to 'the *truth*, that is, to the Light of the Word, truth beheld and known.'[69] The way and the focus of obedience was embodied and made evident by God in Christ. Rather than being immaterial (or *decarnate*), God's will had been enfleshed in Christ as profoundly incarnate. Christ himself holds the secret of life, whom to obey is to know, and whom to know is to obey.[70]

MacDonald understood that some may need to make a timid beginning, but he urged that if people had even the vaguest suspicion that 'Jesus, who professed to have come from God, was a better man than other men, one of your first duties must be to open your ears to his words, and see whether they commend themselves to you as true; then, if they do, to obey them with your whole strength and might, upheld by the hope of the vision promised in them to the obedient.'[71] The will required such engagement with the Truth in order that the intellect may also be able to grow in conformity.

Belief was also not dependent or even greatly helped by the miraculous. MacDonald saw no short cut to assurance of faith: 'God will have us sure of a thing through knowing its source, the heart whence it comes; that is the only worthy assurance. To know, he will have us go in at the grand entrance of obedient faith.'[72] He saw no help coming from a miracle for one 'who could not see him in the face of his Son,' for without a sense of God's character, a demonstration of God's existence would not bring much light.[73] Christ demonstrated in response to the third temptation in the wilderness that doing the will of God was needed for human deliverance, not some external magical power.[74] The way of obedience to Christ requires perseverance and patience, for 'the truth must show itself in God's time and in and by the labour. The kingdom must come in God's holy human way.'[75] God's way has been evident throughout the history of divine interaction with God's people. It is a way of patient transformation with eons of long-suffering love.

Knowing God's will through understanding Christ's ways is a gradual process of enacting what truth one does know, and through this, learning the truth one needs

---

66 MacDonald, 'Salvation from Sin,' *HG*, p. 19.

67 Ibid., p. 20.

68 MacDonald, in *GMAW*, p. 508.

69 'Child in the Midst,' *US*, 1, p. 11.

70 *ML*, pp. 331–2.

71 Ibid., p. 255.

72 *CW*, p. 160.

73 'Child in the Midst,' *US*, 1, p. 151.

74 'Temptation,' *US*, 1, pp. 153–8.

75 Ibid., p. 153.

to know.[76] This included a willingness to trust before one can fully understand: 'He that would always know before he trusts, who would have from his God a promise before he will expect, is the slayer of his own eternity.'[77] Trusting means becoming as a child, placing one's hand in God's hand, and walking with him, 'like a boy with his father, desiring and doing his pleasure – falling in with his design in the making of you, a design that cannot be effected without you.'[78] Through aligning one's will to God's, we become 'fellow workers with him in the affairs of the universe … labourers with him at the heart of [things].'[79]

The work of obedience is anything but boring. It demands more vibrancy and imagination than almost anything else. Obedience to God's will is the 'highest creation of which man is capable … that *has* an element of the purely creative, and then is man likest God.'[80] This is a creativity which is possible by giving way to the 'bit in [one's] mouth' and the 'spur in [one's] flank.'[81] The way of worship through offering oneself as a living sacrifice is the route to one's full and free humanity. This is the way of becoming real and of growing into the fullness of the Real, for it means participation in divine nature. And 'that which is in God alone exists, and alone can become ours.'[82] Any other sense of growth or creativity is illusory.

The key for MacDonald in orthopraxis was not grasping for perfection, but of being in the grasp of perfection, the perfection of Christ.[83] He recognized that the only way the created could embrace the Creator was as God reached 'down a thousand true hands for [one] to grasp' and lifted one up into union with God's self.[84] This meant not trying to define or categorize God, but rather exulting in the privilege of living in God as one's true home.[85] Obedience becomes possible as one abides *in* Christ by his Spirit. Here one learns to be a true child of God to the end that through Christ's tenderness, 'the world will be made great, then children like thee, will all … smile in the face of the great God.'[86]

An illustration of such a way of life is given by MacDonald through the character of Malcolm.[87] So encompassing is Malcolm's faith that his entire life reminds him of God's love and care. When he is fishing, the wind draws him to rejoice in the breath of God, who made the wind and who breathes life into him. Encountering the fiery spirit of his horse or the beauty of a flaming sunset, he stands in awe of God's creativity. When he commands the crew of his boat, before setting forth he reads to

---

76 'Individual Development,' *DO*, p. 76.
77 *CW*, p. 286.
78 Ibid., p. 162.
79 Ibid., p. 280.
80 MacDonald, *Mary Marston*, p. 125.
81 MacDonald, 'Letter to Lady Mount-Temple' (7 October 1897), in *GMAW*, pp. 544–5.
82 Ibid.
83 'A Sermon,' *DO*, p. 286.
84 Ibid., p. 295.
85 Ibid.
86 'Child in the Midst,' *US*, 1, p. 17.
87 Malcolm is the protagonist of *Malcolm* and *The Marquis of Lossie*.

them out of the Gospels, 'striving earnestly to get the truth alive into their hearts.'[88] He seeks continually to pursue Christ's ways in all he does and in every encounter with another, reading and praying on his own and receiving as from a prophet the teaching of one who is more mature than himself. In this way, MacDonald invites his readers into Christ's way of love.

b. Returning to the Value of Goodness

Through *Malcolm* and other narratives, MacDonald earthed the meaning of the love and goodness which flows from an integration of faith and practice. He was able to create a realistic and inviting picture of goodness such that C.S. Lewis commented: 'The "good" characters are always the best and most convincing.'[89] MacDonald's depictions of goodness affected Lewis in a holistic way: 'I know nothing that gives me such a feeling of spiritual healing, of being washed, as to read MacDonald.'[90] Chesterton claimed that MacDonald 'made a difference to my whole existence,'[91] for he was able to make goodness itself attractive without being moralistic. This is considered to be one of his 'supreme and unique gifts.'[92]

MacDonald's emphasis on goodness offers the Church a way to regain its prophetic edge.[93] The temptation is to settle for 'goodness' by viewing distorted reflections in the mud-puddle of the human condition. Or to create abstract conceptions of it, which seem distant, unrealistic, uninteresting, and uninviting. While acknowledging the dilemmas of human sin, MacDonald goes even further back to the original news, that goodness is inherent in the created nature of humankind, and through Christ's redemption has become the only true human state:[94] 'She did not yet know that goodness is the only nature. She regarded it as a noble sort of disease – at least as something of which it was possible to have too much. She had not a suspicion that goodness is simply life and health ... we must have it – not stare at it from the bottom of a broken-rundled, interminable dream-ladder.'[95]

In MacDonald's portrayals of such characters as Gibbie, Annie, Diamond, Margaret, Malcolm, Robert Falconer, Hester, Mary St. John, and so on, he revealed the hardships and challenges of the truly 'good' life. He also depicted so rich a picture

---

88 *ML*, p. 385.

89 C.S. Lewis, 'Introduction,' *George MacDonald: An Anthology* (London, 1955), p. 18.

90 C.S. Lewis, 'To Arthur Greeves' (31 August 1930), in W. Hooper (ed.), *Collected Letters of C.S. Lewis* (New York, 2004), p. 936.

91 *GMAW*, p. 39.

92 Marion Lochhead, *The Renaissance of Wonder* (Edinburgh, 1977), p. 2.

93 Cf. William E. Placher, *Unapologetic Theology* (Louisville, TN, 1989), p. 12. Ron Sider, *The Scandal of the Evangelical Conscience* (Grand Rapids, MI, 2004), and Robert Bellah, *Habits of the Heart* (New York, 1985).

94 In a similar vein, Kathy Triggs wrote: 'MacDonald shows in the story [*A Rough Shaking*] that worldly normality is in fact "deranged" and that Clare's values are those of the one true man, Jesus Christ'; Triggs, *The Stars and the Stillness*, p. 149.

95 *CW*, p. 139.

of freedom and goodness that such a life, redemption, and humanity become more tangible and compelling. Through encountering their lives, one realizes that goodness is dependent on a certain kind of freedom, and that true freedom and goodness are mutually reinforcing. MacDonald dispels ideological frameworks which view them as oppositional and contradictory. The source from which both goodness and freedom grow in harmony and truth is God's Spirit, which Paul describes as not 'a spirit of timidity, but a spirit of power and of love and of self-control.'[96] To create a richer understanding of goodness, MacDonald worked to restore an understanding of freedom consistent with the gift of the Spirit. He demonstrated that goodness is tied to power, love and self-control as known through Jesus Christ, which fosters the freedom to 'lose' oneself, to be a servant, to be holy, to grow out of possessiveness and fearfulness, and into a commitment for community and mission.

c. Restoring an Understanding of Freedom which is Consistent with Goodness

1) Freedom to Lose Oneself

Through the 'inbreathing of God' and the 'love of our neighbour,' one is able to move 'out of the dungeon of the self' and one's own foul air to the 'fair sunlight of God, the sweet winds of the universe.'[97] Rather than seeing life as the knowing, seeking, and enjoying of oneself, MacDonald taught that fullness of life comes with a self-forgetting love which can embrace all forms of life. 'Losing oneself' occurs through giving oneself back to the Father from whom one came: 'Every highest human act is just a giving back to God of that which he first gave to us.'[98] How amazing it is, thought MacDonald, 'that in the Christian law we can offer to God the most deformed and diseased thing we have got – ourselves.'[99] Laying the self, with all of its desires and aspirations on God's altar, produces a profound transformation: 'That altar is in truth the nest of God's heart, and ... there the poor, unsightly, callow offerings shall lie, brooded upon by divinest love, until they come to shape and loveliness, and wings grow upon them to bear them back to the sacrificer divinely precious.'[100] The surrender of self, which resembles a snowflake gently falling on a fountain, was not a facile resignation to fate, nor a passive response, but was dynamic and very intentional.[101] It means a continual battle with everything in a person that resists such a relinquishment, especially with one's emotions.[102]

To be free to lose oneself, one needs the guidance of a higher compass than one's feelings. MacDonald's thoughts in this area challenge the preoccupation with

---

96 2 Timothy 1:7.
97 'Love Thy Neighbour,' *US*, 1, p. 214.
98 'The Hands of the Father,' *US*, 1, p. 182.
99 'Letter to His Wife' (7 March 1861), in *EC*, p. 134.
100 *CW*, p. 234.
101 *PW*, 2, p. 228.
102 A vivid portrayal of such a struggle can be found in Vane's life in *Lilith*. He is repeatedly tempted away from the necessary relinquishment of 'sleeping' through an entire range of feelings, from pride, to fear, to selfish desire.

feelings as the primary guiding force for one's life. In Jesus' response to his first temptation, MacDonald discerned wisdom for how to respond when circumstances and feelings do not reinforce obedience: 'A man does not live by his feelings any more than by bread, but by the Truth, that is, the Word, the Will, the uttered Being of God.'[103] Faith is not confidence, but obedience, and therefore one is not bound to feel, but to arise.[104] This meant to trust in spite of doubts, which MacDonald thought were inevitable until a person is one with God:

> To trust in spite of the look of being forgotten; to keep crying out into the vast whence comes no voice, and where seems no hearing; to struggle after light, where is no glimmer to guide in the direction of it; at every turn to find a doorless wall, yet ever seek a door; to stare at the machinery of the world pauseless grinding on as if self-moved, caring for no life, shifting no hair's-breadth for all entreaty, and yet believe that God is awake and utterly loving; to desire nothing but what comes meant for us from his hand; to wait patiently, willing to die of hunger, fearing only lest faith should fail - such is the victory that overcometh the world; such is very faith.[105]

One's feelings were not seen as unimportant to God, who expresses love for all, and special tenderness to those in the dark who have yet to obey.[106] Knowing God cares was enough for MacDonald, who exhorted: 'Heed not thy feelings: Do thy work.'[107] Obedience was seen as enabling a far deeper satisfaction, through which one begins to experience the delight of the Father's pleasure and an increasing capacity to receive God's gifts of power, love, and self-control.

In this way, one is most able to be oneself and to come closest to the soul of another, for one is released to seek to understand and to love, more than to be understood and loved.[108] No longer being driven so much by feelings, one is granted peace which flows forth to others, along with the freedom to welcome love without necessarily seeking it.[109] Losing oneself and rising above one's feelings is not 'living in denial,' as if in some sort of a state of illusion. Rather, it comes from knowing one lives in the very presence of God, whose 'Yes' in love is greater than any experience which might lead one to feel differently. It is a denial of only the less real, and a willingness to act on a commitment to the reality that God's truth extends beyond all human quandaries. Service that overflows from trust in God can allay the temptation to fill one's inner emptiness through serving others, which tends to spread that emptiness further.

---

103 'The Temptation in the Wilderness,' *US*, 1, pp. 141–2.

104 'The Eloi,' *US*, 1, p. 178.

105 *CW*, p. 288.

106 For example, see the great-grandmother's merciful approach to Lootie and Curdie's inability to believe in her in *The Princess and the Goblin*.

107 'The Eloi,' *US*, 1, p. 178.

108 MacDonald, *Phantastes*, p. 189.

109 *ML*, p. 61.

2) Freedom for Servanthood

Pivotal in MacDonald's view of both freedom and goodness was the idea of power expressed in serving others. He saw in Christ an inversion of all human notions of power which would view others as footstools by which one can climb to one's imagined glorious heights:[110] '... the Son of Man lies at the inverted apex of the pyramid; he upholds, and serves, and ministers unto all, and they who would be high in his kingdom must go near to him at the bottom, to uphold and minister to all that they may or can uphold and minister unto.'[111] There is no symbol in all of life, observes MacDonald, which can reach high enough to express the thought of God's own ministration.[112] Christ's service was the giving of himself entirely. True Lordship was in him disclosed, such that 'to rule is to raise, and a man's rank is in his power to uplift.'[113]

To be like Christ, one seeks not to rule over others, but to come under them and minister to them. The idea of chivalry once held aloft in the Middle Ages, MacDonald noted, has now come to be disdained as sentiment and soppiness.[114] But in such a commitment to serve lies the power and freedom to pursue that which is right, regardless of what may seem best for oneself.[115] Servanthood is the way in which one takes one's place in God's scheme of things and learns to think, feel and discern as God does.[116] MacDonald did not just speak in abstractions about servanthood, but depicted it as often including menial labor. He proclaimed that one who is incapable of drudgery is incapable of the finest work.[117] Thus the beautiful and wise woman in 'The Golden Key' begged Tangle to let her wait on her, saying that serving was her great pleasure.[118] Malcolm, though the laird of the village, joined the women in their toil of cleaning fish. Such service is possible through the worship of God, and through being 'so absorbed in the delight and glory of the goodness that is round about them that they learn not to think much about themselves.'[119]

3) Freedom in Holiness, the Only Real Choice

MacDonald believed that one's only true freedom lies in choosing the good, for it is the 'very necessity of his nature.'[120] To choose otherwise he saw as a submission to slavery and a stealing of the choice. Thus 'freedom is the unclosing of the idea

---

110 'True Christian Ministering,' *DO*, pp. 298–311.

111 Ibid., p. 299.

112 'True Christian Ministering,' *DO*, p. 303.

113 *ML*, p. 330.

114 'True Christian Ministering,' *DO*, p. 309.

115 Cf. Elaine Storkey, who writes: 'For servanthood is not something we choose in opposition to rich independence. It is something we choose in opposition to self-centred arrogance and toil'; Storkey, *Mary's Story, Mary's Song* (London, 1993), p. 17.

116 'True Christian Ministering,' *DO*, p. 309.

117 *HA*, p. 57.

118 'The Golden Key,' in *GCC*, p. 266.

119 'True Christian Ministering,' *DO*, p. 300.

120 *ML*, p. 186.

which lies at our root and is the vital power of our existence. The rose is the freedom of the rose-tree.'[121] One could never be satisfied with 'less than the liberty of a holy heart, less than the freedom of the Lord himself.'[122] Because one has an eternal root as the source of one's being, one is always longing 'for larger existence ... more of God's making, and less of our own unmaking.'[123] This is a freedom found in being ruthless with selfishness (not 'justifying' it under the category of self-acceptance and self-fulfillment), that one may submit one's desires to God's perfect will. So central was this issue to MacDonald that he depicts this battle in various ways in all of his narratives. One example is Molly in *Home Again*, whose gentle being radiated light, like a 'creature born of the sun and ripened by his light and heat ... When she caught selfishness in her, she was down upon it with the knee and grasp of a giant. Strong is man or woman whose eternal life subjects the individual liking to the perfect Will. Such man, such woman, is free man, free woman.'[124]

Moving in contradiction to this 'only' choice, one experiences the loss of one's individuality, the loss of one's unique 'face.' MacDonald illustrated this through the character of Alec, who began to lose his unique identity as he came under the degrading influence of Beauchamp. Increasingly, he resembled his false guide: 'For all wickedness tends to destroy individuality, and declining natures assimilate as they sink.'[125] The pressures of society, peers, and profession soon dictate one's options and one's direction, providing an entire mask and costume for greater societal acceptability.[126] MacDonald viewed individuality and freedom as synonymous, both gifts of God. He marveled at the gift God was able and willing to give in making humankind apart from God's self, a far greater wonder, he thought, than human dependence. Freedom was then the bond between humanity and God, and 'the freer the man, the stronger the bond that binds him to him who made his freedom.'[127]

Freedom in holiness takes one in the opposite direction from that which is commonly associated with both freedom and individuality. At its highest, it means that one is willing to be '*nothing* relatively.'[128] Competitive self-assertion fades away, for being greater or less than another person has no value. With this freedom, the laird of *Castle Warlock* was able truly to serve the drunk lord, and to be thought of and treated as a servant, while ever desiring the best for him.[129] Such individuality

---

121 MacDonald, *DG*, Vol. 3, p. 78, cited in *GMAW*, p. 78.
122 MacDonald, 'Jesus and His Fellow Townspeople,' *HG*, p. 36.
123 *CW*, p. 279.
124 *HA*, p. 276. MacDonald's inclusive language was unusual in his day, and expresses his commitment to enable women as well as men to be all they were created to be.
125 *AF*, p. 315.
126 MacDonald developed the character Cornelius in *Weighed and Wanting*, who demonstrates just such conformity and loss of individuality.
127 'The Eloi,' *US*, 1, p. 175.
128 'Wordsworth's Poetry,' *DO*, p. 225.
129 *CW*, p. 95.

is lived in and satisfied by the 'absoluteness' of the truth, and therefore feels no need to form comparisons of the self with others.[130]

MacDonald was clear that to go in Jesus' name, one must go like him. 'Crucifixion,' wrote MacDonald, 'symbolizes the one Law of life.'[131] It leads to 'unspeakable bliss of the human heart and soul and mind and sense' for the one who is 'crucified with Christ, who lives no more from his own self, but is inspired and informed and possessed with the same faith toward the Father in which Jesus lived and wrought the will of the Father.'[132] This holiness is the supreme expression of freedom and individuality in which God's love alone reigns and motivates. For this reason, MacDonald referred to the saints of God as the 'servants of the Crucified.'[133]

4) Freedom from Possessiveness

To be crucified with Christ and thus becoming a servant like him meant for MacDonald that one's hands and one's heart would be opened wide. Grasping and hoarding were contradictory to new life in Christ, for all things, 'the world and all that God cared about in it,' belong to one born again in him, 'as no miser's gold could ever belong to its hoarder.'[134] MacDonald described possessiveness as the 'cleaving of his soul to the dust.'[135] This attachment to things or to place is a form of idolatry.[136] True love of anything includes a willingness to relinquish it whenever God wills. Entering into the inheritance of the saints occurs when one will not 'receive anything save from the hands that have the right to withhold it, and in whose giving alone lies the good of having.'[137] Therefore, MacDonald proclaimed: 'To be lord of space, a man must be unbound from place. For a heart to be heir of all things, it must have no *things* inside it. The man must be as the one who makes things, not one who puts them in his pocket. He must stand on the upper, not the lower side of them.'[138]

This freedom from materialistic possessiveness also included a freedom from selfish prudence, such that a person is free to give generously to the needs of others even when it might seem to affect one's own security (though he cautioned against any disregard of one's basic responsibilities). The contrast between prudence and charity he saw in terms of the following images: 'Upon one of the prized cabinets was carved *Charity* gazing at the child on her arm, and beside her *Prudence* with a mirror in her hand, contemplating herself.'[139]

130 'Forms of Literature,' *DO*, p. 225.
131 MacDonald, cited by Greville MacDonald, *Reminiscences of a Specialist* (London, 1932), p. 168.
132 George MacDonald, *Thomas Wingfold, Curate* (London, 1887), p. 499.
133 Ibid., p. 497.
134 Ibid., p. 494.
135 *CW,* p. 292.
136 Ibid., p. 290.
137 Ibid., p. 292.
138 Ibid., p. 329.
139 Ibid., p. 295.

5) Freedom from Fear

MacDonald adamantly stressed that the Spirit which God has given people is not a spirit of timidity. One of the key character qualities of his heroes or heroines was the ability to remain faithful in the midst of fearful situations. Though one might at times be afraid, it becomes deleterious to let fear dictate one's thoughts or course of action. Responding to the call for obedience, regardless of danger or consequences, gives force to truth which evokes a sense of peace and of being at home in all situations. In the case of consistent disobedience, however, even the very thought of truth itself evokes 'fear and dismay.'[140] To this end, MacDonald urged that 'God is the only adviser to be trusted, and you must do what he tells you, even if it lead you to a stake, to be burned by the slow fire of poverty.'[141] There is nothing to fear when one dwells in the living God, nothing which can cause God's presence and love to fail: 'To know one's self safe amid storm and darkness, fire and water, disease and pain, violence and death, is to be a follower of the Master, for that is what he knew, even in the hour of his darkness.'[142]

To illustrate this, MacDonald repeatedly depicted protagonists in difficult, even terrifying situations, who were yet able to remain calm and at peace, knowing that whatever happened, they would still be in the hands of God. Thus, for example, blind Tibbie and Annie, who were caught in a life-threatening flood, remained fearless and calm. He also was able to illuminate the problem of the fear of the unknown, showing that often this fear has its basis in illusion more than reality. When Richard in 'Cross Purposes' discovers the only way for him and Alice to move ahead is through a bog swarming with slimy, horrid creatures, he takes her in his arms and jumps in. The creatures vanish, as minnows do when a stone is thrown into the water.[143] At another time, he is forced to jump down from the wall of a tower which seems very high. For love of Alice, he jumps first, only to discover he was but a few feet from the ground. MacDonald revealed in these and other similar situations that fear will often be dispelled when one does what one must. The point was not somehow to try to ascertain the future, for 'Trust is better than foresight.'[144] Similarly, he believed that one would be given enough light to manage the next step: 'Act according to thy faith in Christ, and thy faith will soon become sight.'[145] Princess Irene is utterly surprised to discover where following the thread takes her, but even when dismayed, continues to reflect on her great-grandmother's trustworthy character and to persist in following her thread.

A sense of holy fear, the fear of God, MacDonald saw as efficacious and essential to help with all other fears. This kind of fear is not a cringing and craving fear, but one which acknowledges him to be the Master of all. Before God, one must bow

---

140 Ibid., p. 270.
141 Ibid., p. 289.
142 Ibid., p. 95.
143 MacDonald, 'Cross Purposes,' in *GCC*, p. 251.
144 MacDonald, *Flight of the Shadow* (London, 1891), p. 190.
145 *HA*, p. 286.

down all one's desires, thought, and loves, for God is the life of them, and yearns for their purity.[146] There is no fear of losing one's true life in drawing near to the Consuming Fire, for God *is* one's life.

In this context, MacDonald saw no place for preoccupation with or fear related to one's own safety and welfare. Jesus' response to the first temptation in the wilderness shows that the Father is trustworthy in caring for one's needs, and that one's overriding concern must be to do the Father's will.[147] Jesus revealed God alone to be our refuge. God's care for God's children is 'the divinest thing in the universe,' which Jesus demonstrated must not be exchanged for the 'merest commonplace of self-preservation.'[148] In his work, MacDonald exhorted people repeatedly to cast all their cares on God, that they might dedicate themselves to the only thing worth a person's care – the will of God.[149] To pursue God's will means to pursue Christ, and so to eat of the only bread which satisfies, the Bread of Life.

As noted previously, MacDonald himself worked hard to live out this single-mindedness toward God's will, despite sickness, much poverty, and death of loved ones. Thus in *The Seaboard Parish*, when he spoke words of challenge through the father to the daughter, Connie, after her paralyzing accident, he understood the nature of the relinquishment and courage which he urged: 'You must say to God something like this: "O Heavenly father, I have nothing to offer Thee but my patience. I will bear Thy will, and so offer my will a burnt offering unto Thine. I will be as useless as Thou pleasest."'[150] To believe in the Father's care was to be without any anxiety for one's well-being.

Furthermore, it meant to enter into the joy of the Lord. The joy depicted in the self-giving of the flying rainbow fish in 'The Golden Key' is MacDonald's portrayal of the results of freedom from the kind of fear which continually urges one toward self-preservation. The fish fly into a pot of boiling water in their desire to give nourishment for others. They do not die in so doing, but while leaving delicate-tasting fish behind to be eaten, are also each transformed into 'a lovely little creature in human shape, with large white wings.'[151] This transformation is a conversion realized through love, which enables one to express Christ's love to all around.

---

146 'The Consuming Fire,' *US*, 1, p. 30.
147 'The Temptation in the Wilderness,' *US*, 1, p. 136.
148 Ibid., p. 138.
149 *CW*, p. 162.
150 *SP*, p. 32.
151 'The Golden Key,' in *GCC*, p. 265.

3. Embracing Community and Mission, the Harvest of the Word

Make not of thy heart a casket,
Opening seldom, quick to close;
But of bread a wide-mouthed basket,
And a cup that overflows.[152]

Community was central to MacDonald's descriptions of God's purposes and human identity. He viewed community as possible through the deep implanting of the Word of God, in which God's own love overflows and draws people back together to God's self. In community, one is able to experience the wonder of being a part of God's harvest, the joy of harvesting with God, and the anticipation of the ultimate harvest celebration in which all will dance with faces of love and of laughter.

MacDonald recognized that in the present age, difficulties exist in the community of those who call themselves Christians, such that weeds and wheat grow side by side.[153] He saw God as a long-suffering Master who would patiently abide 'centuries of seeming bafflement' to grow God's people into his sons and daughters.[154] Though he was angered by the paltriness of people's faith and love, which was enough to drive unbelievers away in disinterest or disgust, for the most part he felt the body of believers must be shown the light to help them grow rather than being reminded of their darkness:[155] 'Surely if a man would help his fellow-men, he can do so far more effectually by exhibiting truth than exposing error, by unveiling beauty than by a critical dissection of deformity ... It is the light that makes manifest.'[156] The danger in focusing on error is part of the continual temptation of the Church to place its attention on that which is relative and passing rather than eternal.

Viewing community as God's gift established in Christ, MacDonald challenged relativist and subjectivist tendencies. Just as it did not increase the light to focus on the fallacies of those around, it was also not illuminating to argue on the basis of human opinion. Human opinion he saw as the foliage that changes with the seasons, in contrast to faith, which is rooted in God's self-revelation.[157] To argue for a particular opinion is merely insisting on oneself and drawing attention to the form of the lantern which holds the light: 'Do not talk about the lantern that holds the lamp, but make haste, uncover the light, and let it shine.'[158] He urged people to be 'jealous that the human not obscure the divine,' for the danger of opinions is that

---

152 *CW*, p. 45.
153 Matthew 13:24–30.
154 'The Temptation in the Wilderness,' *US*, 1, p. 153. See also *The Marquis of Lossie*, pp. 77–8.
155 An illustration of MacDonald's criticism of 'poverty-stricken believers' can be found in *Thomas Wingfold*, pp. 498–9.
156 A Sermon,' *DO*, pp. 196–7.
157 Ibid., p. 287.
158 Ibid., p. 293.

they can create obstacles between individuals and God, between oneself and one's neighbor, and even between the self and one's better self.[159]

Opinions, MacDonald thought, are often the death of love, for they are frequently the basis of condemnation in which one becomes 'a wounder, a divider of the oneness of Christ,' rather than one who uplifts.[160] Furthermore, giving priority to one's personal views is self-imprisoning. We 'become such fools of logic and temper that we lie in the prison-houses of our own fancies, ideas and experiences, shut the doors and windows against the entrance of the free spirit, and will not inherit the love of the Father.'[161]

He was concerned about sectarianism which develops from giving undue weight to one's opinions: 'Division has done more to hide Christ from the view of men than all the infidelity that has ever been spoken.'[162] MacDonald reacted to any element of condescension and pride in the church, including that which treated women, the poor, the uneducated, or the elderly as having less to offer. Thus, for example, to offset the condescending attitudes towards women, in MacDonald's collection of poems he included 16 devotional poems lauding New Testament women; he often portrayed women, single or married, as his protagonists; he challenged the double standard with which women were treated in Victorian times as in *Paul Faber, Surgeon*, and he was personally involved in the education of women at various women's colleges. Pride and a sense of superiority had, he felt, also created Church structures which veiled the essential humility of the Lord Jesus Christ. Not only administrative hierarchies, but even church buildings often failed to reflect 'the spirit of His revelation':

> All church forms should be on the other side from show and expense. Let the money go to build decent houses for God's poor, not to give them his holy bread and wine out of silver and gold and precious stones ... I would send all the church plate to fight the devil with his own weapons in our overcrowded cities, and in our villages where the husbandmen are housed like swine, by giving them room to be clean and decent air from heaven to breathe.[163]

MacDonald did not hesitate to admit that each person's thoughts were also a mixture of wheat and weeds, truth and opinions. That which was worthy and good, if nurtured, would endure and would lift one toward God.[164] Preaching on Paul's injunction to be like-minded, MacDonald encourages people who are of differing opinions to seek God, who 'will himself unveil to them the truth of the matter.' He continues: 'God must reveal, or nothing is known.' Once the truth of God's revelation has been affirmed, the key is to act on that truth, which will draw people together in unity: 'With the whole energy of his great heart, Paul clung to unity ... And he knew well

---

159 Ibid., p. 297.
160 Ibid., pp. 291, 293.
161 Ibid., p. 296.
162 *PF*, Vol. 2, p. 126.
163 *SP*, p. 51.
164 'A Sermon,' *DO*, p. 295.

that only by walking in the truth to which they had attained, could they ever draw near to each other.'[165]

As one relinquishes one's rights to one's opinions, an embracing vision of the family of God emerges. God's people are bound together in Christ, rather than divided by ideas which will wither and fade. He desired to approach all people as part of the universal family of God.[166] The inclusiveness of his vision encouraged the acceptance of greater diversity without sacrificing the need for conformity to the revealed will of God. In fact, the possibility of harmony in the midst of such diversity, of a dance of such complexity and variety which does not spin into chaos, was seen as only possible through responsiveness to the choreography of the Lord of the Dance. The unity of this family was an ontological gift possible through Christ's shared humanity, for 'In God alone can man meet man.'[167]

With God as the basis and central unifying force in all relationships, MacDonald wrote that there is now an 'infinitely greater' law to fulfill than to love one's neighbor as oneself. The key is now to 'love [one's] neighbour even as Christ hath loved him.'[168] In this, MacDonald avoids a contemporary pitfall which arises from the avowed need to love one's self in order to love one's neighbor. He thus diffuses the common tension between my needs and my neighbor's and raises the issue to a higher plane. Though indeed loving as Christ loves may lead to martyrdom, as it did with Christ, it means living in harmony with one's deepest need, which is know God and to let God live through one's life. To love as Christ loves is to let oneself slip out of one's preoccupation into the care of the Father. It is to let Christ's own love fill and be poured out of one's life without condition and without differentiation, other than that of obedience to him.

From this basis it is possible to extend Christ's love to all peoples and nations. The universality of the Church is, in MacDonald's thinking, part of her strength and wholeness: 'As he makes families mingle, to redeem each from its family selfishness, so will he make nations mingle, and love and correct and reform and develop each other, till the planet-world shall go singing through space one harmony to the God of the whole earth.'[169] With its basis in Christ's love and Christ's way of loving, the Church is relieved of the burden and the fallacy of seeing herself as a power-wielding body. Additionally, there is no justification for preferential treatment of certain members, for in Christ's love there are 'only the sons and daughters of God, only the brothers and sisters of the Lord.' Furthermore, 'Excuse [of others] ought to be one of the blossoms of love rooted in obedience.'[170]

---

165 Ibid., pp. 289–90.
166 MacDonald wrote of Cosmos that which applied to himself: 'Everybody seems to be of his own family'; *CW*, p. 165.
167 'Love Thy Neighbour,' *US*, 1, p. 196.
168 *ML*, pp. 77.
169 *RF*, p. 134.
170 *CW*, pp. 185, 165.

The truth of the human condition, wrote MacDonald, is that 'We are all good and all bad.'[171] However, loving with Christ's love does not mean a mere tolerance of the bad. It calls for a willingness to 'die to divide evil [from one's] fellows' combined with a gracious willingness to 'make for any one of them all *honest* excuse.'[172] The love which is 'in the image of God's love [is] all-embracing, quietly excusing, heartily commending ... not insensible to that which is foreign to it, but over-coming it with good.'[173]

Forgiveness is so essential to the Christian community that MacDonald emphasized it in all of his works. Even after suffering great offence, those characters who bear the love of God are able humbly to forgive and to welcome back the ones who have offended. Thus Isy, who had been sexually seduced and then abandoned by James, and who almost dies trying to fend for herself and their child, feels ongoing love for him. When he seeks her and expresses deep remorse, she willingly forgives him. She is eager to see the pain removed from his heart, eager for his restoration and for his ability to experience God's forgiveness.[174]

To forgive is to give a person back his own self – cleansed and unburdened.[175] An unwillingness to forgive or to receive forgiveness was seen by MacDonald as shutting God out altogether.[176] If some are too proud to forgive another or themselves, it is necessary that God's forgiveness have its humbling way with them, to drown 'their pride in the tears of repentance, and [to make] their heart come again like the heart of a little child.'[177] Efforts at forgiveness and reconciliation in the family of God were seen as essential, for 'there is that in the depths of every human breast which makes a reconciliation the only victory that can give true satisfaction.'[178] Receiving and extending Christ's forgiveness is the only way to overcome barriers erected by hostilities which otherwise spark endless cycles of revenge.

To love in Christ's way is to be able to see in others, both within the Body of Christ and without, in the midst of their weakness and sin, the image of God to which Christ would restore them completely. It is to be willing to honor 'every image of the living God it had pleased that God to make ... destined to be one day a brother of Jesus Christ.'[179] Because of this, any outreach or mission to others must be as persons

---

171 *RF*, p. 110. Chesterton lauded MacDonald for his realism in his 'recurring theme that even within good persons there always lurks the potentiality for evil.' This he sees portrayed metaphorically in *The Princess and Curdie*, in which there is evil within the castle, and in which one knows but does not fully know his own house; Chesterton, in Leo A. Hetzler, 'George MacDonald and G.K. Chesterton,' *Durham University Journal*, 37 (1976): 176–82.

172 *CW*, p. 165.

173 'Browning's Christmas Eve,' *DO*, pp. 213–14.

174 MacDonald, *Salted with Fire*, pp. 297–8.

175 *AF*, p. 277.

176 'It Shall Not Be Forgiven,' *US*, 1, p. 82.

177 Ibid., p. 80.

178 *AF*, p. 106.

179 *CW*, p. 280.

with persons, rather than the response of an organization toward objects. MacDonald urged that to help others, one must draw near in love to listen to the joys and hurts of their heart, soul, mind, and body.

For its fragmented and impersonal approach to people, MacDonald resisted proselytization, saying: 'If there is one role I hate, it is that of the proselytizer. But shall I not come to you as a brother to brethren?'[180] He condemned the attempt to share doctrine with the poor when they really needed food, clothing, purpose, and love. Thus, for example, he contrasted Robert Falconer, who gave himself to bring sustenance and health to the minds, spirits, and bodies of those in need, with a man who combatively read the Bible to Mr. De Fleuri, who had lost his wife and three children and was trying to nurse his starving daughter.[181] Because in the midst of a mass of people one is surrounded with those bearing the image of God, MacDonald felt one should be able to hear God's word there as easily as when in the peacefulness of nature: 'I canna but think there's something wrang wi' a man gien he canna hear the word o' God as weel i' the mids o' a multitude no man can number, a' made ilk ane i' the image o' the Father – as weel, as i' the hert o' win' an' watter an' the lift an' the starns an' a'.'[182]

Even with those who are excessively selfish and difficult to love, MacDonald urged Christ's love and the will to see Christ in them. Rather than leaving them to perish by seeing only the 'outer falsehood of Satan's incantations,' he called the servants of the Crucified to see the 'dearly lovable reality of them,' and with love to break their bonds.[183] Selfishness and alienation can be diminished, MacDonald felt, in the midst of a loving community that offers a role in caring for others to those who are self-preoccupied. Thus Robert Falconer cared for the bitter Mr. De Fleuri and urged him to begin to seek ways to help others in his slum tenement.[184] Rather than leaving one alienated by sin and selfishness, MacDonald asserted: 'With my love at least shalt thou be compassed about, for thou hast not thy own lovingness to infold thee; love shall come as near thee as it may; and when thine comes forth to meet mine, we shall be one in the indwelling God.'[185] Therefore, he said: 'A man must not choose his neighbour; he must take the neighbour that God sends him. In him, whoever he be, lies, hidden or revealed, a beautiful brother.'[186] In offering love to the unlovely or difficult to love, one is given a unique kind of power in vision which MacDonald described poetically in 'Cross Purposes.' When Richard is able to begin to love the rather condescending Alice, MacDonald wrote, 'his eyes began to send forth light' which illuminated her truer nature and the path ahead of her.[187]

---

180 'A Sermon,' *DO*, p. 291.
181 *RF*, pp. 366–9.
182 *ML*, p. 45.
183 'Love Thine Enemy,' *US*, 1, p. 222.
184 *RF*, p. 369.
185 'Love Thine Enemy,' *US*, 1, p. 223.
186 Ibid., p. 210.
187 'Cross Purposes,' in *GCC*, p. 250.

The gift of community is closely tied with celebration and creativity.[188] He viewed obedience to God in the love of one's neighbor as that which opens the inner door of one's life that God's Spirit of creativity may enter in.[189] Thus a renewed vision of humanity is a vital aspect of both theological understanding and artistic expression. To be able to see the true nature of things and people in love is to see with an inner eye, and by this to be filled with a radiant hope. It is to be able to rejoice, knowing the kingdom is both in one's midst and yet coming with all of its fullness. MacDonald mused: 'Shall we not find thee equal to our faith? One day, we shall laugh ourselves to scorn that we looked for so little from thee ....'[190] The community of believers is not to be characterized as a people of despair, but as those who are active and hopeful, who can say to another as Eve did to Vane in *Lilith*: 'To our eyes ... you were coming all the time.'[191] To be able to see wisdom and loveliness in those who are mentally and physically challenged, such as Steenie Barclay in *Heather and Snow*, the 'mad Laird' in *Malcolm*, the Polwarths in *Paul Faber, Surgeon*, is to approach others humbly, with hope and gratitude that they too are part of the universal family of God. The one who sees with the inner eye can see 'no bliss, no good in being greater than someone else,'[192] and thus, rather than being a person of competition and self-assertion, is able in meekness to identify with all. One worries no longer about having 'time to prepare a face to meet the faces that you meet.'[193] In seeing Christ's face in others, one will be given his face of radiant love. This renewal propels one to approach suffering with resolute hope rather than resignation.

---

188 'Forms of Literature,' *DO,* pp. 233–4.

189 *CW*, p. 36.

190 'The Higher Faith,' *US*, 1, p. 60.

191 *Lilith*, p. 229.

192 MacDonald, 'The Heirs of Heaven and Earth,' *HG,* p. 45.

193 T.S. Eliot, 'The Love Song of J. Alfred Prufrock,' *The Complete Poems and Plays* (New York, 1962), p. 4. In an interesting essay entitled 'George MacDonald and T. S. Eliot Further Consideration,' John Pennington details many similarities between MacDonald and Eliot, and establishes justification supporting fairly significant ways in which MacDonald influenced Eliot; see *North Wind* 8 (London, 1989), pp. 12–24.

Chapter 7

Renewed Vision of Suffering, Aging, and Death

Pain and sorrow,
Plough and harrow,
For the seed its place to find;
For the growing
Still the blowing
Of the Spirit's thinking wind;
For the corn that it will bear,
Love eternal everywhere.[1]

1. Suffering and Evil and the Inversion of Truth

Suffering is often viewed in Western societies as something to be avoided whatever the cost. MacDonald traced this perspective to the assumption that the highest good is 'ease and comfort, and the pleasures of animal and intellectual being,' such that these are 'the only things most people desire.'[2] People questioned God's goodness and God's existence when their comfort was disturbed by suffering: 'The maker who did not care that his creatures should possess or were deprived of such [comforts and pleasures] could not be a good God.'[3] Similarly, the notion that well-being consists in being well-off makes 'the kind-hearted person … tempted to doubt the existence of a God – and perhaps it is well they should be so tempted.'[4] Some would try to explain suffering as God's right to do as God pleases. MacDonald saw this as using a 'very bad argument for God,' for it does not challenge false assumptions, nor does it do justice to the nature of God.[5] He argued that holding such a view of God leads to a sense of what Barth would later call 'uncertainty of the capricious and irrational.'[6]

MacDonald worked to restore people's belief that the God who is truth exists at the heart of all things, and can be trusted to the uttermost. The highest human good is to see and to be one with God. This is what it means to 'stand on the highest point

---

1   MacDonald, 'Poem for Miss Goodwin,' *GMAW*, p. 505.
2   *ML*, p.188.
3   Ibid.
4   Ibid., p. 187.
5   *AF*, p. 284.
6   Karl Barth, *Church Dogmatics*, Vol. 2, Part 1, trans. T.H.L. Parker et al., ed. G.W. Bromiley and T.F. Torrance (Zurich and Edinburgh, 1957), p. 427.

of created being.'[7] The obstacle to this pinnacle of being is not suffering, for to suffer may be to join with God. Rather, the obstacle is evil. MacDonald took evil very seriously, viewing moral evil as the 'cause of every man's discomfort.'[8] Evil aims to separate and the 'parent of all evils' is disjunction between the created and Creating life.[9] Whatever causes separation from God cooperates with evil. In MacDonald's narratives, comfort and ease often feed the illusion that one is like God and therefore should be able to command and domineer rather than serve or draw near to God. Agnes and Rosalind in 'The Wise Woman' have everything they might need in their different circumstances of urban riches and rural humbleness. Both develop odious personalities, though, for each is led to believe that 'she is a Somebody' and the most important around.[10] MacDonald believed that one cannot 'make terms' with evil. Though its existence cannot be denied, it is not a thing in itself, but rather a parasite or corruption of the good:[11] 'It is the strength of human nature itself that makes evil strong. Wickedness could have no power of itself: it lives by the perverted powers of good.'[12]

Just as MacDonald believed it was not helpful to view suffering or God as the source of the world's problems, he also refused to blame the devil for the evil of the world: 'The terrible things that one reads in old histories, or in modern newspapers, were done by human beings, not by demons.'[13] Through sin and disobedience, one moves into darkness and emptiness. MacDonald's story of Anodos defying the warning of the farmer's wife illustrates the way one enters into the realm of evil, which is the inversion of all truth. Anodos ignores all warnings to avoid the house of the ogre and the door from which the shadows rise. He makes himself the center of action and being, and thus encounters the great existential lie: 'darkness had no beginning, neither will it ever have an end. So, then, it is eternal ... Truly, man is but a passing flame, moving unquietly amid the surrounding rest of night; without which he yet could not be, and whereof he is in part compounded.'[14] Here Anodos acquires his shadow, which increases the darkness, distortion, and fear. Rather than living in trust that there is good at the heart of all things, he lives in doubt and destructive cynicism.

For MacDonald, evil is to God like shadows to the sun. The overcoming of evil is experienced as the 'sun' burns up the shadows, and shines through the things

---

7   MacDonald, 'God's Family,' *HG*, p. 56.

8   Ibid., p. 14.

9   Greville MacDonald, *Reminiscences of a Specialist*, p. 323. See also MacDonald, *The Flight of the Shadow*, p. 304.

10 'The Wise Women,' *GCC*, pp. 286–7; 325.

11 Marjorie Wright comments that this perspective on evil was shared by C.S. Lewis, Charles Williams, and J.R. Tolkien; Wright, 'The Vision of Cosmic Order in the Oxford Mythmakers,' in Charles A. Huttar (ed.), *Imagination and the Spirit* (Grand Rapids, MI), p. 268.

12 'St. George's Day,' *DO*, p. 125.

13 MacDonald, *Annals of a Quiet Neighbourhood*, p. 321.

14 *Phantastes*, p. 55.

that cast them, compelling their transparency.[15] The idea that the fire of God's love consumes darkness and evil was central to MacDonald's understanding of the way in which God uses and redeems suffering: 'We must be saved from ourselves by very unpleasant things ....'[16] As long as one seeks refuge from suffering through altering one's circumstances or through escape, the process of the cure of the soul is short-circuited. The nourishment which the soul would otherwise receive is denied it. Rather, a willingness to endure requires the admission that it is sin and evil which are the real problem, rather than suffering.

Thomas Erskine wrote that sin must be approached as one approaches a physical ailment, through seeking a remedy for the removal of the malady, rather than new circumstances into which to carry the ailment.[17] This was not used as a excuse to ignore those who lived in dire conditions. MacDonald expressed deep compassion for those whose lives were battered by the neglect and evil of others.[18] He was also a staunch activist working to relieve the suffering of the poor and the powerless. Yet he believed that each person has access to moral power and can assume a measure of moral responsibility, through God's ever-present Spirit. Regardless of the circumstance, each person is equipped in some way to turn from the darkness and toward the ever-beckoning Light.

For MacDonald, regardless of how depraved one's background, it is possible to grow toward the Light and thus transform suffering into strength and sickness into health. Gibbie, the son of an alcoholic who died of his disease, and Clare Skymer, who was orphaned when tiny and abused in a variety of settings, exemplify this growth. In these portrayals, he also demonstrated that one's suffering is often not in direct relationship to one's sin, but may be a result of human sin and the fall of humankind in general. Furthermore, suffering may be used in the continuing outworking of Christ's defeat of the sinful state of one's 'inhuman' condition. The goodness of God and suffering were thus not viewed as mutually exclusive. If the deprivation of comfort and well-being would lead to 'something in its very nature so much better,' it would be well for God to enable such deprivation.[19]

Suffering can have meaning because God is able to use it and cause it to bear fruit. Yet MacDonald knew that in light of some of life's bitter experiences, 'eternity must be very rich to make up for some such hours.'[20] He perceived that one who fails to understand that God is far beyond 'the intensest presence of bliss or of pain, must have ... many an empty cistern and dried-up river in the world of his being!'[21]

---

15 *CW*, p. 241.

16 'Letter to Louisa' (Summer 1857, ALS Yale), in Raeper, *George MacDonald*, p. 141.

17 Thomas Erskine, 'Letter to Madame de Staël' (29 September 1843), in David Douglas (ed.), *The Fatherhood of God Revealed in Christ: A Lesson from the Letters of Thomas Erskine of Linlathen* (Edinburgh, 1888), pp. 58–9.

18 See, for example, MacDonald's depiction of Shagar's mother or Shagar in *Robert Falconer*, and Nanny in *At the Back of the North Wind*.

19 *ML*, p. 188.

20 *AF*, p. 318.

21 *CW*, pp. 205–6.

2. MacDonald's Perspective on the Place of Suffering

> O Life, why dost thou close me up in death?
> O Health, why make me inhabit heaviness
> I ask, yet know: the sum of this distress,
> Pang-haunted body, sore-dismayed mind,
> Is but the egg that rounds the winged faith;
> When that its path into the air shall find,
> My heart will follow, high above cold, rain, and wind.[22]

a. Suffering Exists within the Realm of God's Love

MacDonald believed that all pain and sorrow exist within the realm of God's love, and are permitted or even appointed by that love. As such, 'under the suffering care of the highest minister, [they] are but the ministers of truth and righteousness.'[23] Furthermore, God's presence is evident in the midst of suffering with gifts expressive of God's tenderness and love. MacDonald conveyed this through Annie in *Alec Forbes of Howglen*, who is granted a vision of the face of God. She realized that Christ had been with her in her father's death and relocation to the home of the cruel Robert Bruce. Christ had offered people of consolation all along the way.[24] Though no sparrow can fall without God, David Elginbrod, knew that the fall of the sparrow was inevitable, for by this did it learn to fly. Through the sorrow and suffering which would inevitably come to his daughter, he knew 'she could be fashioned into the perfection of a child of the kingdom.'[25] So seriously did David take evil that he thought it preferable that Margaret should suffer and die than that she live and turn to evil ways. This was never an excuse to inflict suffering. Rather, the goal was to be willing to trust one's life to God rather than to try to gain more life by denying God. MacDonald's faith affirmed that God's continuing tolerance of suffering itself expresses that it must be worthwhile for God's children.[26]

Divine tolerance of suffering reveals that the goal of life is not 'comfort or enjoyment, but blessedness, yea, ecstasy.'[27] God can actually lead one toward blessedness through the fires of suffering. MacDonald portrayed this powerfully through the story of *The Princess and Curdie*. Curdie is asked to place his hands in the fire of roses by the great-great-grandmother. The suffering is intense and almost unbearable, but Curdie endures until his hands feel nothing at all. He looks up to see the grandmother weeping profusely and learns that she has been bearing this pain with him and for him. His hands become vehicles of a 'second sight,' enabling

---

22 *DOS* (23 January), p. 19.
23 MacDonald, *Mary Marston*, p. 232.
24 *AF*, pp. 374–5.
25 *DE*, p. 82.
26 'Letter to his father' (Hastings, 2 December 1857), in *EC*, p. 124.
27 *US*, 1, p. 122.

him to discern the character of anyone he touches and thus to be a blessing in the kingdom.

With suffering inside the sphere of God's love, it is not an indication of God's absence, but an indication of his compassionate presence. Therefore, when his father died, MacDonald wrote to his step-mother: 'the only thing that can comfort you for the loss of my father' is 'to go nearer to Him ... There is no gift so good, but its chief goodness is that God gives it.'[28] In harmony with this idea, Mother Theresa affirms that 'suffering – pain, humiliation, sickness and failure, is the kiss of Jesus.'[29] 'Sometimes,' writes Kreeft, 'his kiss is full of tears.'[30]

b. Suffering Exists within the Realm of God's Experience

The tears and the suffering of God are integral to the intelligibility of suffering and the ability to trust God in the midst of it. Alister McGrath comments: 'any theology which is unable to implicate God in some manner in the sufferings and pain of the world condemns itself as inadequate and deficient.'[31]

MacDonald recognized a parallel inadequacy in the prevailing atonement theories of his age. God was thought to be removed from suffering through sending the Son to suffer what was impossible for a Holy, Perfect Being to encounter. Part of MacDonald's opposition to this approach was based on Jesus' own statement that 'he came to do what the Father did, and that he did nothing but what he had learned of the Father.'[32] Thus, even his death was that which he had learned from the Father, such that 'the suffering of those three terrible hours was a type of the suffering of the Father himself in bringing sons and daughters through the cleansing and glorifying fires, without which the created cannot be made the very children of God, partakers of the divine nature and peace.'[33] MacDonald concluded from this that in all things God, 'in the simplest, most literal, fullest sense, and not by sympathy alone, suffers *with* his creatures.'[34] In Christ's time of 'unfathomable horror' on the cross, he was surrounded and pierced by a darkness that devoured his sense of the Father's presence. Despite his utter sense of abandonment, he was able to proclaim God, saying: 'My God, My God ....' It was supremely in this, wrote MacDonald, that Divine obedience was perfected through suffering: 'God withdrew, as it were, that the perfect Will of the Son might arise and go forth to find the Will of the Father.'[35] Even so, the Father was all the time sharing in the agony of the Son: 'He against

---

28 'Letter to his Stepmother' (15 October 1858), in *EC*, p. 129.
29 Mother Theresa, *Words to Live By* (Notre Dame, IN, 1983), p. 64.
30 Kreeft, *Making Sense out of Suffering*, p. 149.
31 McGrath, Alister E. 'Resurrection and Incarnation: The Foundations of the Christian Faith,' *Different Gospels*, Andrew Walter, ed., (London, 1988), p. 93.
32 *ML*, p. 193. John 8:28, 29.
33 Ibid., p. 193.
34 Ibid.
35 'The Eloi,' *US*, 1, p. 169.

whom was the sin, became the sacrifice for it; the Father suffered in the Son, for they are one.'[36]

Even as the Father experienced the anguish of the Son, the Triune God experiences the anguish of all those who have been and are being carried home to God in the Son. MacDonald praised the goodness and 'the grandeur of God who can endure to make and see his children suffer,' when 'sorely [does] he long to take them to his bosom and give them everything.'[37] To give them all without their coming to God, though, would only make them care for the gifts without desiring God or God's love. This would be to 'turn their own souls into hells, and the earth into a charnel of murder.'[38] Until one experiences a perfect reunion with God, sorrow is inevitable. Because God bends over God's children with tears of love, human sorrow is not endured alone. It is a shared experience with God, which may also draw one closer to God. When God is invited into the experience of suffering, when one can say with Mary, 'Be it done to me according to Thy will,' the very agony which one encounters may be turned into the kind of pain which gives birth to new life.

3. The Good of Suffering

The year's fruit must fall that the year's fruit may come and
the winter itself is the King's highway to the spring.[39]

Through his use of the imagination, MacDonald is able to convey the very difficult concept of the good which exists behind suffering – that 'sorrow … [is] only the beneficent shadow of Joy.'[40] One sees this vividly in *At the Back of the North Wind*. The safety and shelter Diamond is able to experience as he is carried along behind the damaging and purging North Wind makes suffering seem less formidable. The peace he experiences when he passes through suffering to the realm at her Back fosters hope that suffering may serve a higher purpose. Kathy Triggs writes of this helpful application of imagery and story to deal with suffering: 'In matters of faith and metaphysics, where the imagination leads the way, heart and mind can follow, and even children can understand.'[41] Through his novels and fantasies, MacDonald sought to reveal the good which lay at the back of all the difficulties the characters faced, that people might learn to trust God in times of sorrow. He explained: '… if I had reason for hoping there was a God, and if I found, from my own experience and the testimony of others, that suffering led to valued good, I should think, hope, expect to find that he caused suffering for reasons of the highest, purest and kindest import, such as when understood must be absolutely satisfactory to the sufferers

---

36 *WMM*, p. 111.
37 *ML*, pp. 158–9, 114.
38 Ibid., p. 114.
39 *CW*, p. 286.
40 *AF*, p. 265.
41 Triggs, *The Stars and the Stillness*, pp. 104–5.

themselves.'[42] MacDonald explored five ways in which suffering could lead to valued good. Suffering could draw a person to God, deepen one's relationship with God, purify and strengthen, enable new vision, and deepen one's compassion for others.

a. Serving to Draw a Person to God

'Much of what appears as evil – suffering, illness, distress and misfortune – can, in fact, be shapes of good, sent to bring the sinner back to God.'[43] MacDonald told a parable in *Diary of Old Soul* of a child in the gutter groping for anything valuable, when his Father's palace stands just behind him ready to receive him whenever he should turn and seek entrance.[44] Coming to the end of one's own means is often what is needed to provoke a return to the Father. The parable of the prodigal son demonstrates this, as Erskine notes: 'It is by sorrow that God calls the prodigal to think of his true home, and it is by sorrow that He perfects His saints ....'[45]

Because evil cannot comprehend goodness, there are times when suffering arouses the anger of the unbeliever and is used to justify unbelief. This is the case of Mrs. Catanach in *Malcolm* and *The Marquis of Lossie*. She was a person full of evil and destructive plans, who stole Malcolm as a baby and left him to believe he was the grandson of a blind piper, rather than the son of the laird. When he was an adult, she tried to destroy him with slow poison, for he had grown to be too powerful, too loving of all those around, and too perceptive of her evil ways. She repelled his offer of clemency and forgiveness. Judging his character to be like hers, she suspected that his offer of grace was a plot to destroy rather than to redeem her. She is among those who ascribe to God what is evil and so deny 'the Spirit, and therefore cannot be forgiven. For without the Spirit no forgiveness can enter the man to cast out the satan.'[46]

Malcolm's punishment of her crime is a gift of grace in which, after exposing her crime to the community, he agrees to support her as long as she does not leave the community. Should she leave, he warns that she will be prosecuted. In this way she is forced to live in the light without the possibility of deceiving others. It is his hope that she will finally begin to suspect that she is a sinner who has been offered the gift of gracious forgiveness.

In *Malcolm*, *Lilith*, and other works, MacDonald emphasized that evil is not destroyed when the evildoer is annihilated: 'Only good where evil was, is evil dead. An evil thing must live with its evil until it chooses to be good. That alone is the slaying of evil.'[47] For MacDonald, judicial punishment exists to effect change and

---

42 *ML*, p. 190.

43 Raeper, *MacDonald*, p. 253.

44 *DOS* (26, 27 September), pp. 195, 197. He also began *Sir Gibbie* with Gibbie searching in the gutter for a treasure.

45 Erskine, 'Letter to Madame de Staël' (29 September 1843), in Douglas (ed.), *The Fatherhood of God Revealed in Christ,* pp. 66–7.

46 'It Shall Not Be Forgiven,' *US*, 1, pp. 88–9.

47 *Lilith*, p. 153.

the beginning of a return to the Father of forgiveness and goodness. Even if it means sending a person to the outer darkness, to learn what it is to be without God, all must be done to enable repentance.[48] This is the sense in which MacDonald seems to incorporate the possibility of a place of purgatory, not for the purgation of sins, but rather the purgation of pride and independence, that forgiveness may penetrate and enter in and begin to effect transformation. Suffering has its place in this process of enabling humility and repentance because God is in the midst of it to draw the needy one homeward. MacDonald concurred with Erskine when he affirmed: 'Sorrow alone cannot take man off his own root, and graft him on the true vine. This is work for Him who made us.'[49]

b. Serving to Deepen One's Relationship with God

> Help me, my Father, in whatever dismay,
> Whatever terror in whatever shape,
> To hold the faster by thy garment's hem;
> When my heart sinks, oh, lift it up, I pray ...[50]

For MacDonald, one's response to suffering shapes its impact on one's life. Misery could be 'God unknown' if it remains as misery, or it could be the doorway to prayer:[51] 'There are two doorkeepers to the house of prayer, and Sorrow is more on the alert to open than her grandson Joy.'[52] Spiritual poverty is evident when we only rejoice and desire to draw near to God 'in the sunshine of the mind when we feel him near us. We are poor creatures, willed upon, not willing, reeds, flowering reeds, it may be, and pleasant to behold, but only reeds blown about of the wind ....'[53] The key is to arise and go to the Father, even in the midst of sorrow and emptiness, viewing suffering not as a diminishment of God's love, but as clouds which 'will serve the angels to come down by.'[54]

MacDonald believed it false hope to wait for Time to heal one's wounds, for 'Time can no more cure or cause our ills, than space can unite or divide our souls!'[55] With God alone, the God of all comfort, 'is the only possibility of essential comfort, the comfort that turns an evil into a good.'[56] God is the One who lifts God's people

---

48 'It Shall not be Forgiven,' *US*, 1, p. 97.

49 Erskine, *The Unconditional Forgiveness of the Gospel*, p. 18.

50 *DOS* (14 July), p. 143.

51 *HA*, p. 192. Cf. 'And I can bless thee too for every smart / For every disappointment, ache, and fear / For every hook thou fixest in my heart, / For every burning cord that draws me near'; *PF*, Vol. 3, p. 185.

52 MacDonald, 'Sorrow the Pledge of Joy,' *HG*, p. 49.

53 'The Eloi,' *US*, 1, pp. 172–3.

54 MacDonald, *Mary Marston*, p. 68.

55 *CW*, p. 217.

56 *HA*, p. 191.

up, who heals their hurts and who only can give them their heart's desire.[57] For this reason, in the midst of his own physical and vocational suffering, MacDonald saw it as worth all suffering 'to be at length one with God.'[58] To suffer in pursuit of God's will and God's Kingdom was to share in God's own suffering, and to be drawn into the very life of the Triune God. To seek God's presence and union with God above all things meant such freedom that one would 'choose his will at any expense of suffering!'[59] 'There lies a prayer in every spirit, generally frozen, sometimes only dumb, to be taken like a child, and weakness lets it out sometimes.'[60]

c. Serving to Purify and Strengthen

> I cannot tell why this day I am ill;
> But I am well because it is thy will –
> Which is to make me pure and right like thee.
> Not yet I need escape – 'tis bearable
> Because thou knowest. And when harder things
> Shall rise and gather, and overshadow me,
> I shall have comfort in thy strengthenings.[61]

As one is beckoned by God to draw nearer, the fire of Divine love serves to purify. Purifying love both prepares one for such nearness and results from being in God's presence. One's very weakness and impurity require the fire which consumes. MacDonald knew that for those who cling to their sins, whose very sense of identity is tied to those sins, the idea of God's love as a consuming fire would be unacceptable:

> Can it be any comfort to them to be told that God loves them so that he will burn them clean. Can the cleansing of the fire appear to them anything beyond … a process of torture. And is not God ready to do unto them even as they, fear, though with another feeling and a different end from any which they are capable of supposing? He is against sin: in so far as, and while, they and sin are one, he is against them – against their desires, their aims, their fears, and their hopes; and thus he is altogether and always *for them*.[62]

Though the consuming fire was a recurring image which MacDonald used to describe the purifying way in which God used suffering, he also used a variety of other images to convey this idea. He likened it to the 'friendly aid of a hard winter, breaking up the cold, selfish clods of clay, [that one might] share in the loveliness of a new spring, and be perfected in the beauty of a new summer.'[63] Affliction is that which

---

57 *CW*, p. 217.
58 'Letter to Louisa' (Manchester, 26 September 1853), in *GMAW*, p. 210.
59 *ML*, pp. 188–9.
60 *CW*, p. 193.
61 *DOS* (17 July), p. 145.
62 'The Consuming Fire,' *US*, 1, p. 38.
63 *DE*, p. 78.

can be used as a chisel to bring God's image to the surface.[64] Similarly, in one who combines deep religious feeling with rigid dogmatism, suffering can enable a greater gentleness and a cracking 'of the prisoning pitcher, [to] let some brilliant ray of the indwelling glory out, to discomfit the beleaguering hosts of troublous thoughts.'[65] Furthermore, suffering is the rain needed to renew one into spring until such time as one is filled to overflowing from the well of Christ's living water within.[66]

For MacDonald, suffering was inevitable for both those inclined toward evil and those inclined toward good. Through suffering, one is made 'capable of the blessedness to which all the legends of a golden age point.'[67] Affliction was seen as integral to the building of God's living temple, 'But he who would escape the mill that grinds slow and grinds small, must yield to the hammer and chisel; for those who refuse to be stones of the living temple must be ground into mortar for it.'[68] He did not see suffering in this sense as an annihilation of personality, but as a factor in making one more real, more solid, and more one with the chief cornerstone.

For even the relatively innocent, suffering can enable greater participation in God's own strength and endurance. MacDonald envisioned God sharing in and absorbing the suffering of God's creatures and empowering them with strength: 'I believe that the endurance of God goes forth to uphold, that his patience is strength to his creatures, and that while the whole creation may well groan, its suffering is more bearable therefore than it seems to the repugnance of our regard.'[69] The innocent children in MacDonald's works, Diamond, Gibbie, and the Little Ones (*Lilith*), all suffer blamelessly, but are strengthened through their suffering to join with God in bearing hope and life to others. The 'fool,' Feel Jock in 'Wow O-Rivven,' has little cognizance of life around him, but shares in God's ministry of giving to the orphan, Elsie, hope of an eternal home. In addition, the elderly (like Grannie in *Castle Warlock*) may find the usefulness of physical ailments, such as 'rheumatism,' to teach patience, 'sent to start them well in the next world.'[70]

The fearsomeness of God on Mt. Sinai was to inhibit human evil, and so give room for grace to grow, that they might see that 'evil and not fire is the fearful thing; yea, so transform them that they would gladly rush up into the trumpet-blast of Sinai to escape the flutes around the golden calf.'[71] MacDonald recognized that purity of heart is worth any suffering, for then alone can one see and be united with the God of Mt. Sinai who reveals God's self in the face of Jesus Christ.

---

64 MacDonald cited a poem of Donne's which illustrates this idea: 'As perchance carvers do not faces make, / But that away, which hid them there, do take, / Let Crosses so take what hid Christ in thee, / And be his Image, or not his, but He'; 'On Polish,' *DO,* p. 191.

65 *AF*, p. 203.

66 *CW*, p. 107.

67 *AF*, p. 173.

68 *CW*, p. 143.

69 *ML*, p. 193.

70 *CW*, p. 65.

71 'The Consuming Fire,' *US*, 1, p. 39.

d. Serving to Enable New Vision

> The rainbow is the colour light-gendered of the dark tear-drops of the world; hope is the shimmer on the web of history, whose dingy warp of trouble is shot with the golden wool of God's intent. 'Nothing almost sees miracle but misery.'[72]

Suffering, more than anything else, can clear the fog from one's settled routine to grant vision of what is worthwhile: 'As misery alone sees miracles, so is there many a truth into which misery alone can enter.'[73] One must value truth above comfort to affirm the good in being awakened from an alluring dream. MacDonald writes: 'All who dream life instead of living it require some similar shock [as from a great dash of cold water] ... every disappointment, every reverse, every tragedy of life ... [can drive one] a trifle nearer to the truth of being, of creation, of God.'[74]

Joy and happiness are what we naturally desire. However, 'Joy cannot unfold the deepest truths, although truth must be deepest joy. Cometh white-robed Sorrow, stooping and wan, and flingeth wide the doors she may not enter.'[75] The vision which sorrow enables is to lay bare the 'simple, truer deeps' such that even nature becomes more accessible through the experience of it.[76] Through the clarifying power behind suffering, barriers that exist between oneself and God and oneself and one's neighbor may be broken down. When the soul is 'ploughed with the plough of suffering,' greater understanding of others' brokenness is possible, and God's identification in Christ with that brokenness becomes vitally meaningful.[77]

e. Serving to Deepen Relationships and Compassion for Others

MacDonald had seen the ravages of evil in people's lives and the anguish of suffering especially in inner city London. For him, it was not acceptable to offer spiritual platitudes and ignore the suffering of others because God can use it efficaciously. A Christian response to the suffering of others must reflect Christ, who bore human suffering and in this demonstrated his love. Because Christ is the One who has carried human grief, his people no longer need to fear or avoid it. They may enter into the suffering of others with him, to bear it with them and when possible to lift it off their shoulders. God is able to bond people together through suffering and to teach them to help God's other children.[78] The misery of others, MacDonald wrote, may be the 'devil' one has to fight, and cannot be left to consume those who can see no light

---

72 *CW*, p. 156.
73 MacDonald, *Flight of the Shadow*, p. 320.
74 *WMM*, p. 227.
75 MacDonald, *Phantastes*, p. 67.
76 *ML*, pp. 296–7; Cf. 'I doubt if [nature] will open to you at all except through sorrow'; *WMM*, p. 216.
77 *WMM*, p. 177.
78 MacDonald, cited in *GMAW*, p. 213.

or hope in the midst of it.[79] Though MacDonald did not view sorrow or suffering as good in themselves, when 'allied to good' they 'may open the door of the heart for any good.'[80] Misery loses its some of its dark side when Christ's suffering love penetrates through his own suffering servants.

MacDonald's perspective on suffering is much needed for those who hope in a prosperity gospel where increased faith results in decreased suffering. There was no hint in MacDonald's thinking that a Christian should in any way be exempt from suffering (though he in no way advocated intentionally seeking it). It is a potent and sometimes exceedingly bitter medicine, but it can be used by God both as a cure of the soul, and when willingly shared, as a means of expressing great love for others.

Thus MacDonald urged people first to seek to gain from suffering, rather than to be delivered from it. Freedom was seen as possible in the midst of pain and strife, when one by God's help chooses 'a mighty, conscious, willed repose.'[81] This is a call to active love and hopefulness, rather than to mere resignation. Such repose is possible knowing that in God's will alone is perfect peace.[82] Through confidence in the glory of God's love and will, one may trust that the shadows will not linger forever: 'Just because you are eternal, your trouble cannot be ... Be such while it lasts that, when it passes, it shall leave you loving more, not less.'[83]

MacDonald never clearly defined or explained evil and suffering. Neither did he try to solve them as one would a problem. Rather, he reflected on these issues more in terms which acknowledged the essential mystery innate in life's struggles.[84] For him, the controlling center from which light radiated to illumine this mystery was Jesus Christ, whose life was ever directed toward Calvary. His hands and His feet were nailed to human misery and suffering, and thus He triumphed over them. To turn toward the cross of suffering is the only way to live out this conquest over human sin which would ever urge comfort over truth and 'happiness' over goodness. This is the path to becoming real and true, and thus it is the only way to gain a face with which to see the face of the Living God.

---

79 MacDonald, *At the Back of the North Wind*, p. 122.

80 MacDonald, 'Sorrow the Pledge of Joy,' *HG*, p. 49.

81 'Rest,' *PW*, pp. 293–5.

82 This idea is found throughout the writing of MacDonald, and is evident in the work of one of his favorite writers, Dante: 'His will is our peace' (Canto III), cited by T.S. Eliot, *Selected Essays of T S. Eliot* (New York, 1964), p. 226.

83 *CW*, p. 127.

84 As Leonardo Boff expresses in *The Maternal Face of God*: 'Problems have solutions. Once solved, they are gone for good. But mystery has no solution. The deeper we probe, the more challenging it becomes. Mystery is not dark; it is altogether too light. But light attracts light, and we can understand more and more'; Boff, *The Maternal Face of God*, trans. Robert R. Barr (San Francisco, CA, 1987), p. 253.

4. The Nature of Death and the Life Beyond

Tolkien wrote that the theme which most inspired MacDonald was that of death, a theme which in itself was not unusual for Victorian writers.[85] However, MacDonald approached it unlike many of his own contemporaries and unlike many today. Death for him was not a problem to be solved or a fear to be assuaged. Rather, in the midst of the pain, anguish, and loss that death brings, it may also be perceived as a gift, a final unveiling when one may actually see God face to face.[86]

Like suffering, it also was a mystery for him of too much light to be able to fathom or logically to analyze. For this reason, he approached the themes of death and the life beyond with richer imagery than any other themes. After presenting some of his images for aging and death, his understanding of death will be summarized. From this, his view of hell will be discussed, which seems at times to cross over the line of traditional orthodoxy. Hell did not inspire the use of many images in MacDonald's writing. Whereas horrific images of hell abounded in the preaching of his contemporaries, he spent far more time and energy presenting imagery which alluded to heaven. A description of his vision of heaven will be followed by a summary of his thinking on eternal life. Finally, a conclusion will discuss the value of MacDonald's theology as a whole, along with the contribution it makes to the contemporary theological quest.

a. Aging

> Be welcome years! with your rich harvest come;
> Wither the body, and make rich the heart;
> For who that bears the golden corn-sheaves home
> Will heed the paint rubbed from his groaning cart?[87]

MacDonald's perspective on aging is a refreshing challenge to contemporary cultures where growing old is feared and disdained. Old age is something which, like all of God's gifts, may be received with gratitude and hope. MacDonald questioned how old age could be thought to be an evil thing when, like Love and Death, it too makes all people into children, a necessity for entering the Kingdom of God.[88] He saw the feebleness of a person in old age as the matrix of God's divine strength, from which one would soon enter into inestimable glory.

MacDonald cautioned against preoccupation with pampering and sheltering the body, which he saw as making the body 'thicker and thicker, lessening the room within, [such that] it squeezes the life out of the soul, and when such a body dies, the soul inside it is found a poor shrivelled thing.'[89] He saw the weakening of the body

---

85 Tolkien, 'On Fairy-stories,' *Tree and Leaf*, p. 62.
86 See Prickett, *Victorian Fantasy*, p. 59.
87 *PW*, 2, p. 210, cited in *GMAW*, p. 488.
88 *AF*, p. 240.
89 *CW*, p. 88.

as that which frees the soul to grow larger and more solid 'until it bursts the body at length, as a growing nut breaks its weakening shell.'[90] A faith-filled perspective reveals that 'age is not all decay; it is the ripening, the swelling of the fresh life within, that withers and bursts the husk.'[91] To yearn for a return to one's youth made no sense to MacDonald, when one could instead look forward to 'the better, the truer, the fuller childhood' yet to come.[92]

b. Images of Death and Dying

> I was like Peter when he began to sink,
> To Thee a new prayer therefore have I got –
> That when death comes in earnest to my door,
> Thou wouldst thyself go, when the latch doth clink,
> And lead him to my room, up to my cot;
> Then hold thy child's hand, hold and leave him not,
> Till death has done with him for evermore …[93]

Though in his own life MacDonald knew both death's 'terror and its comfort,' his images of it express more the promise in it than the anguish.[94] His perspective was not of naive optimism, as is evident in his depiction of the death-like figure Lilith, who like a leech slowly sucks the life out of Vane. But the feeling of 'sinking' in the face of death was greatly tempered by his confidence in the lifting and sustaining power of the Father for those who know and love him and will receive his help.

   Thus death was also seen as a friend or a being of striking beauty:

> Behind me comes a shining one indeed:
> Christ's friend, who from life's cross did take him down,
> And set upon his day night's starry crown!
> *Death*, say'st thou? Nay – thine be no caitiff creed! –
> A woman-angel! see – in long white gown!
> The mother of our youth! – she maketh speed.[95]

Similarly, MacDonald wrote of death as a beautiful woman, named Athanasia, who spoke in a voice 'sweet though worn and weary.'[96] In 'The Golden Key,' it is the 'Old Man of the Sea' who represents death, who after sending Mossy and Tangle into the bath of their deaths, reveals a face of majesty and beauty.[97] Before they each

---

90 Ibid.
91 *ML*, p. 177.
92 Ibid.
93 *DOS* (28 January), p. 23.
94 'Letter to his Step-mother' (18 August 1879), in *EC*, p. 298. He wrote of learning about death's 'terror and comfort' after losing two of his own children in the same year.
95 'Death,' *PW*, 1, p. 267.
96 MacDonald, *Wilfrid Cumbermede*, in Raeper, *George MacDonald*, p. 205.
97 'The Golden Key,' *GCC*, pp. 275–6, 281.

had arrived at this place of 'bathing,' they had turned gray and withered, and had lost hold of each other's hands. The experience through which the Old Man takes each of them is one which MacDonald described as having the renewing quality of a rich sleep. Tangle arose from her bath feeling that 'all the fatigue and aching of her long journey had vanished.'[98] The taste of death Mossy declares as 'good' and 'better than life.' The Old Man of the Sea corrects him, saying: 'No, it is only more life.'[99]

Death is a friend because it is that which takes a person from the darkness and carries him/her over the hill to the sunrise.[100] It is that which is the 'final failure of all sickness, the clearing away of the very soil in which the seeds of the ill plants take root.'[101] In death, one is liberated from the slavery of 'low-bred habits of unbelief and self-preservation' to join with loved ones who have begun the process of learning to be children afresh and to speak the language of the old world.[102]

To die was seen as awakening from a dream, and yet entering a world hinted at in the very best of all dreams. MacDonald did not diminish the beauty or the reality of the present life, but he could embrace death because he was so convinced of the more solid reality yet to come. The image of the dream was used in reference to this world, to suggest the passing nature of it. It was also used to describe the next life as a place of fulfilling and even surpassing all deep human longings. To allay the fear of death in others, he felt it was imperative to challenge the misconception that somehow eternal life was a vague ephemeral reality, in contrast to the more solid existence of the present time: 'People talk about death,' he wrote, 'as the gosling might about life before it chips its egg.'[103] He stressed that death has two sides to it, similar to the dark and light sides of the earth. What appears as loss and grievous from this side is a celebration and a grand birthday reunion on the other side. He cited Cowley in *Phantastes*, who used a similar image: 'When we, by a foolish figure say, / Behold an old man dead! then they / Speak properly, and cry, behold a man-child born.'[104]

Though MacDonald, even at the age of 26, saw no blessing in a prolonged life, he also knew that death, like suffering, was not something to be sought. Death was but a necessary and inevitable step in the pursuit of God's Kingdom to be taken at God's appointed time: 'We seek not death, but still we climb the stair where death is one wide landing to the rooms above.'[105] For MacDonald, the human body was significant as a means of relationship and revelation through which to perceive the world around. He had a high view of the body being 'no less of God's making than the spirit that is clothed therein.'[106] But in its aging it became as a cage, the doors of

---

98 Ibid., p. 275.
99 Ibid., p. 281.
100 'Letter to Ruskin' (30 May 1875), in *EC*, p. 243.
101 *CW*, p. 301.
102 Ibid., p. 353.
103 MacDonald, *A Rough Shaking*, p. 87.
104 Cowley, in MacDonald, *Phantastes*, p. 179.
105 'Letter to Louisa' (5 November 1878), *GMAW*, p. 485.
106 'The God of the Living,' *US*, 1, pp. 238–9.

which death would open wide that 'our heavy bodies ... [might] fly free in his high liberty.'[107] He referred to the body as a 'vital evanescence ... a slow glacier-like flow of clothing and revealing matter' which in death is cast aside as a old garment at night is thrown aside for a new and better one in the morning.[108] It would be as silly to desire to keep the old body, wrote MacDonald, as to have the accumulation of all of one's shorn hair restored to one in the Resurrection.[109] Thus he wrote to a friend after the death of her son: 'The loss of the body is not more to his being, than the loss of the little curl of hair would have been to his body, had that yet been alive.'[110] A person at death's door he saw as a 'seed waiting for the Summer, to which this Summer is but a Winter.'[111] To die is to get through, to move from the discord of pain to the place of right tuning.[112]

Though MacDonald knew the horrors and grief of the grave, having spent many hours beside his daughter Lilia's grave especially, he also knew that death was the only doorway to ultimate peace. In *Rampolli*, a collection of many of his favourite poems, he cited 'The Grave' by Von Salis-Seewis, which encapsulates much of MacDonald's feeling about death:

> The grave is deep and soundless,
> Its brink is ghastly lone;
> With veil all dark and boundless
> It hides a land unknown ...

> Yet nowhere else for mortals
> Dwells their implored repose;
> Through none but those dark portals
> Home to his rest man goes.

> The poor heart, here for ever
> By storm on storm beat sore,
> Its true peace gaineth never
> But where it beats no more.[113]

c. Understanding of Death

For MacDonald, death was a comma in life, rather than a period after life. He affirmed death as powerless to separate those who are united in God, 'for where He dwells

---

107 'Letter to Louisa' (regarding his daughter Lilia's life-threatening illness, 27 October 1891), *GMAW*, p. 524.

108 The God of the Living,' *US*, 1, pp. 237–8.

109 Ibid., p. 238.

110 'Letter to Mrs. David Matheson' (14 January 1863), in *EC*, p. 142.

111 'Letter to Louisa' (regarding his sister's dying, 5 July 1855), *EC*, p. 90.

112 *CW*, p. 377.

113 Von Salis-Seewis, 'Grave,' in MacDonald (ed.), *Rampolli*, p. 93.

in us and we in Him, there can be no more separation.'[114] Yet he eagerly looked forward to being carried through death's door and to be totally present with those whom he loved. This attitude toward death is, according to Calvin, basic to spiritual maturity, the opposite of which is allowing fear to dominate one's perspective on it: 'But monstrous it is that many who boast themselves Christians are gripped by such a great fear of death ... that they tremble at the least mention of it ... no man has made progress in the school of Christ who does not joyfully await the day of death and final resurrection.'[115]

Similar to Calvin, MacDonald did not view death as final in the sense of extinguishing the lives of unbelievers. His confidence in God as the source and sustainer of all life convinced him that death opened other doorways than one leading to nothingness: 'Let death do what it may, there is one thing it cannot destroy, and that is just life. Never in itself, only in the unfaith of man does life recognize any sway of death.'[116] There can be no seeming refuge in death for the unbeliever, for death does not lead away from God or from life, but to life in its most potent and confronting form.

Diverging from both Arminian and Calvinist traditions, MacDonald's hopeful anticipation of death was possible for him because he neither accepted the Arminian idea that one's faith decision in life (no longer alterable after death) made all the difference for one's eternal salvation, nor the Calvinist view that one was established in everlasting damnation or salvation from all eternity, a state finally confirmed and irrevocably established with all of its consequences at death. He rejected Calvin's belief that 'God does not indiscriminately adopt all into the hope of salvation but gives to some what he denies to others.'[117] He believed that in Christ, all have truly been offered the hope of salvation, through grace given 'in Christ before the beginning of time,' for Christ has now been revealed, having destroyed death and brought life eternal.

So rich is this offer of salvation that for MacDonald, physical death could not be the ultimate threat to it or the decisive watershed. MacDonald, like Erskine, affirmed the ongoing possibility of spiritual education after death, which Erskine wrote: 'relieves me ... from the agonising thought that twenty-six years of negligence are to fix the eternal condition of the soul for good or evil.'[118] For those who die unredeemed, MacDonald based his hope in God, who has extended grace to all and whose 'hatred to evil cannot be expressed by injustice, itself the one essence of evil – for certainly it would be nothing less than injustice to punish infinitely what was

---

114 MacDonald, 'Letter to Helen Powell' (17 September 1870), in Raeper, *George MacDonald*, p. 270.

115 Calvin, *Institutes of the Christian Religion*, Vol. 1 (Vol. 20 in *LCC*), 50, Bk. 3, Ch. 9.5, pp. 717–18.

116 *CW*, p. 136.

117 Calvin, *Institutes of the Christian Religion*, Vol. 2, Bk. 2, Ch. 21.1, p. 921.

118 Erskine, 'Letter to Captain Paterson' (21 March 1839), *The Fatherhood of God Revealed in Christ*, p. 41.

finitely committed.'[119] Death was seen as neither the end of the possibility for growth and change, nor the end of hope.

Because God's nature is love and God desires all to be saved (1 Timothy 2:4), MacDonald felt called to hope for every person. MacDonald's 'universalism' was based on God's willingness in Christ to seek out prodigals in the far country, and his conviction that the divine Father would not be less merciful than the most loving human parent. What loving parent would want to punish her child forever? In a portrayal of one eagerly following Jesus, Robert Falconer never gives up his search for his lost and degenerate father, and in the end sacrifices his entire ministry of inner-city healing and care for the redemption of that one. In this way he is shown to be one with the will of his heavenly Father, who seeks lost sheep, 'not willing that any should perish but that all should come to repentance' (2 Peter 3:9, KJV).

Though MacDonald could not accept the idea of people being irrevocably consigned to everlasting hell from all eternity through the waywardness of their earthly life, he felt it was a equally a mistake to deny the existence of hell: 'In these days has arisen another falsehood – less, yet very perilous: thousands of half-thinkers imagine that since it is declared with such authority that hell is not everlasting, there is then no hell at all. To such folly I for one have never given enticement or shelter.'[120] Because of the nature of human freedom and human evil, hell was seen as both inevitable and essential: 'I see no hope for many, no way for the divine love to reach them, save through a very ghastly hell. Men have got to repent; there is no other escape for them, and no escape from that.'[121]

However, MacDonald, Maurice and Erskine approached hell as something which would not endure forever.[122] For them, 'eternal' was a more appropriate word to describe both salvation and damnation, than the commonly used word, 'everlasting.' Whereas everlasting expresses duration and a continuation of a time-orientation, eternal lifts one up into a dimension beyond space or time. Erskine defined 'eternal' as 'essential in opposition to phenomenal.'[123] It was possible to experience eternal life and eternal punishment even at the present time: 'So eternal life is God's own life; it is essential life; and eternal punishment is the misery belonging to the nature of sin, and not coming from outward causes.'[124] Hell is eternal in the sense that choices for

---

119 MacDonald, Preface to L.W.J.S., *Letters from Hell* (London 1890), p. viii.

120 Ibid.

121 Ibid.

122 C.S. Lewis described hell in MacDonald's perspective as something itself which would give way to Reality, for in the final state 'only the unshakeable remains,' and 'there are no more possibilities left but only the Real'; C.S. Lewis, *The Great Divorce* (London, 1945), pp. 63, 115.

123 Erskine, 'Letter to Madame Forel' (24 April 1862), *The Fatherhood of God Revealed in Christ*, pp. 143–5.

124 Ibid.

evil cause the essence of hell to overshadow one's past and future, contaminating every aspect of them.[125]

Hell is existence in the darkest shadows of God's kingdom, such 'that men, in defacing the image of God in themselves, construct for themselves a world of horror and dismay; that *the outer darkness* of our own deeds and character are the informing or inwardly creating cause; that if a man will not have God, he never can be rid of his weary and hateful self.'[126] For MacDonald, hell was not so much a place as a state, which he illustrated in *Lilith*.[127] Vane is able to stand alongside Mr. Raven as he explains that though neither of them is in hell, the skeletons whom they observe are.[128] To be in hell is to be skeletal and face-less, without essential humanity.

MacDonald found it difficult to imagine that all could repent in this life. Some, like the reprobate Beauchamp, have 'such an unfavourable start in life' that MacDonald doubts whether they 'could arrive at the goal of repentance in this life.'[129] For one who refuses the cleansing fire of God's love in this life, the next life brings the possibility of repentance through the Judgment, and finally through being sent into the outer darkness. There, one comes to experience the consuming fire of God in its most dreadful form, 'the fire without light – the darkness visible, the black flame. God hath withdrawn himself, but not lost his hold.'[130] Even into this pit, C.S. Lewis envisioned MacDonald saying, the One who can save has descended, for 'there is no spirit in prison to whom He did not preach.'[131]

The only basis of continuing existence at all for those in hell is because God holds on and continues to grant life. Outside of this there is no life. Thus MacDonald conjectured that hell existed within the confines of God's kingdom, and was allowed

---

125 'And that is why, at the end of all things, when the sun rises here and the twilight turns to blackness down there … the Lost [will say], "We were always in Hell." And ...will speak truly'; Lewis, writing as if MacDonald is speaking, *The Great Divorce*, p. 62.

126 MacDonald, Preface to *Letters from Hell*, pp. vi–vii.

127 This is similar to the belief of Dante, whose writing greatly influenced MacDonald. Thus, T.S. Eliot wrote, the *Inferno* 'reminds us that Hell is not a place but a *state*; that man is damned or blessed in the creatures of his imagination as well as in men who have actually lived; and that Hell, though a state, is a state which can only be thought of, and perhaps only experienced, by the projection of sensory images; and that the resurrection of the body has perhaps a deeper meaning than we understand'; Eliot, *Selected Essays of T.S. Eliot*, pp. 211–12. This relates obviously to the figures in MacDonald's fantasies who are in hell, who have no faces, and/or no bodies – only skeletons. It also clarifies the urgency MacDonald felt regarding a healing and cleansing which reached the very depths of the imagination.

128 *Lilith*, p. 93.

129 MacDonald, *AF*, p. 348.

130 'The Consuming Fire,' *US*, 1, p. 48. Though C.S. Lewis's portrayal of hell in *The Great Divorce* expresses many similar emphases to MacDonald, it lacks the sense of torment of self which MacDonald is convinced is inevitable for one who refuses to repent and to return to God.

131 Lewis, *The Great Divorce*, p. 114.

existence for the purpose of enabling repentance at last.[132] Whereas those who repent are given to die once and to die into life (in their very repentance through which they join with Christ in his dying and rising), those who refuse 'die many times, die constantly, keep dying deeper, never have done dying ....'[133]

Yet even then death and hell do not have the final word. Once evil is seen for the horror that it is, MacDonald found it difficult to imagine that a 'swine-keeping son of the father will be able to help repenting at last.'[134] His hope was that the scales would finally fall from the inward eyes of the unrepentant, that they might experience 'absolute revulsion' in themselves, if not in this life, then at the Final Judgment, and if not then, through the stark and terrifying mirror of their evil which hell would provide.[135] For those who do repent, hell would be to them not so much like purgatory, but even as part of heaven's own gracious way.[136] At some point, though, death itself will die everlastingly, and hell, like snow falling on a river, will 'vanish in the fire of God.'[137]

MacDonald has been both criticized as a universalist and defended against this charge, for though he proclaimed that 'death alone can die everlastingly,' he refrained from dogmatically stating that all would be redeemed.[138] Universalism is the logical conclusion of his thinking, for if death and hell alone vanish, it seems consistent to assume that previous to this all will have repented. Logic, however, is not the foundation upon which MacDonald built his understanding of heaven and hell. His foundation was on the unconditional love of God as the source of all of life, as well as God's freedom and the freedom granted to God's creatures.

One wonders if he does justice to that freedom at times, however. He found it hard to imagine that one who shares in God's love, and who has extended that love to his neighbor, could ever experience heaven completely without his/her loved ones being there. Furthermore, in the end a person who pursues the 'non-choice' of independence from God seems to have little 'choice' but to return to God. Yet in making that 'non-choice,' in opting for non-freedom, MacDonald perceived that

---

132 MacDonald, 'A Thanksgiving for F.D. Maurice,' in *GMAW,* p. 398. MacDonald saw in Jesus' words, recorded in Luke 20:38, an affirmation of God's ongoing life-giving sustenance of all: 'He is not the God of the dead, but of the living, for to him all are alive.'

133 *Lilith*, p. 239.

134 *AF*, pp. 361–2.

135 Ibid., p. 348

136 Lewis, *The Great Divorce*, p. 62: 'Not only this valley, but all their earthy past will have been Heaven to those who are saved'; Lewis again is writing as if MacDonald is speaking.

137 Ibid., pp. 63, 130.

138 After hearing MacDonald preach, Henry Dexter wrote to the paper of which he was the editor, *The Boston Congregationalist*: 'There was very little tendency toward Universalism in the discourse; and ... it rather confirms a report which I have heard, that Mr. MacDonald, if he ever leaned in that direction, has seen the error of his ways'; cited in Hindmarsh, 'The Faith of George MacDonald,' p. 164.

one's being could so shrivel that it could dwindle into near or perhaps real non-existence.[139] Thus MacDonald asserted: 'For my part, believing with my whole heart that to know God is, and alone is, eternal life, and that he only knows God who knows Jesus Christ, I would gladly, even by a rational terror of the unknown probable, rouse any soul to the consciousness that it does not know Him, and that it must approach Him or perish.'[140]

The evil queen Lilith is MacDonald's depiction of how even the most destructive person could be made to repent when faced with the reality of her own evil. Lilith is near to the point of perishing, of dying into nothingness, when Vane interposes his own life, and she revives through becoming a parasite of his blood.[141] Lilith expresses only resentment and hatred in return for his rescue of her and for his months of gentle, sacrificial nursing. Her life continues as a source of chaos and destruction for her people and her land. She is a symbol of those who rebel against God and God's purposes. Lilith gloats that she has been able to dry up the land with her hand as the rebel nation of Israel is depicted in 2 Kings 19:24, claiming: 'I dried up with the sole of my foot all the streams of Egypt.'

After spending a terrifying night in the house of Sorrow, where Lilith is forced into the 'hell of her self-consciousness,' she sees the hideousness of her self-centeredness and relinquishes her crushing grip on life's source of renewal. She submits to the need for change, which she realizes she is powerless to effect. From self-loathing, Lilith is moved to sorrow, to deep repentance, and finally to utter self-abandonment. This book, one of his last, reveals MacDonald's hope that God's limitless love would pursue each person to the very limits of their rebellion and bring them home, using even hell itself to awaken people to their need for God. MacDonald admitted his ideas were speculative, however, and urged people to go to Jesus for understanding: 'he will lead us into all truth.'[142]

Among those deemed orthodox throughout the history of the Church, MacDonald is not alone in his universalistic tendencies. As Robert Grano points out, MacDonald's views are similar to those Eastern Orthodox theologians like Gregory of Nyssa – not that 'everyone will automatically be saved, but the idea that all will ultimately repent and be restored to God. Although Gregory's universalism was rejected by the Church, he is Orthodox in his other views and is still considered a saint.'[143] Hans Urs Von Balthasar offers a contemporary example of a theologian who alludes to MacDonald and is sympathetic with his views.[144]

---

139 This is evident of Watho in 'The Day Boy and The Night Girl,' who through evil and
       wrath devolves into a wolf, is killed by an arrow, and finally is devoured by wild beasts.
140 MacDonald, Preface to *Letters from Hell*, p. ix.
141 *Lilith*, pp. 96–108.
142 'It Shall Not be Forgiven,' *US*, 1, p. 97.
143 Robert Grano, 'An Orthodox Appreciation of George MacDonald,' Touchstone, 12(2)
       (1999), p. 16.
144 Hans Urs Von Balthasar, *Dare We Hope 'That All Men be Saved?'* (San Francisco, CA,
       1988).

d. Images of Eternal Life

It is not surprising that C.S. Lewis envisioned MacDonald as his guide through heaven. MacDonald's thinking was so deeply anchored there through his faith in Jesus Christ that heaven colored all of his writing. One has the abiding sense in encountering his work and his life that he was a person moving from death to life, rather than from life to death. Thus he urged that one not remain transfixed, staring out the window of one's life-house into the once-lovely back garden, now trampled and torn: 'Open the window on the other side, where the great mountains shoot heavenward, and the stars rising and setting, crown their peaks. Down those stairs look for the descending feet of the Son of Man coming to comfort you.'[145] Heaven is not at a great distance, but just up the stairs, where those who have died have gone to be with God. The task now is diligently to serve downstairs, even though one may yearn like MacDonald, to join loved ones who have gone before. In Christ these loved ones remain close at hand.[146]

In his images of heaven, MacDonald expressed the presence, yet deferral of the full experience, of eternal life while on earth. Because God is home for the believer, one may be with God and at home each moment. To love God is to be 'clasped to the bosom of love and fed daily from the heart of the Father, whether here or in the other world.'[147] For MacDonald, the day of death is actually a birthday. Yet 'there is a better grander birthday than that, which we may have every day – every hour that we turn away from ourselves to the living love that makes us love, and so are born again.'[148] The ultimate and transcendent birthday occurs when one desires nothing but God's will, and in so doing participates in God's very life.

However. for one who embraces God as one's home, there is a sense of disjunction with the world. 'If we would but understand,' wrote MacDonald, 'that we are pilgrims and strangers! It is no use trying to nestle down.'[149] To dwell in God is to begin to be 'expanded and enlarged,' and to be filled with a good 'too big for this world to hold.'[150] He described this growth in terms of souls blossoming into the full sunshine, in which the daily loves of one's life, the deeper yearnings of one's being, will all be joined in one. His portrayals conveyed a greater sense of reality along with the wondrous sense of walking in a glorious dream.[151]

While in this life, however, there will always be a sense in which one is only half-awake, seeing 'the universe in great measure only by reflection from the dull coffin-

---

145 MacDonald, 'Unpublished Letter' (7 April 1878), in Phillips, *George MacDonald*, p. 326.
146 *DE*, p. 55.
147 'Letter to his father' (Arundel, 5 April 1853), in *EC*, p. 57.
148 'Letter to Lilia' (22 December 1872), in *EC*, p. 235.
149 'Letter to W. C. Davies' (19 June 1879), in *GMAW*, p. 487.
150 'Letter to his father' (5 April 1853), in *GMAW*, p. 172, and 'Letter to his father' (27 October 1891), in *GMAW*, p. 524.
151 'Letter to Louisa' (26 September 1853), *GMAW*, p. 202.

lid over us.'[152] MacDonald perceived that the wonder of eternity is 'impenetrably hidden from us for a time, lest we should by the glory of it miss the door into it.'[153] The doorway is the freedom found in choosing Christ and his way of obedience without inhibition from the fear of death. Much time and discipline is needed to be fully formed into the likeness given to humankind in Jesus Christ. God labors patiently and hiddenly to form humankind into God's own children, that they might be able to possess all of the universe in utter freedom. Thus MacDonald prayed: 'Besmirched and ragged, Lord, take back thy own / A fool I bring thee to be made a child.'[154] It is as a child that one will learn to treasure, far more than any glory, joy, or reward, the very love and presence of the Father:

> So, Lord, if thou tak'st from me all the rest,
> Thyself with each resumption drawing nigher,
> It shall but hurt me as the thorn of the briar,
> When I reach to the pale flower in its breast.
> To have thee, Lord, is to have all thy best ...[155]

5. Understanding of Heaven

MacDonald viewed heaven as utterly dynamic and glorious beyond all imagining.[156] It is the 'place' from which all shadows have fallen, including the shadow of the static nature of unending sameness. Heaven is seen to be a place of wondrous creativity with ongoing possibilities in humankind for growth and development. Relationships begun and developed in love on earth would experience both a sense of continuity and transformation. People would be recognizable, for in the putting on of the immortal in place of the mortal, in becoming more like Christ, each becomes truly more him/ herself.[157] 'Our God is an unveiling, a revealing God,' and in God's unveiling of the truth of each person, lies the delight of glorious reunions and relationships which are finally set right.[158] MacDonald imagined such a reunion after Mossy and Tangle's death in 'The Golden Key.' Mossy enters into the great hall and sees Tangle:

> Her face was beautiful, like her grandmother's, and as still and peaceful as that of the Old Man of the Fire. Her form was tall and noble. Yet Mossy knew her at once.
> 'How beautiful you are, Tangle!' he said, in delight and astonishment.

---

152 'Letter to J. Ruskin' (30 May 1875), in *EC*, p. 243.
153 'Letter to Mrs. Russell Gurney,' on the death of her husband (5 June 1878), in *EC*, p. 282.
154 'A Prayer,' *PW*, 1, p. 321.
155 *DOS* (26 October), p. 217.
156 MacDonald, *Flight of the Shadow*, p. 77.
157 'The God of the Living,' *US*, 1, p. 244.
158 Ibid., p. 242, and *HA*, p. 76.

'Am I?' she returned. 'Oh, I have waited for you so Long! But you, you are the Old Man of the Sea. No. You are like the Old Man of the Earth. No, No. You are like the oldest man of all. You are like them all. And yet, you are my own old Mossy!'[159]

Thus it is together, 'younger and better, and stronger and wiser, than they had ever been before,' they climb up the stairs of a rainbow beside other beautiful beings of all ages, up to where the shadows are no more, to the glorious marriage feast.[160]

MacDonald believed that 'Love ... has a lasting quarrel with time and space: the lower love fears them, while the higher defies them.'[161] In the midst of present separations and difficulties, he saw the love given by God as 'the bond, the oneness,' which enables eternity to penetrate even into the deepest sorrow.[162] Thus, even to the very end of a life filled with endless struggle, loss of loved ones, and of his own health, he could affirm: 'Oh how we shall love him at last! And that we may love him truly, infinitely, let us trust him now, when we find it most difficult!'[163]

---

159 'The Golden Key,' in *GCC*, p. 282.
160 Ibid., p. 120.
161   *DE*, p. 183.
162 'Letter to Mrs. Russell Gurney' (5 June 1878), in *EC*, p. 282.
163 'Letter to Mrs. A.J. Scott' (11 May 1896), in *GMAW*, p. 544.

Conclusion

An Assessment of MacDonald's Imaginative Approach to Theology and His Theology of the Imagination

George MacDonald's life and theology express a bold pilgrimage into the realms of theology and imagination. As with most pilgrims, he opened up new territory and also took some wrong turns. The crucial issue for this book is not the quality of MacDonald's literary contribution, but the extent to which his use of the imagination enables him to truthfully and effectively convey the nature of God as revealed in Jesus Christ, the nature of humans created and re-created in God's image, the role of the imagination, and the nature of the human pilgrimage, both now and eternally.

This book has endeavored to demonstrate that MacDonald's theology has much to offer because God's revealed face in Christ was that which in fact did shape and inform not only his content, but also his entire approach to theology and life.[1] The crux of MacDonald's contribution derives from his deep faith in the greatness and goodness of God, which inspired him to broaden and deepen perspectives both on theology and imagination. Even as he became a mentor for Lewis in these areas, and in Lewis's fictional portrayal of the afterlife, MacDonald can offer wisdom for contemporary pilgrims who seek guidance. He reveals that the way in which pilgrims, theology, and imagination can develop a face with which to face God and reflect God's face is through faith-filled worship, obedience to God's Word, and responsiveness to the universal family of God. Before expounding on these three areas, it is important briefly to acknowledge some questionable turns MacDonald took along the way.

Though rich in evocative imagery, MacDonald's style leaves both theological and literary thinkers somewhat dissatisfied. His non-systematic approach in conveying theological insight left him open to being misunderstood, and in some cases expresses inconclusiveness and lack of clarity. One has to read extensively to glean his theological perspectives, since in only a few of his books did he include a logical progression and ordered treatment of theological issues. Where he did try to amend that by clarifying certain theological perspectives within his narratives, it offends the literary specialist as being didactic.

---

1   Cf. William Burns, 'Abridgement: Profit and Loss in Modernizing George MacDonald,' in *Seven: An Anglo-American Literary Review,* 9 (1988): 123.

The question arises whether his contribution to theology itself would have been more extensive had he produced more works of a systematic nature. His ideas offered helpful correctives to the theology of his era, and yet were for the most part lost to academic theologians because he generally refused to speak their 'language,' or engage in debate with them. Though his contributions to the Church and the general populace were extensive because of his narrative methodology, academic theologians have generally not taken him very seriously.

David Ford speaks of three basic categories necessary for Christian theology: 'system, story, and performance.' The danger, he writes, of giving narrative too important a role is that it 'becomes too exclusively literary and also too exclusively interpersonal in its conception of reality.' He continues: 'Both "system" and "performance" must be in continual, critical interaction with "story" if it is to maintain its rational, moral and spiritual integrity, and in this exchange apologetics takes place.'[2] Interplay of these three is evident in MacDonald's work, such that story and performance are informed and shaped by the distinctive *loci* of the gospel. However, a weaker emphasis on system leaves an imbalance which seems to have inhibited his advancement of theological understanding. Though he evidences a strong theology of the imagination and incorporates this into much of his writing, the brevity of his own conceptual arguments on this particular subject meant that no real trumpet was sounded to alert theologians to the dangers of overlooking this area, and the richness of exploring it. Thus it is only in contemporary theological discussions that a theological perspective on the imagination is seen as of value and necessity.[3]

Flowing from this absence of 'system,' inconsistencies in MacDonald's theological views are evident which a more systematic approach might have diminished. For example, his views on forgiveness and freedom seem at times to conflict with his ideas about judgment, purgatory, and hell. Christ, who is the turning-point for his theology (rooting him in the ground of trinitarian belief), is on occasion more subject to his theology than *the* subject of it. Rather than being the free expression of God's forgiving and reconciling love, Christ is at times approached as offering what God is bound to offer, for God 'is bound in his one divinely willed nature to forgive.'[4]

Furthermore, some would question whether his theology offers an adequate view of biblical inspiration. Because he felt so strongly God's ability to communicate to and through the imagination, he at times placed the inspiration of certain artistic endeavors on the same level as the Bible: 'When I read the Bible or Shakspere [*sic*], I am listening to the word of God, uttered in each after its kind.'[5] Also, with his

---

2   David Ford, ' System, Story, Performance ...,' in Stanley Hauerwas and L. Gregory Jones (eds.), *Why Narrative? Readings in Narrative Theology* (Grand Rapids, MI, 1989), pp. 191, 200.

3   Cf. 'Working out a theological theory of metaphor is an urgent desideratum for both dogmatics and practical theology'; E. Jüngel, *Theological Essays*, trans. J.B. Webster (Edinburgh, 1989), p. 71.

4   MacDonald, *US*, 3, p. 160.

5   *ML* (with his hero Malcolm speaking), p. 332. Cf. 'In implying that revelation exists as a body of free-floating truths that can be picked up anywhere indifferently, they

strong emphasis on communicating through the imagination primarily to the heart, he seems to express a lack of confidence in Christ's ability to reach and transform the intellect directly.

That said, MacDonald's theology was not aimed at reducing the wonder of the gospel in any way, but of expanding appreciation and wonder for all of life in light of the expansiveness of God's nature and love. One of MacDonald's chief contributions to a Christian theology of the imagination was the Trinitarian 'lens' through which he viewed life. He affirmed and explored the imagination in its relationship to the Triune God, and therefore understood it in the context of creation, incarnation, redemption, and sanctification. As a result, he challenged the dualistic thinking of his period. He freed the imagination from the trap of dichotomies between subjectivist and objectivist, realist and idealist. Jesus Christ, God's own *Metaphor*, was for MacDonald not only the elucidation of God, but of all of life. He became a bridge on which the baptized imagination could hold these dichotomies together in a dynamic tension: 'The one originating, living, visible truth, embracing all truths in all relations, is Jesus Christ.'[6] The way God had offered self-revelation in Christ becomes the way for his people to communicate about him and about life. It is the way of relationships, of integration, of unity and diversity, and the way of mystery. Three areas in which MacDonald contributes to current discussions bear summary comment.

1. Theology through Faith and Worship Rather than Fear

MacDonald's desire to write and preach about God emerged from a passionate love and adoration of God. God was not a distant reality to be examined, but a beloved Father/Mother (of both strength and tenderness) whom he wanted all to meet. Because MacDonald approached knowing God with an enduring confidence in God's love, he was freed from some of the snares of fear into which the human theological endeavor – and human life of faith – can fall. With little fear for his own reputation, he was freed from giving primacy to his own logic, to public opinion, or to the internal consistency of his arguments. Neither he nor his theology was central. He sought rather for God to make known God's own divine logic through him and to maintain consistency with God's astounding and limitless truth.

Similarly, he did not fear Enlightenment marginalization of theology *per se*, and the presumed need to establish it on other more philosophically acceptable grounds. His primary drive was not to make it culturally palpable, but to discern appropriate and accessible cultural metaphors which harmonized with the 'clothing' which Jesus, the Eternal Truth, clothed himself. God was seen for the most part as the determining subject of Theology, the Thou, rather than its object, and as the One upon whom theology depends, not the reverse. God's divine purposes established humankind,

---

misunderstand the sense in which Christianity is a "a religion of the book"'; Janet Martin Soskice, *Metaphor and Religious Language* (Oxford, 1987), p. 154.

6   *US*, 3, p. 79.

and were accepted as that which establishes theology. Human purposes or theology did not establish God.

For MacDonald, God not only shapes the content of theology, but also guides the form and way people are to think and speak about God. Christian theologians are obligated to ensure that their use of metaphors is consistent with the revelation of Jesus Christ and not somehow distorted or limited by years of abstract debate. This is also applicable to the imagination itself, which MacDonald argued is rooted in the very Being of God, and therefore gains its fullest significance and freedom in relationship to God. Furthermore, MacDonald offers forms of theological communication which are more consistent with the form of God's self-revelation. This includes forms which honor both the transcendence and immanence of God, and the objective and subjective realities of human life.

The concreteness of God's self-revelation in Christ calls for theological expressions which themselves lean more toward concreteness than abstraction. Thus MacDonald endeavored to center his theology on the self-communication of God in Jesus Christ as both the true human and the crucified and resurrected Son of God. He would have concurred with Jüngel's assertion that 'the basic aporia into which European theology has blundered' under the dictatorship of metaphysics is to 'think of God without thinking of him simultaneously as the Crucified.'[7] Avoiding this 'dictatorship' requires careful use of language. MacDonald's ability to hold the Sovereignty of God together with the suffering of God was intimately related to his taking Scripture and the language and images of Scripture seriously. God's self-giving in Christ becomes the window on God's eternal nature: 'For in self-giving, if anywhere, we touch a rhythm not only of all creation but of all being. For the Eternal Word also gives Himself in sacrifice; and that not only on Calvary. For when He was crucified He "did that in the wild weather of His outlying provinces in the torture of the body of his revelation, which He had done at home in glory and gladness."'[8] Theological communication that harmonizes with God's self-revelation will be more invitational than impositional, more compelling than controlling.

Similarly, MacDonald allowed the incarnational nature of truth to shape his expressions of human life and nature. By conveying theological perspectives through narratives, MacDonald communicated a 'middle-distance' which David Ford affirms as central and vital to the testimony of Jesus Christ.[9] A middle distance between general truths and the subjective orientation of a person's inner world is expressed through portrayals of persons in the midst of life and realistic relationships. This includes the mediation of realism, 'finding,' and of idealism, 'fashioning,' a dialectic

---

7   Eberhard Jüngel, *God as the Mystery of the World* (Grand Rapids, MI, 1983), p. 39. '... the cross of Jesus Christ is the ground and measure of the formation of metaphors which are appropriate to God'; Jüngel, *Theological Essays*, p. 65.

8   *US*, 3, pp. 11–12.

9   Ford, ' System, Story, Performance ...,' pp. 195–6. Ford affirms that 'in its multiplicity of functions, its characteristic style, its sensuality and indirectness, the novel is wholly different from the philosophical treatise' and may be 'best equipped to incarnate a philosophy which a treatise could not adequately set down'; ibid., p. 205.

that honors and stretches both to capacity in order to convey both the concreteness and openness of life.[10] MacDonald challenges dichotomizing approaches which would sink either into over-systematized theology or to overly idealized, subjective, or individualized theology.[11] In the midst of this he included both reflections of a somewhat systematic nature in his theological books, and expressions of his own personal piety, especially through his poetry. He recognized that both the objective knowledge 'content' of Christianity and one's personal faith experience are essential, and neither one has any rights to exclusivity with regards to the communication of Truth.

MacDonald's use of the baptized imagination provides a bridge between the visible and invisible and between being and language that challenges both contemporary fundamentalist and deconstructionist tendencies. It was through this approach that he was able to affirm the *indirectness* or *mystery* in the relationship between language, the world and God. This indirectness plus his worshipful acknowledgement that we are *trouvères* of God's meanings rather than co-creators calls forth an orientation of listening humility.

It is because imaginative language can hold onto the tension created by polarities that it is most appropriate to expressing the truth.[12] In theology, the ultimate tension is confessing 'Jesus *as* true God and God *as* true man,' which remained for MacDonald always at the heart of his thinking precisely because he combined gospel-centeredness and imaginative openness. Holding fast to the dialectic of worshipful consistency with Christ and faith-filled creativity, MacDonald encouraged visionary faithfulness which is much needed today: 'Be not afraid to build upon the rock Christ, as if thy holy imagination might build too high and heavy for that rock ...' .[13]

One other implication of MacDonald's communication of theology through faith rather than fear bears comment. Not only did MacDonald's deep faith shape the form of his communication as noted above, it also restrained him from exploiting

---

10 Ibid., pp. 195–196. Cf. Metaphors 'participate in truth, by leading the actual beyond its actuality without asserting anything false about it, and precisely because they lead the actual beyond its actuality, they specify and emphasize this actuality. So metaphor does say more than is actual, and yet precisely in so doing it is true'; Jüngel, *Theological Essays*, pp. 51, 57.

11 Ford points out that 'cognitive-propositionalism is more in line with the type of revelation represented by the Koran as understood by most Muslims,' and 'experientialism-expressivism is more congenial to Buddhists or Hindus. ... if persons and events are crucial to a religion's identity ... then it will have an advantage if the primary account is to be in terms of "thick description"'; 'System, Story, Performance ....,' p. 213.

12 'In all this, there is a combination of openness and mystery, speech and silence, which makes the clarity and distinctness aimed at by the rationalist tradition positively hostile to the truth. Thus the tables are turned: metaphor rather than being the cinderella of cognitive language becomes the most rather than the least appropriate means of expressing the truth'; Colin E. Gunton, *The Actuality of Atonement* (Grand Rapids, MI, 1989), pp. 38–9.

13 *US*, 3, p. 173.

people's fears. He cautioned against inspiring fear in his readers, convinced that inspiring confidence in the faithfulness of God is a more life-giving approach. His work offers a prophetic word today, when the provocation of fear has become major entertainment and big business and risks doing more to spread darkness than bear light. MacDonald cautioned artists in their portrayal of evil and suffering, saying: 'There are facts in human life which human artists cannot touch. The great Artist can weave them into the grand whole of his Picture, but to the human eye they look too ugly and too painful.'[14]

Through an approach of love and faith, MacDonald's theology paints a vision of a trustworthy God as the center of all things. Rather than seeking to be trusted as an artist, MacDonald desired for people to trust the Artist, who could weave all things together for good. He demonstrates that theological illumination depends more on a relationship of deepening love for God rooted in Scripture than it does on the accumulation and dissemination of information. In this way, his work conveys the poetic nature of theology, which is perhaps nearer to a love song than has been adequately acknowledged. This love song nourishes the mind through more fully addressing the hunger of the heart.

2. Theology through Obedience

Jesus' words in John 8:31–2 formed much of the basis of MacDonald's theological approach and content: 'If you hold to my teaching you are really my disciples. Then you will know the truth, and the truth will set you free.' His theology was nurtured through constant intersection of his actions and his thoughts, which he sought to conform to God's will. In this way, his entire life was engaged in theology, rather than just his intellect. His theological methodology expressed obedience to God's will and nature as well, issuing forth a personal, relational expression of theology through story and narrative.

As William Bausch confirms: 'Systematic theology engages the intellect; storytelling engages the heart and indeed the whole person. Systematic theology is a later reflection on the Christ story; the story is the first expression of Christ. Logic is one avenue of truth, however limited. Imagination as myth and story is another avenue, but one that involves, disturbs and challenges us and as such is to be preferred.'[15] MacDonald demonstrates that such an approach is not necessarily non-systematic, but embraces patterns of reflection and truth flowing more directly and immediately from the life story of Jesus Christ. In this way, it overcomes two drawbacks which Bausch attributes to standard systematic theology: (1) dependence on 'limited and conditioned' modes of thought, often tied to dated philosophical assumptions, which form the structure of normal systematic theologies, and (2) the

---

14 *AF*, p. 338. Cf. 'Dull are those, little at least can they have of Christian imagination, who think that where all are good, things must be dull'; *US*, 2, p. 228.

15 William J. Bausch, *Storytelling, Imagination and Faith* (Mystic, CT, 1993), p. 27.

closed nature of a system which means being closed off to other systems and thus only part of the whole.[16]

Through his commitment to an obedient theology, MacDonald's work addresses the void left by moral relativism, cheap grace, and situation ethics. In narratives, MacDonald lifts matters of character and integrity out of their confinement as private preferential options into the clarifying light of social interactions and implications. He offers holistic ethical guidance to Churches reeling from following leaders whose professional credentials may be excellent, but whose character is unformed by adherence to Christian convictions. Exploring the lives of individuals who seek to be obedient to Christ offers vision and motivation for discipleship. Exemplars of the character of Christ reveal the artfulness, relevance, and necessity of such character today. They also offer alternatives that challenge hopeless resignation to broken ways of living that flood movie and television screens. The consequences of such brokenness are not romanticized or normalized in MacDonald's work. The moral imagination is given a host of encouraging options, and the call to obedience is extended in a way that impacts both the mind and the heart.

Faith and actions were shown to be integrated through the lives of individuals, such that the heart of theology could more deeply penetrate into the understanding of each person who encountered his work. Though his Victorian writing style has limitations for the twentieth-century reader, the methodology of theology, as enfleshed in lives and living, offers a necessary corrective to theology that keeps God at a distance and ushers muted ethical claims. MacDonald willingness to conform his theology to the living Lord who is personal and relational, who communicated through making the Word flesh, conveys theological obedience.

3. Theology Formed in the Midst of Community

Much of the strength of MacDonald's theology emerges from his commitment to honor truth which flowed from a diversity of people and spheres. The range of languages he understood, material he read and people he encountered and from whom he learned is astounding. His appreciation of certain German thinkers was part of the reason he was branded heretical. Yet that which he gleaned from others was not embraced because of its current or exotic appeal, but because he believed it conveyed something of the light of truth emanating from Jesus Christ. He did not fear a personal loss of face in embracing and espousing truth from any quarter as long as he believed it to be consistent with the Trinitarian faith. He neither desired to defeat theological opponents nor to avoid opposition, but to remain true.

He offers guidance and hope for this current age in which Christians are often combatively polarized or innocuously undifferentiated from those around them. MacDonald was both open, through his faith that God graciously speaks through whomever and whatever God wills, and anchored in the central convictions of

---

16 Ibid., p. 16.

Christian faith. His willingness to learn from all people challenges Christian sectarian dismissal of other Christians, and people, outside of one's own tradition. MacDonald refused to accept that any human perspective, corporate or individual (including his own), had a full grasp of the truth. On the other hand, his call to remain obedient to Christ can awaken an indulgent Church sleepily resigned to fitting in and accepting every kind of spirituality as valid, regardless of its connection to central Christian truths. To arouse the Church, he used narrative to demonstrate the power of the gospel to confront poverty and abuse, doubt and intellectual strife, selfishness and greed, death and evil. In this way, he reversed the impression Christianity at times has left of being inhibiting, irrelevant and escapist. His was not and is not 'a subjectivist [capitulation] to modernity that leaves its difficulties unexplored,' but is rather a response to the need for 'relentless engagement with modernity.'[17] To a culture which asks with Nietzsche 'Where is God gone?'[18] MacDonald gives vital evidence through human lives of God's suffering and authoritative presence with them to draw them homeward. Released from the need to build a logically consistent structure for individual doctrines, MacDonald pursued a pluralistic interpenetration of Christian doctrines which mutually inform each other and harmonize with the *logos* of Jesus Christ. His more sacramental theology also challenges the historic dichotomy between science and the arts, faith and practice, imagination and intellect.

Through MacDonald's openness to truths which were considered heretical by peers, he offers insight and challenges relevant to this age. For example, the image of the crucified God who died for all people, whose Lordship is tender, uplifting and nurturing, and whose celebrative Life engages all parts of creation in God's eternal dance was radical in his context, but is recognized today as reflecting enduring truth. His convictions about continuing progressive growth after death and his determined hope for the eventual salvation of all people after eons of time and 'purgatorial' confrontation are obvious points of contention, then and now. In not establishing a rigid or closed system, MacDonald acknowledged his own imperfect and incomplete knowledge. He did not resent criticism, for he saw himself in pilgrimage and only knowing and seeing in part 'as through a glass darkly.' Therefore, about these after-death issues he was not dogmatic, only hopefully suggestive.

He remains far more prophetic than heretical because there were certain anchors, consistent with the theological creeds of the Church, to which he adhered and which formed the basis of his imaginative theological approach. Imaginativeness did not mean relinquishment of objective truth and a collapse into subjective relativism. His determined affirmation of the Fatherhood of God in Jesus Christ was prophetic, yet thought to be heretical in his age just as it is even for many today. There are those who would wish to re-imagine God cleansed of what is considered an image tied to patriarchal, militaristic, chauvinism of past ages. MacDonald revealed through imaginative honesty that Fatherhood goes beyond its broken refractions throughout history. The challenge is not to re-imagine God, but to allow God to reshape human

---

17 Brian Hebblethwaite, *The Ocean of Truth*, p. 59.
18 Ibid., p. 49.

imaginations which can perceive and reflect God truly. His vivid portrayals of a Fatherhood which is sacrificial, maternal, and abounding in grace can begin to reform distorted understandings of power and leadership associated with horrific wars, tyrannical rulers, and abusive fathers.

Without an imaginatively restored sense of God as the motherly Father, humanity and theology remain faceless and floundering. MacDonald has shown that theology and humanity will only find their face as they bring all they are, in love and adoration and wonder, nearer to the Father who through the Spirit unveils God's self truly in the face of Jesus Christ.

Throughout this book, MacDonald has often been allowed to speak for himself, that the weight of his insight and manner of communication be more fully and truly apparent. Thus it is appropriate that the book conclude with his words. Just as he guided many from the nineteenth into the twentieth century, so he is a worthy guide in the twenty-first century, and even beyond into eternity:

Better to love than be beloved,
Though lonely all the day;
Better the fountain in the heart,
Than the fountain by the way.

Better than thrill a listening crowd,
Sit at a wise man's feet;
But better teach a child, than toil
To make thyself complete.

Better a death when work is done,
Than earth's most favoured birth;
Better a child in God's great house,
Than the King of all the earth.[19]

---

19 *GMAW*, p. 279.

Bibliography

Works by George MacDonald

A Dish of Orts (Whitehorn, CA: Johannesen, 1996; orig. London, 1893).

(ed.), *A Threefold Cord* (London: W. Hughes, 1883).

Adela Cathcart (London: Sampson Low, Marston, Searle, and Rivington, 1882).

Alec Forbes of Howglen (London: Hurst and Blackett, 1865).

Annals of a Quiet Neighbourhood (London: Kegan Paul, Trench, and Trübner, 1893; orig. 1867).

At the Back of the North Wind (London: Blackie and Son, n.d.).

Castle Warlock (London: Kegan Paul, Trench, and Trübner, n.d.; orig., 1882).

Creation in Christ, ed. Rolland Hein (Wheaton: Harold Shaw, 1976).

Cross Purposes and Other Stories (London: Chatto and Windus, 1902).

David Elginbrod (London: Hurst and Blackett, 1863).

Donal Grant (London: Kegan Paul, 1884).

(ed.), *England's Antiphon* (London: Macmillan, n.d.).

Exotics (London: Strahan, 1876).

Flight of the Shadow (London: Kegan Paul, Trench, and Trübner, 1891).

Heather and Snow (2 vols., London: Chatto and Windus, 1893).

Home Again (London: Kegan Paul, and Trench, 1887).

Letters and Manuscripts at Brander Library, Huntly.

Letters and Manuscripts at Kings College Special Collection, University of Aberdeen.

Letters at Huntington Library, San Marino, California, Manuscripts 4 384–6, 6 322–51.

Life Essential: The Hope of the Gospel, ed. Rolland Hein (Wheaton, IL: Harold Shaw, 1974).

Lilith (Chatto and Windus, 1895; reprint Tring: Lion, 1986).

Malcolm (London: Henry S. King, 1877).

Mary Marston (Whitehorn, CA: Johannesen, 1995, orig. 1881)

'Preface,' in L.W.J.S., *Letters from Hell* (London: Richard Bentley and Son, 1890).

Paul Faber, Surgeon (3 vols., London: Hurst and Blackett, 1879).

Phantastes (Tring: Lion, 1982; orig. 1858).

Proving the Unseen, ed. William J. Petersen (New York: Ballantine Books, 1989).

Ranald Bannerman's Boyhood (London: Blackie and Son, n.d.).

(ed.) *Rampolli* (London: Longmans, Green, 1897 and 1899).

Robert Falconer (London: Hurst and Blackett, 1868).

Salted with Fire (London: Hurst and Blackett, 1897).

Sir Gibbie (London: J.M. Dent and Sons, 1914).

St. George and St. Michael (London: Kegan Paul, and Trench, 1886).

The Christmas Stories of George MacDonald, ed. Linda Hill Griffith (Elgin, IL: David C. Cook, 1981).

The Diary of an Old Soul (London: W. Hughes, 1882; orig. 1880).

The Elect Lady (London: Kegan Paul, and Trench, 1888).

The Marquis of Lossie (London: Cassell, 1927).

The Miracles of Our Lord, ed. Rolland Hein (Wheaton: Harold Shaw, 1980).

The Poetical Works of George MacDonald (2 vols., London: Chatto and Windus, 1893).

The Portent and Other Stories (London: T. Fisher Unwin, n.d.).

The Princess and Curdie (London: Chatto and Windus, 1883).

The Princess and the Goblin (London: J.M. Dent and Sons, 1949).

The Seaboard Parish (Whitehorn, CA: Johannesen, 1995; orig. 1868).

The Tragedie of Hamlet, Prince of Denmarke. Study with text of folio of 1623 (London: Longmans, Green, 1885).

The Wise Woman and Other Fantasy Stories (Grand Rapids, MI: Eerdmans, 1980).

Thomas Wingfold, Curate (London: Kegan Paul, and Trench, 1887).

Unspoken Sermons (3 vols., Eureka, CA: J. Joseph Flynn, 1989; republishing of all original material, from London: Longmans, Green, 1889).

Weighed and Wanting (3 vols., London: Samson, Low, Marston, Searle, and Rivington, 1882).

What's Mine's Mine (London: Chatto and Windus, 1883).

Wilfrid Cumbermede, An Autobiographical Story (London: Hurst & Blackett/ Scribener, 1872).

Within and Without (London: Longman, Brown, Green, Longmans, and Roberts, 1857).

Anthologies of MacDonald's Works

Bubier, G.B. (ed.), *Hymns and Sacred Songs* (Manchester: Septimus Fletche, 4th edn., 1866).

Escott, Harry (ed.), *A History of Scottish Congregationalism* (Glasgow: Congregational Union of Scotland, 1960).

——, *God's Troubadour* (London: Epworth Press, 1940).

—— (ed.), *In My Father's House* (London: Epworth Press, 1943).

——, *George MacDonald: An Anthology* (London, Geoffrey Bles, 1955).

Neuhouser, David L., *George MacDonald* (selections) (Wheaton: Victor Books, 1990).

Phillips, Michael, *A Time to Harvest* (Minneapolis, MN: Bethany House, 1991).

——, *Knowing the Heart of God* (Minneapolis, MN: Bethany House, 1990).

Sadler, Glenn Edward (ed.), *An Expression of Character: The Letters of George MacDonald* (Grand Rapids, MI: Eerdmans, 1994).

—— (ed.), *The Gifts of the Child Christ and Other Stories and Fairy Tales* (Grand Rapids, MI: Eerdmans, 1996 edn.).

Yates, Elizabeth, *Gathered Grace: A Short Selection of George MacDonald's Poems* (Cambridge: W. Heffer and Sons, n.d.).

Biographies, Books, Articles, or Letters Related to MacDonald

Aichele, George, Jr., 'Literary Fantasy and Postmodern Theology,' *Journal of the American Academy of Religion*, 59(2) (1991): 323–37.

Aiura, Reiko, 'Recurring Symbols in the Fantasies and Children's Stories of George MacDonald,' unpublished M.Litt. thesis (Aberdeen: University of Aberdeen, 1986).

Ankeny, Rebecca, *The Story, the Teller and, the Audience in George MacDonald's Fiction* (Lewiston, NY: Edwin Mellen, 2000).

Boaden, Ann, 'Falcons and Falconers: Vision in the Novels of George MacDonald,' *Christianity and Literature*, 31(1) (1981): 7–17.

Burnside, William H., 'Abridgement: Profit and Loss in Modernizing George MacDonald,' *Seven: An Anglo-American Literary Review*, 9 (1988): 117–28.

Fink, Larry E. and Hein, Rolland, *George MacDonald: Images of His Word* (Texas: Pasture Springs Press, 2004).

Gaarden, Bonnie Lou, 'The Goddess of George MacDonald,' unpublished thesis (Buffalo, NY: University of New York at Buffalo, 1995).

——, 'Cosmic and Psychological Redemption in George MacDonald's Lilith,' *Studies in the Novel*, 37(1) (Spring 2005): 20–36.

Geddes, Wm. D., 'Letter to MacDonald' (29 February 1868), MS. 2167/1-3 (Special Collections, University of Aberdeen).

Gonzalez Davies, Maria, 'A Spiritual Presence in Fairyland: The Great-Great Grandmother in the Princess Books,' *North Wind*, 12 (1993): 60–65.

Grano, Robert, 'An Orthodox Appreciation of George MacDonald,' *Touchstone*, 12(2) (1999): 15–16.

Gray, George, 'Recollections of Huntly,' *Banffshire Journal* (1929), reprinted in *Local History* (1953) (Special Collections, University of Aberdeen).

Grierson, H.J.C., 'George MacDonald,' *The Aberdeen University Review*, 12(34) (1924): 1–13.

Gunther, Adrian, '"Little Daylight": An Old Tale Transfigured,' *Children's Literature in Education*, 26(2) (June 1995): 107–17.

Hayward, Deidre, 'George MacDonald and Jacob Boehme: Lilith and the Sevenfold Pattern of Existence,' *Seven: An Anglo-American Literary Review*, 16 (1999): 55–72.

Hein, Rolland Neal, 'Faith and Fiction: A Study of the Effects of Religious Convictions in the Adult Fantasies and Novels of George MacDonald,' unpublished Ph.D. dissertation (West Lafayett, IN: Purdue University, 1971).

——, 'George MacDonald: A Portrait from His Letters,' *Seven: An Anglo-American Literary Review*, 7 (1986): 5–19.

——, *George MacDonald: Victorian Mythmaker* (Nashville, TN: Star Song, 1993).

——, *The Harmony Within: The Spiritual Vision of George MacDonald* (Grand Rapids, MI: Christian University Press, 1982).

——, *The Harmony Within: The Spiritual Vision of George MacDonald* (Chicago, IL: Cornerstone, 1999).

Hetzler, Leo A., 'George MacDonald and G.K. Chesterton,' *Durham University Journal*, 68 (new series 37) (1975): 176–82.

Hindmarsh, Douglas Bruce, 'The Faith of George MacDonald,' unpublished Masters dissertation (Vancouver, BC: Regent College, 1989).

Holbrook, David, 'George MacDonald and Dreams of the Other World,' *Seven: An Anglo-American Literary Review*, 4 (1983): 27–37.

Horsman, Gail, 'C. S. Lewis and George MacDonald: A Comparison of Styles,' *C.S. Lewis Society Bulletin*, 13(2) (146) (1981): pp. 105f.

Huttar, Charles A. (ed.), *Imagination and the Spirit* (Grand Rapids, MI: Eerdmans, 1971).

Hutton, Muriel, 'The George MacDonald Collection,' *Yale University Library Gazette*, 51 (1976): 74–85.

Jenkins, Ruth Y, '"I am spinning this for you, my child": Voice and Identity Formation in George MacDonald's Princess Books,' *The Lion and the Unicorn*, 28(3) (September 2004): 325–44.

Johnson, Joseph, *George MacDonald* (London: Sir Isaac Pitman and Sons, 1906).

Johnson, Rachel, 'Pilgrims: The MacDonalds and John Bunyan's The Pilgrim's Progress,' *North Wind*, 21 (London, 2002): 15–25.

King, Don, 'The Childlike in George MacDonald and C. S. Lewis,' *Mythlore: A Journal of J.R.R. Tolkien, C.S. Lewis, Charles Williams*, 46 (1986): 17–26.

Lochhead, Marion, *The Renaissance of Wonder* (Edinburgh: Canongate, 1977).

McCann, Janet, 'George MacDonald's Romantic Christianity in Lilith,' *Renascence*, 54(2) (Winter, 2002): 109–18.

MacDonald, Greville, *George MacDonald and His Wife* (London: George Allen and Unwin, 1924).

——, *Reminiscences of a Specialist* (London: George Allen and Unwin, 1932).

MacDonald, Ronald, *From a Northern Window* (London: James Nisbet, 1911).

Manlove, Colin, *Christian Fantasy* (Notre Dame, IN: University of Notre Dame Press, 1992).

——, 'George MacDonald's Early Scottish Novels,' in Ian Campbell (ed.), *Nineteenth-century Scottish Fiction* (Manchester: Carcanet New Press, 1979), pp. 68–88.

Mann, Nancy Elizabeth Dawson, 'George MacDonald and the Tradition of Victorian Fantasy,' unpublished Ph.D. dissertation (Stanford, CT: Stanford University, 1973).

Matthews, Betsy, 'Mara and Galadriel: MacDonald's and Tolkien's Vehicles for Spiritual Truth,' *Premise*, 5(3) (July 1998): 18–25.

Maurice, Frederick Denison, *Testimonials to George MacDonald. Candidate for Chair of English, Edinburgh University* (Huntly: Brander Library, 1865).

Neuhouser, David, 'God as Mother in George MacDonald's "The Wise Woman,"' *Christianity and the Arts*, 4(4) (2000): 42–4.

Pennington, John, 'From fact to fantasy in Victorian fiction: Dicken's Hard Times and MacDonald's Phantastes,' *Extrapolation*, 38(3) (1997): 200–206.

——, 'George MacDonald and T. S. Eliot: Further Consideration,' *North Wind* 8 (1989): 12–24.

Petzold, Dieter, 'Beasts and Monsters in MacDonald's Fantasy Stories,' *North Wind*, 14 (1999: 4–21).

——, 'Maturation and education in George MacDonald's fairy tales,' *North Wind*, 12 (1993): 10–24.

Phillips, Michael R., *George MacDonald: Scotland's Beloved Storyteller* (Minneapolis, MN: Bethany House, 1987).

Pridmore, John, 'George MacDonald and the Languages of Liberal Spirituality,' *Modern Believing*, 39 (1998): 28–34.

——, 'George MacDonald's Transfiguring Fantasy,' *Seven: An Anglo-American Literary Review*, 20 (2003): 49–65.

——, 'Nature and Fantasy,' *North Wind*, 19 (2000): 2–8.

——, 'Talking of God and Talking of Faeries: Discourses of Spiritual Development in the Works of George MacDonald and in the Curriculum,' *International Journal of Children's Spirituality*, 7(1) (2002): 24–35.

Raeper, William, *George MacDonald* (Tring: Lion, 1987).

——, (ed.), *North Wind: Journal of the George MacDonald Society*, 4–8 (1985–89).

——, (ed.), *The Gold Thread* (Edinburgh: Edinburgh University Press, 1990).

Reed-Nancarrow, Paula Elizabeth, 'George MacDonald, Remythologizing the Bible: Fantasy and the Revelatory Hermeneutic of George MacDonald,' unpublished Ph.D. dissertation (Minneapolis, MN: University of Minnesota, 1988).

Reis, Richard, *George MacDonald* (New York: Twayne, 1972).

Robb, David S., *George MacDonald* (Edinburgh: Scottish Academic Press, 1987).

——, 'George MacDonald and Animal Magnetism,' *Seven: An Anglo-American Literary Review*, 8 (1987): 9–24.

——, 'The Fiction of George MacDonald,' *Seven: An Anglo-American Literary Review*, 6 (1985): 35–44.

Robertson, F.W., *Lectures on the Influence of Poetry and Wordsworth* (London: Kennikat Press, 1906; reissued 1970).

Sadler, Glenn Edward, 'The Cosmic Vision: A Study of the Poetry of George MacDonald,' unpublished Ph.D. dissertation (Aberdeen: University of Aberdeen, 1966).

——, 'The Fantastic Imagination in George MacDonald,' in Charles Huttar (ed.), *Imagination and the Spirit* (Grand Rapids, MI: Eerdmans, 1971).

Saffi, Aurelio, 'Letter to MacDonald. My dear Friend' (21 July 1859), from Ms. 2167/1/25 (Special Collections, University of Aberdeen).

Saintsbury, Elizabeth, *George MacDonald: A Short Life* (Edinburgh: Canongate Publishing, 1987).

Schenke, Elmar, 'Antigravity: Matter and the Imagination in George MacDonald and Early Science Fiction,' *North Wind*, 14 (1999): 46–56.

Scott, A.J., 'Letter of Recommendation of MacDonald for Chair of English Language and Literature at Bedford Square Ladies' College' (5 July 5 1857), from Ms 2167/1/26 (Special Collections, University of Aberdeen).

——, *Testimonials to George MacDonald. Candidate for Chair of English Edinburgh University* (Huntly: Brander Library, 1865).

Shaberman, Raphael B., *George MacDonald, A Bibliographical Study* (Winchester: St. Paul's Bibliographies, 1990).

——, 'Lewis Carroll and George MacDonald,' *Jabberwocky*, 5 (1976): 67–87.

Shideler, Mary McDermott, *George MacDonald* (Grand Rapids, MI: Eerdmans, 1972).

Soto, Fernando, 'Chtonic Aspects of MacDonald's Phantastes: From the Rising of the Goddess to the *Anodos* of Anodos,' *North Wind*, 19 (2000): 19–49.

Thorpe, Douglas, 'A Hidden Rime: The World View of George MacDonald,' unpublished Ph.D. dissertation (Toronto, Ontario: University of Toronto, 1981).

Tolkien, J.R.R., *Tree and Leaf* (London: HarperCollins, 1992; orig. 1964).

——, *The Silmarillion*, ed. Christopher Tolkien (Boston, MA: Houghton Mifflin, 1977).

Trexler, Robert, 'George MacDonald: Merging Myth and Method,' *The Bulletin of the New York C.S. Lewis Society*, 34(4) (July/August 2003): 1–13.

Triggs, Kathy, *The Seeking Heart* (Basingstoke: Pickering and Inglis, 1984).

——, *The Stars and the Stillness: A Portrait of George MacDonald* (Cambridge: Lutterworth Press, 1986).

Troup, Robert, *The Missionar Kirk of Huntly* (Edinburgh: John Menzies, 1901).

Webb, William, 'George MacDonald: A Study of Two Novels,' in James Hogg (ed.), *Salzburg Studies in English Literature* (Salzburg: Institut für Englische Sprache und Literatur, Universität Salzburg, 1973). pp. 57–118.

Willcox, Louise Collier, 'A Neglected Novelist,' *North American Review*, 183 (September 1906): 394–403.

Willis, Lesley, 'Born Again: The Metamorphosis of Irene in George MacDonald's The Princess and the Goblin,' *Scottish Literary Journal*, 12(1) (1985): 24–39.

Wolfe, Gregory, 'C. S. Lewis's Debt to George MacDonald,' *C.S. Lewis Society Bulletin*, 2(170) (December 1983): 1–7.

Wolff, Robert Lee, *The Golden Key: A Study of the Fiction of George MacDonald* (New Haven, CT: Yale University Press, 1961).

Wright, Marjorie Evelyn, 'The Vision of Cosmic Order in the Oxford Mythmakers,' in Charles Huttar (ed.), *Imagination and the Spirit* (Grand Rapids, MI: Eerdmans, 1971), pp. 259–76.

Writers or Works about Writers Influencing MacDonald

Barfield, Owen, *What Coleridge Thought* (Middletown, CT: Wesleyan University Press, 1971).

Campbell, John McLeod, *The Nature of the Atonement* (6th edn., London: Macmillan, 1915).

Christensen, Torben, *The Divine Order: A Study in F.D. Maurice's Theology* (Leiden: E.J. Brill, Gullanders Bogtrykkeri A.-S. Skjern, 1973).

Coleridge, Samuel Taylor, *Aids to Reflection*, ed. Henry Nelson Coleridge, Esq. (Burlington, VT: Chauncery Goodrich, 1840).

——, *Biographia Literaria and Two Lay Sermons* (London: George Bell & Sons, 1894 reprint).

——, *Miscellanies, Aesthetic and Literary*, ed. T. Ashe (London: George Bell and Sons, 1892).

——, *The Friend: A Series of Essays to Aid in the Formation of Fixed Principles in Politics, Morals and Religion* (London: Bell and Daldy, 1866).

——, *The Poetical Works of Samuel Taylor Coleridge*, ed. James Dykes Campbell (London: Macmillan, 1938).

——, *Theologia Germanica*, trans. Susanna Winkworth (New York: Pantheon, 1949).

Corapi, Wayne, 'History and Trinitarian Thought: The Impact of Samuel Taylor Coleridge's Understanding of History on His Conversion to Trinitarian Orthodoxy,' unpublished thesis, (Vancouver, BC: Regent College, 1997).

Davison, James E., 'Can God Speak a Word to Man? Barth's Critique of Schleiermacher's Theology,' *Scottish Journal of Theology*, 37 (1984): 189–211.

Douglas, David (ed.), *The Fatherhood of God Revealed in Christ: A Lesson from the Letters of Thomas Erskine of Linlathen* (Edinburgh, 1888).

Erskine, Thomas, *The Unconditional Forgiveness of the Gospel* (Edinburgh: Edmonston and Douglas, 1870).

Flesseman-van Leer, Ellen, *Grace Abounding: A Comparison of Frederick Denison Maurice and Karl Barth* (Lectures Given in King's College, London, 1968).

Hanna, William (ed.), *The Letters of Thomas Erskine of Linlathen* (Edinburgh: David Douglas, 1884).

Haywood, Bruce, *Novalis: The Veil of Imagery. A Study of the Poetic Works of Freidrich von Hardenberg (1772–1801)* ('s-Gravenhage: Mouton, 1959).

Hogg, James, *The Private Memoirs and Confessions of a Justified Sinner* (London: A.M. Philpot, 1926).

Jackson, H.J. (ed.), *Samuel Taylor Coleridge* (Oxford: Oxford University Press, 1985).

Logan, John B., 'Thomas Erskine of Linlathen: Lay Theologian of the "Inner Light,"' *Scottish Journal of Theology*, 37 (1984): 23–40.

Maurice, Frederick Denison, *The Doctrine of Sacrifice* (London: Macmillan, 1879).

——, *The Kingdom of Christ* (4th edn., London: Macmillan, 1891).

——, *The Prayer Book and the Lord's Prayer* (London: Macmillan, 1880).

——, *The Religions of The World* (London: Macmillan, 1877).

——, *The Word 'Eternal' and The Punishment of the Wicked: A Letter to the Rev. Dr. Jelf, Canon of Christ Church, and Principal of King's College* (Cambridge: Macmillan, 1853).

Needham, Nicholas R., *Thomas Erskine of Linlathen: His Life and Theology* (Edinburgh: Rutherford House, 1990).

Neubauer, John, *Novalis* (Boston, MA: Twayne Publishers, 1980).

Novalis, *Hymns to the Night and Other Selected Writings*, trans. Charles E. Passage (Indianapolis, IN: Bobbs-Merrill, 1960).

——, *Twelve of the Spiritual Songs*, trans. and ed. George MacDonald (issued privately, 1851).

Oliphant, Mrs. (Margaret), *The Life of Edward Irving* (2 vols, London: Hurst and Blackett, 1862).

Pfefferkorn, Kristin, *Novalis* (New Haven, CT: Yale University Press, 1988).

Prickett, Stephen, *Romanticism and Religion* (Cambridge: Cambridge University Press, 1976).

——, *Victorian Fantasy* (Brighton: Harvester Press, 1979).

Reardon, Bernard M.G., *Religious Thought in the Victorian Age* (London: Longman, 1971).

Robertson, F.W., *Lectures on the Influence of Poetry and Wordsworth* (London: Kennikat Press, 1906; reissued 1970).

Root, Michael, 'Schleiermacher as Innovator and Inheritor: God, Dependence and Election,' *Scottish Journal of Theology*, 43(1) 1990: 87–110.

Ruskin, John, *Unto This Last* (London: George Allen, 1901).

Saul, Nicholas, *History and Poetry in Novalis and in the Tradition of the German Enlightenment* (London: University of London, Institute of Germanic Studies, Bithell Series of Dissertations, Vol. 8, 1984).

Scott, A.J., 'Hints on 1 Corinthians XIV,' *Neglected Truths*, Vol. 1 (London: L.B. Seeley and Sons, 1830).

——, 'On the Divine Will,' *The Morning Watch*, Vol. 7 (Greenock: RB. Lusk, 1830): 15.

Story, R.H., 'Lecture 7: Edward Irving,' *St. Giles' Lectures, Scottish Divines* (Edinburgh: MacNiven and Wallace, 1883).

Torrance, James, 'Introduction,' in J. McCleod Campbell, *The Nature of the Atonement* (Grand Rapids, MI: Eerdmans, 1996).

Vidler, Alec R., *The Theology of F.D. Maurice* (London: SCM Press, 1948).

Wordsworth, William, 'The Prelude,' in Carlos Baker (ed.), *Selected Poems and Sonnets* (New York: Holt, Rinehart, and Winston, 1954).

General Theological and Other Related Texts

Arnold, Matthew, 'The Study of Poetry,' in Eliot W. Eliot (ed.), *Essays English and American, The Harvard Classics* (New York: P.F. Collier and Son, 1910).

Athanasius, *On the Incarnation*, trans. and ed. A Religious of C.S.M.V., *De Incarnatione Verbi Dei* (London: A.R. Mowbray, 1979 reprint).

Barth, Karl, *Church Dogmatics, Volume 2: The Doctrine of God*, Part 1, trans. T.H.L. Parker et al., ed. G.W. Bromiley and T.F. Torrance, *Die Kirchliche Dogmatik. 2: Die Lehre von Gott. 1* (Zurich: Evangelischer Verlag AG; Edinburgh: T. and T. Clark, 1957).

——, *Dogmatics in Outline* (New York: Harper and Row, 1959).

——, *From Rousseau to Ritschl*, trans. Brian Cozens (London: SCM Press, 1959).

——, *The Knowledge of God and the Service of God*, trans. J.L.M. Haire and Ian Henderson (London, 1938), pp. 13–21, in R. Ellmann, and C. Feidelson (eds.), *The Modern Tradition* (New York: Oxford University Press, 1965), pp. 939–43.

——, *The Word of God and the Word of Man,* trans. Douglas Horton (New York: Harper and Row, 1957).

Bausch, William J., *Storytelling, Imagination and Faith* (Mystic, CT: Twenty-third Publishers, 1993).

Begbie, Jeremy, *Beholding the Glory* (Grand Rapids, MI: Eerdmans, 2000).

——, *Voicing Creation's Praise* (Edinburgh: T. and T. Clark, 1991).

Boff, Leonardo, *The Maternal Face of God*, trans. Robert R. Barr (San Francisco, CA: Harper and Row, 1987).

Brueggemann, Walter, *Interpretation and Obedience* (Minneapolis, MN: Fortress Press, 1991).

——, *The Prophetic Imagination* (Philadelphia, PA: Fortress Press, 1978).

Buckley, Jerome Hamilton, *The Triumph of Time* (Cambridge: Penguin, 1966).

——, *The Victorian Temper* (London: George Allen and Unwin, 1952).

Calvin, John, *Institutes of the Christian Religion*, Vol. 1, trans. and ed. John T. McNeill and Ford Lewis Battles (Philadelphia, PA: Westminster Press, 1960).

Chryssavgis, John, *Soul Mending: The Art of Spiritual Direction* (Brookline, MA: Holy Cross Press, 2000).

Copleston, Frederick, S.J., *A History of Philosophy*, Vol. 1, Part 1 (Garden City, NY: Image Books, 1962).

Downes, David Anthony, *The Temper of Victorian Belief* (New York: Twayne, 1972).

Eliot, T.S., *Selected Essays of T.S. Eliot* (New York: Harcourt, Brace, and World, 1964).

Ellmann, Richard and Feidelson, Charles, Jr., (eds.), *The Modern Tradition* (New York: Oxford University Press, 1965).

Filmer, Kath (ed.), *The Victorian Fantasists* (London: Macmillan, 1991).

Ford, David. F., *The Modern Theologians* (2 vols, Oxford: Blackwell, 1989).

Fowler, James, 'Future Christians and Church Education,' in Theodore Runyon (trans. and ed.), *Hope for the Church* (Nashville, TN: Abingdon, 1979).

Gunton, Colin E., *The Actuality of Atonement* (Grand Rapids, MI: Eerdmans, 1989).

Hauerwas, Stanley and Jones, L. Gregory (eds.), *Why Narrative? Readings in Narrative Theology* (Grand Rapids, MI: Eerdmans, 1989).

Hebblethwaite, Brian, *The Ocean of Truth: A Defence of Objective Theism* (Cambridge: Cambridge University Press, 1988)

Horsman, Alan, *The Victorian Novel*, Vol. 8, in John Buxton, and Norman Davis (eds.), *The Oxford History of English Literature* (Oxford: Clarendon Press, 1990).

Jens, Walter and Küng, Hans, *Literature and Religion*, trans. Peter Heinegg (New York: Paragon House, 1991).

Jones, John Miriam, *With an Eagle's Eye* (Notre Dame, IN: Ave Maria Press, 1998).

Jüngel, Eberhard, *God as the Mystery of the World* (Grand Rapids, MI: Eerdmans, 1983).

——, *Theological Essays*, trans. J.B. Webster (Edinburgh: T. and T. Clark, 1989).

Kreeft, Peter, *Making Sense out of Suffering* (London: Hodder and Stoughton, 1986).

——, *Three Philosophies of Life* (San Francisco, CA: Ignatius, 1989).

Lewis, C.S., *Collected Letters of C.S. Lewis*, ed. Walter Hooper (New York: HarperSanFrancisco, 2004).

—— (ed.), *Essays Presented to Charles Williams* (Grand Rapids, MI: Eerdmans, 1966).

——, *The Great Divorce* (London: Geoffrey Bles, Centenary Press, 1945).

——, *The Weight of Glory and Other Addresses* (Grand Rapids, MI: Eerdmans, 1949).

Lochhead, Marion, *The Renaissance of Wonder* (Edinburgh: Canongate, 1977).

McClendon, James, *Biography as Theology* (Philadelphia, PA: Trinity Press, 1990).

McCormack, Bruce L., 'Divine Revelation and Human Imagination: Must We Choose Between the Two?,' *Scottish Journal of Theology*, 37 (1984): 431–455.

McFague, Sallie, *Metaphorical Theology* (Philadelphia, PA: Fortress, 1982).

McIntyre, John, *Faith, Theology and Imagination* (Edinburgh: Handsel, 1987).

McLaren, Peter, *Critical Pedagogy and Predatory Culture: Oppositional Politics in a Postmodern Age* (New York: Routledge, 1995).

Milton, John, *The Latin Poems of John Milton*, trans. and ed. Walter MacKellar (London: Oxford University Press, 1930).

Moltmann, Jürgen, *The Trinity and the Kingdom of God*, trans. Margaret Kohl (London: SCM Press, 1981).

Mother Theresa, *Words to Live By* (Notre Dame, IN: Ave Maria Press, 1983).

Newell, Roger J., 'Participatory Knowledge: Theology as Art and Science in C.S. Lewis and T.F. Torrance,' unpublished Ph.D. thesis (Aberdeen: University of Aberdeen, 1983).

Pattison, George, *Art, Modernity and Faith* (Hong Kong: Macmillan, 1991).

Placher, William E., *Unapologetic Theology* (Louisville, TN: Westminster/John Knox Press, 1989).

Plato, *The Republic* (New York: Charles Scribner's Sons, 1956).

Ricoeur, Paul, *The Rule of Metaphor*, trans. Robert Czerny (Toronto, Ontario: University of Toronto Press, 1977).

Runyon, Theodore (ed.), *Hope for the Church* (Nashville, TN: Abingdon, 1979).

Sartre, Jean-Paul, *Imagination: A Psychological Critique*, trans. Forrest Williams (Ann Arbor, MI: The University of Michigan Press, 1962).

Sayers, Dorothy, *The Mind of the Maker* (San Francisco, CA: Harper, 1987).

Scudder, Vida, *Social Ideals in English Letters* (New York: Houghton Mifflin, 1898).

Shaw, Lucy, *The Sighting* (Wheaton, IL: Harold Shaw, 1981).

Sine, Tom, *Wild Hope* (Dallas, TX: Word, 1991).

Soskice, Janet Martin, *Metaphor and Religious Language* (Oxford: Clarendon Press, 1987).

Stahl, E.L. and Yuill, W.E., *Introductions to German Literature*, Vol. 3 (London: Cresset Press, 1970).

Storkey, Elaine, *Mary's Story, Mary's Song* (London: Fount, HarperCollins, 1993).

Thrall, William Flint; Hibbard, Addison, and Holman, C. Hugh, *A Handbook to Literature* (Indianapolis, IN: Odyssey Press, 1960).

Tillich, Paul, *Theology of Culture*, ed. Robert C. Kimball (New York: Oxford University Press, 1959).

Torrance, James, 'The Incarnation and 'Limited Atonement,' *Evangelical Quarterly*, 55 (1983): 83–94.

Torrance, T.F., *Karl Barth: Biblical and Evangelical Theologian* (Edinburgh: T. and T. Clark, 1990).

——, *The Trinitarian Faith* (Edinburgh: T. and T. Clark, 1988).

Tournier, Paul, *The Gift of Feeling*, trans. Edwin Hudson (Atlanta, GA: John Knox Press, 1981).

Tozer, A.W., *The Root of the Righteous* (Chicago, IL: Moody, 1955).

Valdés, Mario J, (ed.), *A Ricoeur Reader: Reflection and Imagination* (Toronto, Ontario: University of Toronto Press, 1991).

Vidler, Alec R., *The Church in an Age of Revolution: 1789 to the Present Day* (New York: Penguin, 1981).

Walker, Andrew (ed.), *Different Gospels* (London: Hodder and Stoughton, 1988).

Walsh, Brian J. and Keesmaat, Sylvia C., *Colossians Remixed: Subverting the Empire* (Downers Grove, IL: InterVarsity Press, 2004).

Warnock, Mary, *Imagination* (London: Faber and Faber, 1976).

——, 'Imagination and Knowledge,' *Theology* (September 1989): 363–5.

Waterhouse, Gilbert, *A Short History of German Literature* (London: Methuen, 1942).

Wilder, Amos Niven, *Theopoetic* (Philadelphia, PA: Fortress, 1976).

Wright, T.R., *Theology and Literature* (Oxford: Blackwell, 1988).

Zizioulas, John D., *Being as Communion* (London: Darton, Longman, and Todd, 1985).

Indices

References to MacDonald's Works